MEMOIRS

OF

CAPT. GEORGE CARLETON,

AN ENGLISH OFFICER;

INCLUDING

ANECDOTES OF THE WAR IN SPAIN UNDER
THE EARL OF PETERBOROUGH,

AND

MANY INTERESTING PARTICULARS RELATING
TO THE MANNERS OF THE SPANIARDS IN THE BEGIN-
NING OF THE LAST CENTURY.

WRITTEN BY HIMSELF.

The Naval & Military Press Ltd

in association with

The National Army Museum, London

Published jointly by

The Naval & Military Press Ltd
Unit 10 Ridgewood Industrial Park,
Uckfield, East Sussex,
TN22 5QE England

Tel: +44 (0) 1825 749494
Fax: +44 (0) 1825 765701

www.naval-military-press.com
www.military-genealogy.com
www.militarymaproom.com

and

The National Army Museum, London
www.national-army-museum.ac.uk

In reprinting in facsimile from the original, any imperfections are inevitably reproduced and the quality may fall short of modern type and cartographic standards.

PREFACE

TO

CARLETON'S MEMOIRS,

CONTAINING

BIOGRAPHICAL NOTICES

OF

THE EARL OF PETERBOROUGH.

From an anecdote in Boswell's Life of Johnson, we are referred to the following Memoirs for the best account of the military achievements of the Earl of Peterborough. " The best account of Lord Peterborough that I have happened to meet with, is in Captain Carleton's memoirs. Carleton was descended of an officer who had distinguished himself at the siege of

Derry.* He was an officer, and, what was rare at that time, had some knowledge in engineering. Johnson said he had never heard of the book. Lord Elliot had a copy at Port Elliot; but after a good deal of enquiry, procured a copy in London, and sent it to Johnson; who told Sir Joshua Reynolds, that he was going to bed when it came, but was so much pleased with it, that he sat up till he read it through, and found in it such an air of truth, that he could not doubt its authenticity; adding, with a smile, in allusion to Lord Elliot's having recently been raised to the peerage, I did not think a young Lord could have mentioned to me a book in the English history that was not known to me."—*Boswell's Life of Johnson.*

A short sketch of the life of this celebrated General may be no unpleasing introduction to a

* Mackenzie in his " Narrative of the Siege of Londonderry," mentions no officer called Carleton. There is indeed a Colonel Crofton frequently spoken of. But as Carleton himself served in the great Dutch war of 1665, we can hardly suppose him *descended* of a person distinguished by feats of arms in 1688.

volume, which derives its chief value from narrating his glorious successes.

Charles Mordaunt, afterwards Earl of Peterborough, was born in 1658; and in June 1675, succeeded to the title of Lord Mordaunt and estate of his family. He was educated in the navy, and in his youth served with the Admirals Torrington and Narborough in the Mediterranean. In 1680 he accompanied the Earl of Plymouth in the expedition to Tangier, where he distinguished himself against the Moors.

In the succeeding reign, Lord Mordaunt opposed the repeal of the Test Act in the House of Lords; and having thus become obnoxious to the court, obtained liberty to go into the Dutch service. When he arrived in Holland, he was, as we learn from Burnet, amongst the most forward of those who advised the Prince of Orange to his grand enterprise. But the cold and considerate William saw obstacles which escaped the fiery and enthusiastic Mordaunt; nor although that prince used his services in the Revolution, does he appear to have reposed entire confidence in a character so opposite to his own. Yet Mordaunt reaped the reward of his zeal, being in 1688 created Earl of Monmouth, lord of the bedchamber, and first commissioner of the treasury, which last office he did not long retain. He accompanied William in his campaign of 1692; and in 1697 succeeded to the title, which he has so highly distinguished, by the death of his uncle Henry, the second Earl of Peterborough.

In the first year of Queen Anne's reign, Peterborough was to have been sent out as Governor General of Jamaica, but the appointment did not take place. In 1705 he was appointed General and Commander in Chief of the forces sent to Spain, upon the splendid and almost romantic service of placing Charles of Austria on the throne of that monarchy. The wonders which he there wrought, are no where more fully detailed than in the simple pages of Carleton.* Barcelona was

---

* See also the "Earl of Peterborough's conduct in Spain," by Dr John Freind. London, 1707.

taken by a handful of men, and afterwards relieved in the face of a powerful enemy, whom Peterborough compelled to decamp, leaving their battering artillery, ammunition, stores, provisions, and all their sick and wounded men. He drove before him, and finally expelled from Spain, the Duke of Anjou, with his army of twenty-five thousand French, although his own forces never amounted to half that number. All difficulties sunk before the creative power of his genius. Doomed as he was, by the infatuated folly of Charles, and by the private envy of his enemies at home, to conduct a perilous expedition, in a country ill affected to the cause, without supplies, stores, artillery, reinforcements, or money; he created substitutes for all these deficiencies,—even for the last of them. He took walled towns with dragoons, and stormed the caskets of the bankers of Genoa, without being able to offer them security. He gained possession of Catalonia, of the kingdoms of Valencia, Arragon, and Majorca, with part of Murcia and Castile, and thus opened the way for the Earl of Galway's marching to Madrid without a blow. Nor was his talent at conciliating the natives less remarkable than his military achievements. With the feeling of a virtuous, and the prudence of a wise man, he restrained the excesses of his troops, respected the religion, the laws, even the prejudices of the Spaniards; and, heretic as he was, became more popular amongst them than the Catholic prince, whom he was essaying to place on their throne. Yet, as Swift has strongly expressed it, " the only General, who, by a course of conduct and fortune almost miraculous, had nearly put us into possession of the kingdom of Spain, was left wholly unsupported, exposed to the envy of his rivals, disappointed by the caprices of a young unexperienced prince, under the guidance of a rapacious German ministry, and at last called home in discontent."* The cause of this strange step it would be tedious here to investigate. One ostensible reason was, that Peterborough's parts were of too lively and mercurial a quality, and that his letters shewed more wit than became a General; a common-place objection,

* Conduct of the Allies.

raised by the dull malignity of common-place minds against those whom they see discharging with ease and indifference the tasks which they themselves execute (if at all) with the sweat of their brow, and in the heaviness of their heart. It is no uncommon error of judgment to maintain *à priori*, that a thing cannot possibly be well done, which has taken less time in doing than the person passing sentence had anticipated. There is also a certain hypocrisy in business, whether civil or military, as well as in religion, which they will do well to observe, who, not satisfied with discharging their duty, desire also the good report of men. To the want of that grave, serious, business-like deportment, which admits of no levity in the exercise of its office; but especially to the envy excited by his success, Britain owed the recal of the Earl of Peterborough from Spain, during the full career of his victories. The command of the troops devolved on the Earl of Galway; a thorough-bred soldier, as he was called; a sound-headed, steady, solid General, who proceeded, with all decency, decorum, and formal attention to the discipline of war, to lose the battle of Almanza, and to ruin the whole expedition to Spain.

In June 1710-11, the thanks of the House of Peers were returned to the Earl of Peterborough for his services in Spain; and the chancellor used these remarkable words in expressing them:— " Had your Lordship's wise counsels, particularly your advice at the council of war in Valentia, been pursued in the following campaign, the fatal battle of Almanza, and our greatest misfortunes which have since happened in Spain, had been prevented, and the design upon Toulon might have happily succeeded."

In the years 1710 and 1711, the Earl was employed in embassies to Turin, and other courts of Italy, and finally at Vienna. He returned from the German capital with such expedition, that none of his servants were able to keep up with him, but remained scattered in the different towns where he had severally out-stripped them. He out-rode, upon this same occasion, several expresses which he had himself dispatched to announce his motions. Swift at this time received

PREFACE. ix

a letter from him, dated Hanover, and desiring an answer to be sent to him at his country house in England.* Indeed, Peterborough's characteristic rapidity of travelling was about this time celebrated by the Dean, in a little poem inscribed to him:—

> Mordanto fills the trump of fame,
> The Christian world his deeds proclaim,
> And prints are crowded with his name.
>
> In journies he outrides the post,
> Sits up till midnight with his host,
> Talks politics, and gives the toast.
>
> Knows every prince in Europe's face,
> Flies like a squib from place to place,
> And travels not, but runs a race.
>
> From Paris Gazette a-la-main,
> This day arrived, without his train,
> Mordanto in a week from Spain.
>
> A messenger comes all a-reek,
> Mordanto at Madrid to seek;
> He left the town above a week.

---

* Swift's Journal to Stella, 24th June, 1711.

Next day the post-boy winds his horn,
And rides through Dover in the morn:
Mordanto's landed from Leghorn.

Mordanto gallops on alone,
The roads are with his followers strown,
This breaks a girth, and that a bone.

His body active as his mind,
Returning sound in limb and wind,
Except some leather lost behind.

A skeleton in outward figure;
His meagre corpse, though full of vigour,
Would halt behind him, were it bigger.

So wonderful his expedition,
When you have not the least suspicion,
He's with you like an apparition.

Shines in all climates like a star;
In senates bold, and fierce in war;
A land commander, and a tar:

Heroic actions early bred in,
Ne'er to be matched in modern reading,
But by his namesake, Charles of Sweden.

Peterborough's haste was, in 1711, probably stimulated by the interest he took in the great public discussions on the policy of continuing the war with France. He argued in the affirmative with great ability, but without success. Although a strenuous Whig in principle, he was disliked by most of his own party, and greatly caressed in consequence by the Tories. After his return to England, he obtained the regiment of Royal Horse Guards, and the honours of the Garter, being installed 4th August, 1713. In November following, we find the Earl British Plenipotentiary to the King of Sicily and other Italian potentates; and in March 1713-14, he was appointed governor of the island of Minorca.

Under George I. and George II. the Earl of Peterborough was General of the marine forces in Great Britain.

In October 1735, he found it necessary to set sail for Lisbon for recovery of his health; " no body," to use Pope's expression, " being so much wasted, no soul being more alive." He was cut in the bladder for a suppression of urine ; immediately after which cruel operation, he took coach, and travelled no less a journey than from

Bristol to Southampton, " like a man," says the same poet, " determined neither to live nor die like any other mortal " He died on his voyage to Lisbon, 25th October, 1735, aged seventy-seven.

The Earl of Peterborough was twice married, and left two sons and a daughter by his first wife.

To all the talents of a General and negociator, this wonderful man added those belonging to a literary character. He associated with all the wits of Queen Anne's reign, was a lively poet, and his familiar letters are read to advantage amongst those of Gay, Arbuthnot, Swift, and Pope. He lived in great intimacy with the last, who boasts, that

> He whose lightning pierced the Iberian lines,
> Now forms my quincunx, and now ranks my vines,
> Or tames the genius of the stubborn plain,
> Almost as quickly as he conquered Spain.

To Pope, Peterborough bequeathed on his death-bed his watch, a present from the King of Sardinia, that, as he expressed it, his friend might have something to put him every day in mind of him.

The frame in which were lodged such comprehensive talents, was thin, short, spare, and well calculated to endure the eternal fatigue imposed by the restless tenant within. The famous lines of Dryden might be happily applied to the Earl of Peterborough :

> A fiery soul, which, working out its way,
> Fretted the pigmy body to decay,
> And o'er informed the tenement of clay.

His face, judging from the print in Dr Birch's Lives, was thin; his eye lively and penetrating. Such was Charles, Earl of Peterborough, one of those phenomena, whom nature produces once in the revolution of centuries, to shew to ordinary men what she can do in a mood of prodigality.

To this short sketch of the principal character in these Memoirs, the publishers would willingly have added some particulars of the author; but they are unable to say more on the subject than may be collected from the work itself, and the original preface. It is obvious that Captain George Carleton was one of those men who chuse the path of military life, not from a wish to indulge either indolent or licentious habits, but with a feeling of duty, which should be deeply impressed on all to whom their country commits the charge of her glory, and of the lives of their fellow subjects. There is a strain of grave and manly reflection through the work, which speaks the author accustomed to scenes of danger, and familiar with the thoughts of death. From his studies in mathematics, and in fortification, he is entitled to credit for his military remarks, which are usually made with simple modesty. His style is plain and soldier-like, without any pretence at ornament; though in narrating events of importance, its very simplicity gives it occasional dignity. Of the fate of the author after deliverance from his Spanish captivity, we know nothing; but can gather from some passages in his Memoirs, that it did not correspond with his merit. * While we hope that our present army pos-

---

* The Memoirs were first printed in 1743, with the following comprehensive title page:—" The Memoirs of Captain George Carleton, an English officer, who served in the two last wars against France and Spain, and was present in several engagements, both in the fleet and army. Containing an account of the conduct of the Earl of Peterborough, and other general Officers, Admirals, &c. and several remarkable transactions both by sea and land.

sesses many such characters, as the reflecting, manly, and conscientious Carleton, we heartily wish them better fortune.

In which the genius, pride, and barbarity of the Spaniards, during the author's being a prisoner of war among them, are set in a true light. Together with a description of many of their cities, towns, &c. particularly Valencia, Barcelona, Molviedro, Saguntum, Alicant, Montserat, Denia, St Clement de la Mancha, Madrid, Valladolid, Bilboa, St Jean de Luz, Bayonne, Pont d'Esprit, Pampeluna, Saragoza, &c. Their manners and customs, both religious and civil; observations on their monasteries and nunneries, and their manner of investing nuns. Likewise their bull-feasts, and other public diversions."

TO

THE RIGHT HONOURABLE

SPENCER LORD COMPTON,

BARON OF WILMINGTON,

KNIGHT OF THE BATH, AND ONE OF HIS MAJESTY'S
MOST HONOURABLE PRIVY COUNCIL.

It was my fortune, my Lord, in my juvenile years, *Musas cum marte commutare ;* and truly I have reason to blush, when I consider the small advantage I have reaped from that change. But lest it should be imputed to my want of merit, I have wrote these Memoirs, and leave the world to judge of my deserts. They are not set forth by any fictitious stories, nor embellished with rhetorical flourishes; plain truth is certainly most becoming the character of an old soldier. Yet let them be never so meritorious, if not protected by some noble patron, some persons may think them to be of no value.

To you, therefore, my Lord, I present them; to you, who have so eminently distinguished yourself, and whose wisdom has been so conspicuous to the late representatives of Great Britain, that each revolving age will speak in your praise; and if you vouchsafe to be the Mecænas of these Memoirs, your name will give them sufficient sanction.

An old soldier I may truly call myself, and my family allows me the title of a gentleman; yet I have seen many favourites of fortune, without being able to discern why they should be so happy, and myself so unfortunate. But let not that discourage your Lordship from receiving these my Memoirs into your patronage; for the unhappy cannot expect favour, but from those who are endued with generous souls.

Give me leave, my Lord, to congratulate this good fortune, that neither Whig nor Tory (in this complaining age) have found fault with your conduct. Your family has produced heroes, in defence of injured kings; and you, when it was necessary, have as nobly adhered to the cause of liberty.

My Lord,
Your Lordship's most obedient,
And most devoted humble Servant,
G. Carleton.

TO

THE READER.

The Author of these Memoirs began early to distinguish himself in martial affairs, otherwise he could not have seen such variety of actions, both by sea and land. After the last Dutch war he went into Flanders, where he not only served under the command of his Highness the Prince of Orange, whilst he was Generalissimo of the Dutch forces, but likewise all the time he reigned King of Great Britain. Most of the considerable passages and events, which happened during that time, are contained in the former part of this book.

In the year 1705, the regiment, in which he served as captain, was ordered to embark for the West Indies; and he, having no inclination to go thither, changed with an half-pay captain; and being recommended to the Earl of Peterborough by the late Lord Cutts, went with him upon that noble expedition into Spain.

When the forces under his Lordship's command were landed near Barcelona, the siege of that place was thought by several impracticable, not only for want of experienced engineers, but that the besieged were as numerous as the besiegers; yet the courage of that brave earl surmounted those difficulties, and the siege was resolved upon.

Our author having obtained, by his long service, some knowledge of the practic part of an engineer, and seeing at that critical time the great want of such, readily acted as one, which gave him the greater opportunity of being an eye-witness of his Lordship's actions; and consequently made him capable of setting them forth in these his Memoirs.

It may not be, perhaps, improper to mention, that the Author of these Memoirs was born at Ewelme in Oxfordshire, descended from an ancient and an honourable family. The Lord Dudley Carleton, who died secretary of state to King Charles I., was his great uncle; and in the same reign his father was envoy at the court of Madrid, whilst his uncle, Sir Dudley Carleton, was ambassador to the States of Holland; men in those days respected both for their abilities and loyalty.

MEMOIRS

OF

CAPTAIN CARLETON.

In the year one thousand six hundred and seventy-two, war being proclaimed with Holland, it was looked upon, among nobility and gentry, as a blemish, not to attend the Duke of York* aboard the fleet, who was then declared admiral. With many others, I, at that time about twenty years of age, entered myself a volunteer on board the London, commanded by Sir Edward Sprage, Vice-Admiral of the Red.

---

* Afterwards James II. By the treaty betwixt England and France, 6000 of the British troops were to assist the French army against the Dutch. The two fleets of France and England joined the 2d May. The English consisting of 100, and the French of 40 sail. The States had 72 large ships and 40 frigates.

The fleet set sail from the buoy of the Nore about the beginning of May, in order to join the French fleet, then at anchor in St Helen's Road, under the command of the Count de Estrée. But in executing this design, we had a very narrow escape: For De Ruyter, the admiral of the Dutch fleet, having notice of our intentions, waited to have intercepted us at the mouth of the River, but by the assistance of a great fog we pass'd Dover before he was aware of it; and thus he miscarried, with the poor advantage of taking only one small tender.

A day or two after the joining of the English and French, we sailed directly towards the Dutch coast, where we soon got sight of their fleet; a sand called the Galloper lying between. The Dutch seemed willing there to expect an attack from us; but in regard the Charles man of war had been lost on those sands the war before, and that our ships drawing more water than those of the enemy, an engagement might be rendered very disadvantageous, it was

CAPTAIN CARLETON. 3

resolved in a council of war, to avoid coming to a battle for the present, and to sail directly for Solebay, which was accordingly put in execution.

We had not been in Solebay above four or five days, when De Ruyter, hearing of it, made his signal for sailing, in order to surprize us; and he had certainly had his aim, had there been any breeze of wind to favour him. But though they made use of all their sails, there was so little air stirring, that we could see their fleet making towards us long before they came up; notwithstanding which, our admirals found difficulty enough to form their ships into a line of battle, so as to be ready to receive the enemy.

It was about four in the morning of the 28th of May, being Tuesday in Whitson week, when we first made the discovery; and about eight the same morning, the blue squadron, under the command of the Earl of Sandwich, began to engage with Admimiral Van Ghent, who commanded the

English and Dutch Fleets engaged in Solebay.

Amsterdam squadron; and about nine, the whole fleets were under a general engagement. The fight lasted till ten at night, and with equal fury on all sides, the French excepted, who appeared stationed there rather as spectators than parties; and as unwilling to be too much upon the offensive, for fear of offending themselves.

During the fight, the English admiral had two ships disabled under him; and was obliged, about four in the afternoon, to remove himself a third time into the London, where he remained all the rest of the fight, and till next morning. Nevertheless, on his entrance upon the London, which was the ship I was in, and on our hoisting the standard, De Ruyter and his squadron seemed to double their fire upon her, as if they resolved to blow her out of the water. Notwithstanding all which, the Duke of York remained all the time upon quarter-deck; and as the bullets plentifully whizzed around him, would often rub his hands, and cry, " Sprage, Sprage, they follow us still."

I am very sensible latter times have not been over favourable in their sentiments of that unfortunate Prince's valour; yet I cannot omit the doing a piece of justice to his memory, in relating a matter of fact, of which my own eyes were witnesses, and saying, that if intrepidity, and undauntedness, may be reckoned any parts of courage, no man in the fleet better deserved the title of courageous, or behaved himself with more gallantry than he did.

The English lost the Royal James, commanded by the Earl of Sandwich, which about twelve (after the strenuous endeavours of her sailors to disengage her from two Dutch fire-ships placed on her, one athwart her hawsers, the other on her starboard side) took fire, blew up, and perished; and with her a great many brave gentlemen, as well as sailors; and amongst the rest the Earl himself, concerning whom I shall further add, that in my passage from Harwich to the Brill, a year or two after, the master of the packet boat told me, that, having observed a great flock of gulls hovering in one particular part of the sea, he ordered his boat to make up to it; when, discovering a corpse, the sailors would have returned it to the sea, as the corpse of a Dutchman; but keeping it in his boat, it proved to be that of the Earl of Sandwich. There was found about him between twenty and thirty guineas, some silver, and his gold watch; restoring which to his lady, she kept the watch, but rewarded their honesty with all the gold and silver.

This was the only ship the English lost in this long engagement. For although the Katherine was taken, and her commander, Sir John Chicheley, made prisoner, her sailors soon after finding the opportunity they had watched for, seized all the Dutch sailors, who had been put in upon them, and brought the ship back to our own fleet, together with all the Dutchmen prisoners; for which, as they deserved, they were well rewarded. This is the same ship which the Earl of Mulgrave (afterwards Duke of Buckingham) commanded the next sea fight, and has caused to be painted in his house in St James's Park.

I must not omit one very remarkable occurrence which happened in this ship: There was a gentleman aboard her, a volunteer, of a very fine estate, generally known by the name of Hodge Vaughan. This person received, in the beginning of the fight, a considerable wound, which the great confusion during the battle would not give them leave to inquire into, so he was carried out of the way, and disposed of in the hold. They had some hogs aboard, which the sailor, under whose care they were, had neglected to feed; these hogs, hungry as they were, found out, and fell upon the wounded person, and between dead and alive, eat him up to his very skull, which, after the fight was over, and the ship retaken as before, was all that could be found of him.

Another thing, less to be accounted for, happened to a gentleman volunteer, who was aboard the same ship with myself. He was of known personal courage in the vulgar notion of it, his sword never having failed him in many private duels. But notwithstanding all his land-mettle, it was observed of him at sea, that whenever the bullets whizzed over his head, or any way incommoded his ears, he immediately quitted the deck, and ran down into the hold. At first he was gently reproached; but after many repetitions, he was laughed at, and began to be despised; sensible of which, as a testimonial of his valour, he made it his request to be tyed to the main mast. But had it been granted him, I cannot see any title he could have pleaded from hence, to true magnanimity; since to be tyed from running away can import nothing less, than that he would have still continued these signs of cowardice, if he had not been prevented. There is a bravery of mind, which I fancy few of those gentlemen duellists are possessed of. True courage cannot proceed from what Sir Walter Raleigh finely calls the art or philosophy of quarrel. No! It must be the issue of principle, and can have no other basis than a steady tenet of religion. This will appear more plain, if those artists in murder will give themselves leave coolly to consider, and answer me this question,—Why he, that had ran so many risques at his sword's point, should be so shamefully intimidated at the whiz of a cannon ball?

The Names of those English Gentlemen who lost their lives, as I remember, in this Engagement.

Commissioner Cox, captain of the Royal Prince, under the command of the admiral; and Mr Travanian, gentleman to the Duke of York; Mr Digby, captain of the Henry, second son to the Earl of Bristol; Sir Fletchvile Hollis, captain of the Cambridge, who lost one of his arms in the war before, and his life in this; Captain Saddleton of the Dartmouth; the Lord Maidstone, son to the Earl of Winchelsea, a volunteer on board the Charles, commanded by Sir John Harman, Vice-Admiral of the Red.

Sir Philip Carteret, Mr Herbert, Mr Cotterel, Mr Poyton, Mr Gose, with several other gentlemen unknown to me, lost their lives with the Earl of Sandwich, on board the Royal James; Mr Vaughan, on board the Katherine, commanded by Sir John Chicheley.

In this engagement, Sir George Rook was youngest lieutenant to Sir Edward Sprage; Mr Russel, afterwards Earl of Orford, was captain of a small fifth rate, called the Phœnix; Mr Herbert, afterwards Earl of Torrington, was captain of a small fourth rate, called the Monck; Sir Harry Dutton Colt, who was on board the Victory, commanded by the Earl of Ossory, is the only man now living that I can remember was in this engagement.

But to proceed; the Dutch had one man of war sunk, though so near the shore, that

I saw some part of her main-mast remain above water; with their Admiral Van Ghent, who was slain in the close engagement with the Earl of Sandwich. This engagement lasted fourteen hours, and was looked upon the greatest that ever was fought between the English and the Hollander.

I cannot here omit one thing, which to some may seem trifling, though I am apt to think our naturalists may have a different opinion of it, and find it afford their fancies no undiverting employment in more curious and less perilous reflections. We had on board the London, where, as I have said, I was a volunteer, a great number of pigeons, of which our commander was very fond. These, on the first firing of our cannon, dispersed, and flew away, and were seen no where near us during the fight. The next day it blew a brisk gale, and drove our fleet some leagues to the southward of the place where they forsook our ship, yet the day after they all returned safe aboard; not in one flock, but in small parties of four or five at a time. Some persons at that time aboard the ship, admiring at the manner of their return, and speaking of it with some surprize, Sir Edward Sprage told them, that he brought those pigeons with him from the Streights; and that when, pursuant to his order, he left the Revenge man of war, to go aboard the London, all those pigeons, of their own accord, and without the trouble or care of carrying, left the Revenge likewise, and removed with the sailors on board the London, where I saw them: all which many of the sailors afterwards confirmed to me. What sort of instinct this could proceed from, I leave to the curious.

Soon after this sea engagement I left the fleet. And the parliament, the winter following, manifesting their resentments against two of the plenipotentiaries, viz. Buckingham and Arlington, who had been sent over into Holland, and expressing, withal, their great umbrage taken at the

CAPTAIN CARLETON. 13

prodigious progress of the French arms in the United Provinces; and warmly remonstrating the inevitable danger attending England in their ruin; King Charles from all this, and for want of the expected supplies, found himself under a necessity of clapping up a speedy peace with Holland.   *Peace with Holland.*

This peace leaving those youthful spirits, that had by the late naval war been raised into a generous ferment, under a perfect inactivity at home; they found themselves, to avoid a sort of life that was their aversion, obliged to look out for one more active, and more suitable to their vigorous tempers abroad.

I must acknowledge myself one of that number; and therefore, in the year 1674, I resolved to go into Flanders, in order to serve as volunteer in the army commanded by his highness the Prince of Orange. I took my passage accordingly at Dover for Calais, and so went by way of Dunkirk for Brussels.

Arriving at which place, I was informed that the army of the confederates lay encamped not far from Nivelle, and under the daily expectation of an engagement with the enemy. This news made me press forward to the service; for which purpose I carried along with me proper letters of recommendation to Sir Walter Vane, who was at that time a major-general. Upon further enquiry I understood, that a party of horse, which was to guard some waggons that were going to Count Montery's army, were to set out next morning; so I got an Irish priest to introduce me to the commanding officer, which he readily obliged me in; and they, as I wished them, arrived in the camp next day.

I had scarce been there an hour, when happened one of the most extraordinary accidents in life. I observed in the east a strange dusty coloured cloud, of a pretty large extent, riding, not before the wind, (for it was a perfect calm) with such a precipitate motion, that it was got over our heads almost as soon as seen. When the skirts of that cloud began to cover our camp, there suddenly arose such a terrible hurricane, or whirlwind, that all the tents were carried aloft with great violence into the air; and soldiers hats flew so high and thick, that my fancy can resemble it to nothing better than those flights of rooks, which at dusk of evening, leaving the fields, seek their roosting places. Trees were torn up by the very roots, and the roofs of all the barns, &c. belonging to the Prince's quarters, were blown quite away. This lasted for about half an hour, until the cloud was wholly past over us, when as suddenly ensued the same pacific calm as before the cloud's approach. Its course was seemingly directly west; and yet we were soon after informed, that the fine dome of the great church at Utrecht had greatly suffered by it the same day. And, if I am not much mistaken, Sir William Temple, in his Memoirs, mentions somewhat of it, which he felt at Lillo, on his return from the Prince of Orange's camp, where he had been a day or two before.

As soon after this as I could get an opportunity, I delivered, at his quarters, my recommendatory letters to Sir Walter Vane; who received me very kindly, telling me at the same time, that there were six or seven English gentlemen, who had entered themselves volunteers in the Prince's own company of guards : and added, that he would immediately recommend me to Count Solmes, their colonel. He was not worse than his word, and I was entered accordingly. Those six gentlemen were as follows :—
—— Clavers, who since was better known by the title of Lord Dundee; Mr Collier, now Lord Portmore; Mr Rooke, since Major-General; Mr Hales, who lately died, and was for a long time governor of Chelsea Hospital : Mr Venner, son of that Venner remarkable for his being one of the fifth-monarchy men; and Mr Boyce. The four first rose to be very eminent ; but Fortune is not to all alike favourable.

In about a week's time after, it was resolved in a council of war, to march towards Binch, a small walled town, about four leagues from Nivelle; the better to cut off the provisions from coming to the Prince of Condé's camp that way.

The army marcheth towards Binch.

Accordingly, on the first day of August, being Saturday, we began our march; and the English volunteers had the favour of a baggage waggon appointed them. Count Souches, the Imperial general, with the troops of that nation, led the van; the main body was composed of Dutch, under the Prince of Orange, as Generalissimo; and the Spaniards, under Prince Vaudemont, with some detachments, made the rear guard.

As we were upon our march, I being among those detachments which made up the rear guard, observed a great party of the enemy's horse upon an ascent, which, I then imagined, as it after proved, to be the Prince of Condé taking a view of our forces under march. There were many defiles, which our army must necessarily pass; through which that Prince politically enough permitted the Imperial and Dutch forces to pass unmolested. But when Prince Vaudemont, with the Spaniards, and our detachments, thought to have done the like, the Prince of Condé fell on our rear guard; and, after a long and sharp dispute, entirely routed them; the Marquis of Assentar, a Spanish lieutenant-general, dying upon the spot.

Prince of Condé entirely routs the rear of the confederate army.

Had the Prince of Condé contented himself with this share of good fortune, his victory had been uncontested: But being pushed forward by a vehement heat of temper, (which he was noted for,) and flushed with this extraordinary success, he resolved to force the whole confederate army to a battle. In order to which, he immediately led his forces between our second line, and our line of baggage; by which means the latter were entirely cut off, and were subjected to the will of the enemy, who fell directly to plunder; in which they were not a little assisted by the routed Spaniards themselves, who did not disdain at that time to share with the enemy in the plundering of their friends and allies.

The English volunteers had their share of this ill fortune with the rest; their waggon appointed them being among those intercepted by the enemy; and I, for my part, lost every thing but life, which yet was saved almost as unaccountably as my fellow-soldiers 'had lost theirs. The baggage, as I have said, being cut off, and at the mercy of the enemy, every one endeavoured to escape through, or over, the hedges. And as in all cases of like confusion, one endeavours to save himself upon the ruins of others; so here, he that found himself stopt by another in getting over the gap of a hedge, pulled him back to make way for himself, and perhaps met with the same fortune from a third, to the destruction of all. I was then in the vigour of my youth, and none of the least active, and perceiving how it had fared with some before me, I clapt my left leg upon the shoulders of one who was thus contending with another, and with a spring threw myself over both their heads and the hedge at the same time. By this means I not only saved my life, (for they were all cut to pieces that could not get over,) but from an eminence, which I soon after attained, I had an opportunity of seeing, and making my observations upon the remaining part of that glorious conflict.

It was from that advantageous situation, that I presently discovered that the Imperialists, who led the van, had now joined the main body. And, I confess, it was with an almost inexpressible pleasure, that I beheld, about three o'clock, with what intrepid fury they fell upon the enemy. In short, both armies were universally engaged, and with great obstinacy disputed the victory till eleven at night. At which time the French, being pretty well surfeited, made their retreat. Nevertheless, to secure

The battle of Seneff.

French quit the field.

it by a stratagem, they left their lighted matches hanging in the hedges, and waving with the air, to conceal it from the confederate army.

About two hours after, the confederate forces followed the example of their enemies, and drew off. And though neither army had much reason to boast, yet, as the Prince of Orange remained last in the field, and the French had lost what they before had gained, the glory of the day fell to the Prince of Orange; who, although but twenty-four years of age, had the suffrage of friend and foe, of having played the part of an old and experienced officer.

Confederate army drawn off.

There were left that day on the field of battle, by a general computation, not less than eighteen thousand men on both sides, over and above those who died of their wounds: The loss being pretty equal, only the French carried off most prisoners. Prince Waldeck was shot through the arm, which I was near enough to be an eye-witness of: and my much lamented friend, Sir Walter

Vane, was carried off dead. A wound in the arm was all the mark of honour, that I as yet could boast of, though our cannon in the defiles had slain many near me.

The Prince of Condé (as we were next day informed) lay all that night under a hedge, wrapped in his cloak; and, either from the mortification of being disappointed in his hopes of victory, or from a reflection of the disservice, which his own natural over heat of temper had drawn upon him, was almost inconsolable many days after. And thus ended the famous battle of Seneff.

But though common vogue has given it the name of a battle, in my weak opinion, it might rather deserve that of a confused skirmish; all things having been forcibly carried on without regularity, or even design enough to allow it any higher denomination: for, as I have said before, notwithstanding I was advantageously stationed for observation, I found it very often impossible to distinguish one party from another. And this was more remarkably evident on the part of the Prince of Orange, whose valour and vigour having led him into the middle of the enemy, and being then sensible of his error, by a peculiar presence of mind, gave the word of command in French, which he spoke perfectly well. But the French soldiers, who took him for one of their own generals, making answer, that their powder was all spent, it afforded matter of instruction to him to persist in his attack; at the same time, that it gave him a lesson of caution, to withdraw himself as soon as he could, to his own troops.

Prince of Orange in the midst of the French army.

However, the day after, the Prince of Orange thought proper to march to Quarignan, a village within a league of Mons; where he remained some days, till he could be supplied from Brussels with those necessaries which his army stood in need of.

Marches to Quarignan.

From thence we marched to Valenciennes, where we again encamped, till we could receive things proper for a siege.

Marches to Valenciennes, and besieges Oudenard.

Upon the arrival whereof, the Prince gave orders to decamp, and marched his army with a design to besiege Aeth. But having intelligence on our march, that the Mareschal De Humiers had reinforced that garrison, we marched directly to Oudenard, and immediately invested it.

This siege was carried on with such application and success, that the besiegers were in a few days ready for a storm; but the Prince of Condé prevented them, by coming up to its relief. Upon which the Prince of Orange, pursuant to the resolution of a council of war the night before, drew off his forces in order to give him battle; and to that purpose, after the laborious work of filling up our lines of contravallation, that the horse might pass more freely, we lay upon our arms all night. Next morning we expected the Imperial General, Count Souches, to join us; but instead of that, he sent back some very frivolous excuses, of the inconveniency of the ground for a battle; and after that, instead of joining the Prince, marched off quite another way; the Prince of Orange, with the Dutch and Spanish troops, marched directly for Ghent; exclaiming publicly against the chicanery of Souches, and openly declaring, that he had been advertised of a conference between a French Capuchin and that General, the night before. Certain it is, that that General lay under the displeasure of his master, the Emperor, for that piece of management; and the Count de Sporck was immediately appointed general in his place.

The Prince of Orange was hereupon leaving the army in great disgust, till prevailed upon by the Count de Montery, for the general safety, to recede from that resolution. However, seeing no likelihood of any thing further to be done, while Souches was in command, he resolved upon a post of more action, though more dangerous; wherefore ordering ten thousand men to march before, he himself soon after followed to the siege of Grave.

Prince of Orange going to leave the army in disgust.

The Grave, a strong place, and of the first moment to the Hollanders, had been blocked up by the Dutch forces all the summer; the Prince of Orange, therefore, leaving the main army under Prince Waldeck at Ghent, followed the detachment he had made for the siege of that important place, resolving to purchase it at any rate. On his arrival before it, things began to find new motion; and as they were carried on with the utmost application and fury, the besieged found themselves, in a little time, obliged to change their haughty summer note for one more suitable to the season.

Carries on the siege of Grave,

The Prince, from his first coming, having kept those within hotly plied with ball, both from cannon and mortars, Monsieur Chamilly, the governor, after a few days, being weary of such warm work, desired to capitulate; upon which hostages were exchanged, and articles agreed on next morning. Pursuant to which, the garrison marched out with drums beating and co-

And takes it.

lours flying, two days after, and were conducted to Charleroy.

By the taking this place, which made the Prince of Orange the more earnest upon it, the French were wholly expelled their last year's astonishing conquests in Holland. And yet there was another consideration, that rendered the surrender of it much more considerable. For the French being sensible of the great strength of this place, had there deposited all their cannon and ammunition, taken from their other conquests in Holland, which they never were able to remove or carry off, with tolerable prospect of safety, after that Prince's army first took the field.

The enemy being marched out, the Prince entered the town, and immediately ordered public thanksgivings for its happy reduction. Then having appointed a governor, and left a sufficient garrison, he put an end to that campaign, and returned to the Hague, where he had not been long, before he fell ill of the small-pox. The consternation this threw the whole country into, is not to be expressed : any one that had seen it would have thought, that the French had made another inundation greater than the former. But when the danger was over, their joy and satisfaction for his recovery, was equally beyond expression.

<small>Limburgh besieged and taken by the French.</small>

The year 1675 yielded very little remarkable in our army. Limburgh was besieged by the French, under the command of the Duke of Enguien, which the Prince of Orange having intelligence of, immediately decamped from his fine camp at Bethlem, near Louvain, in order to raise the siege. But as we were on a full march for that purpose, and had already reached Ruremond, word was brought, that the place had surrendered the day before. Upon which advice, the Prince, after a short halt, made his little army (for it consisted not of more than thirty thousand men) march back to Brabant. Nothing of moment, after this, occurred all that campaign.

In the year 1676, the Prince of Orange having, in concert with the Spaniards, resolved upon the important siege of Maestrich, (the only town in the Dutch Provinces then remaining in the hands of the French,) it was accordingly invested about the middle of June, with an army of twenty thousand men, under the command of his Highness Prince Waldeck, with the grand army covering the siege. It was some time before the heavy cannon, which we expected up the Maes, from Holland, arrived, which gave occasion to a piece of raillery of Monsieur Calvo, the governor, which was as handsomely reparteed. That governor, by a messenger, intimating his sorrow to find we had pawned our cannon for ammunition bread; answer was made, that in a few days we hoped to give him a taste of the loaves, which he should find would be sent him into the town in extraordinary plenty. I remember another piece of raillery, which passed some days after between the Rhingrave and the same Cal-

Maestrich besieged by the Prince of Orange.

vo. The former sending word, that he hoped within three weeks to salute that governor's mistress within the place; Calvo replied, he would give him leave to kiss her all over, if he kissed her any where in three months.

But our long expected artillery being at last arrived, all this jest and merriment was soon converted into earnest. Our trenches were immediately opened towards the Dauphin Bastion, against which were planted many cannon, in order to make a breach; myself, as a probationer, being twice put upon the forlorn hope to facilitate that difficult piece of service. Nor was it long before such a breach was effected, as was esteemed practicable, and therefore very soon after it was ordered to be attacked.

The disposition for the attack was thus ordered; two serjeants with twenty grenadiers, a captain with fifty men, myself one of the number; then a party carrying wool sacks, and after them two captains with one hundred men more; the soldiers in the trenches to be ready to sustain them, as occasion should require.

The signal being given, we left our trenches accordingly, having about one hundred yards to run, before we could reach the breach, which we mounted with some difficulty and loss; all our batteries firing at the same instant to keep our action in countenance, and favour our design. When we were in possession of the Bastion, the enemy fired most furiously upon us with their small cannon through a thin brick wall, by which, and their hand grenadoes, we lost more men than we did in the attack itself.

But well had it been had our ill fortune stopped there; for as if disaster must needs be the concomitant of success, we soon lost what we had thus gotten, by a small, but very odd accident. Not being furnished with such scoopes as our enemies made use of, in tossing their hand grenadoes some distance off, one of our own soldiers aiming to throw one over the wall into the counterscarp among the enemy, it so happened, that he unfortunately missed his aim, and the grenade fell down again on our side the wall, very near the person who fired it. He starting back to save himself, and some others, who saw it fall, doing the like, those who knew nothing of the matter fell into a sudden confusion, and imagining some greater danger than there really was, every body was struck with a panic fear, and endeavoured to be the first who should quit the Bastion, and secure himself by a real shame from an imaginary evil. Thus was a Bastion, that had been gloriously gained, inadvertently deserted; and that too, with the loss of almost as many men in the retreat, as had been slain in the onset, and the enemy most triumphantly again took possession of it.

Among the slain on our side in this action, was an ensign of Sir John Fenwick's regiment; and as an approbation of my services, his commission was bestowed upon me.

A few days after it was resolved again to storm that bastion, as before; out of three English, and one Scotch regiments, then in the camp, a detachment was selected for a fresh attack. Those regiments were under the command of Sir John Fenwick, (who was afterwards beheaded,) Colonel Ralph Widdrington, and Colonel Ashley of the English; and Sir Alexander Collier, father of the present Lord Portmore, of the Scotch. Out of every of these four regiments, as before, were detached a captain, a lieutenant, and an ensign, with fifty men: Captain Anthony Barnwell, of Sir John Fenwick's regiment, who was now my captain, commanding that attack.

At break of day the attack was begun with great resolution; and though vigorously maintained, was attended with the desired success. The bastion was again taken, and in it the commanding officer, who in service to himself, more than to us, told us, that the centre of the bastion would soon be blown up, being to his knowledge undermined for that purpose. But this secret proved of no other use, than to make us, by way of precaution, to keep as much as we could upon the rampart. In this attack Captain Barnwell lost his life, and it happened my new commission was wetted (not, as too frequently is the custom, with a debauch) but with a bullet through my hand, and the breach of my collar-bone with the stroke of a halbert.

After about half an hour's possession of the bastion, the mine under it, of which the French officer gave us warning, was sprung; the enemy at the same time making a furious sally upon us. The mine did a little, though the less execution, for being discovered; but the sally no way answered their end, for we beat them back, and immediately fixed our lodgment; which we maintained during the time of the siege. But to our double surprize, a few days after, they fired another mine under, or aside the former, in which they had placed a quantity of grenadoes, which did much more execution than the other: notwithstanding all which, a battery of guns was presently erected upon that bastion, which very considerably annoyed the enemy.

The breach for a general storm was now rendered almost practicable; yet before that could be advisably attempted, there was a strong horn-work to be taken. Upon this exploit the Dutch troops only were to signalize themselves; and they answered the confidence reposed in them; for, though they were twice repulsed, at the third onset they were more successful, and took possession, which they likewise kept to the raising of the siege.

There was a stratagem laid at this time, which, in its own merit, one would have thought, should not have failed of a good effect; but, to shew the vanity of the highest human wisdom, it miscarried. On the other side of the Maes, opposite to Maestrich, lies the strong fortress of Wyck, to which it is joined by a stone-bridge of six fair arches. The design was, by a false attack on that regular fortification to draw the strength of the garrison to its defence, which was but very natural to imagine would be the consequence. Ready to attend that well-concerted false attack, a large flat-bottomed boat, properly furnished with barrels of gun-powder, and other necessaries, was to fall down under one of the middle arches, and when fixed there, by firing the powder, to have blown up the bridge, and by that means to have prevented the return of the garrison, to oppose a real attack at that instant of time to be made upon the town of Maestrich by the whole army.

The false attack on Wyck was accordingly made, which, as proposed, drew the main of the garrison of Maestrich to its defence, and the boat so furnished fell down the river, as projected; but unfortunately, before it could reach the arch, from the darkness of the night, running upon a shoal, it could not be got off; for which reason, the men in the boat were glad to make a hasty escape for fear of being discovered; as the boat was, next morning, and the whole design laid open.

This stratagem thus miscarrying, all things were immediately got ready for a general storm, at the main breach in the town; and the rather, because the Prince of Orange had received incontestible intelligence, that Duke Scomberg, at the head of the French army, was in full march to relieve the place: but before every thing could be rightly got ready for the intended storm, (though some there were who pretended to say, that a dispute raised by the Spaniards with the Dutch, about the propriety of the town, when taken, was the cause of that delay,) we heard at some distance several guns fired as signals of relief; upon which, we precipitately, and, as most imagined, shamefully drew off from before the place, and joined the grand army under Prince Waldeck. But it was matter of yet greater surprize to most on the spot, that when the armies were so

Prince of Orange's army retreats from before Maestrich.

joined, we did not stay to offer the enemy battle. The well known courage of the Prince, then Generalissimo, was so far from solving this riddle, that it rather puzzled all who thought of it; however, the prevailing opinion was, that it was occasioned by some great misunderstanding between the Spaniards and the Dutch. And experience will evince, that this was not the only disappointment of that nature, occasioned by imperfect understandings.

Besides the number of common soldiers slain in this attack, which was not inconsiderable, we lost here the brave Rhingrave, a person much lamented, on account of his many other excellent qualifications, as well as that of a general. Colonel Ralph Widdrington, and Colonel Doleman, (who had not enjoyed Widdrington's commission above a fortnight) Captain Douglas, Captain Barnwell, and Captain Lee, were of the slain among the English; who, indeed, had borne the whole brunt of the attack upon the Dauphin's bastion.

I remember the Prince of Orange, during the siege, received a shot through his arm; which giving an immediate alarm to the troops under his command, he took his hat off his head with the wounded arm, and smiling, waved it, to shew them there was no danger. Thus, after the most gallant defence against the most courageous onsets, ended the siege of Maestrich; and with it all that was material that campaign.

Early in the spring, in the year 1677, the French army, under the Duke of Orleans, besieged at once, both Cambray and Saint Omers. This last, the Prince of Orange seemed very intent and resolute to relieve. In order to which, well knowing, by sad experience, it would be to little purpose to wait the majestic motions of the Spaniards, that Prince got together what forces he could, all in Dutch pay, and marching forward with all speed, resolved, even at the hazard of a battle, to attempt

Cambray and St Omers besieged by the French.

Prince of Orange attempts to raise the siege of St Omers, but is forced to retreat.

the raising the siege. Upon his appearing, the Duke of Orleans, to whose particular conduct the care of that siege was committed, drew off from before the place, leaving scarce enough of his men to defend the trenches. The Prince was under the necessity of marching his forces over a morass; and the Duke, well knowing it, took care to attack him near Mont Cassel, before half his little army were got over. The dispute was very sharp, but the Prince being much out-numbered, and his troops not able, by the straitness of the passage, to engage all at once, was obliged at last to retreat. which he did in pretty good order. I remember the Dutch troops did not all alike do their duty; and the Prince seeing one of the officers on his fullest speed, called to him over and over to halt; which the officer in too much haste to obey, the Prince gave him a slash over the face, saying, " By this mark I shall know you another time." Soon after this retreat of the Prince, Saint Omers was surrendered.

St Omers surrenders.

Upon this retreat, the Prince marching back, lay for some time among the boors, who, from the good discipline which he took care to make his troops observe, did not give us their customary boorish reception. And yet as secure as we might think ourselves, I met with a little passage that confirmed in me the notions, which the generality, as well as I, had imbibed of the private barbarity of those people, whenever an opportunity falls in their way. I was strolling at a distance from my quarters, all alone, when I found myself near one of their houses; into which, the doors being open, I ventured to enter. I saw nobody when I came in, though the house was, for that sort of people, well enough furnished, and in pretty decent order. I called, but, nobody answering, I had the curiosity to advance a little farther, when, at the mouth of the oven, which had not yet wholly lost its heat, I spied the corpse of a man so bloated, swoln, and parched, as left me little room to doubt, that the oven had been the scene of his destiny. I confess the sight struck me with horror; and as much courage and security as I entered with, I withdrew in haste, and with quite different sentiments, and could not fancy myself out of danger till I had reached our camp. A wise man should not frame an accusation on conjectures; but, on inquiry, I was soon made sensible, that such barbarous usage is too common among those people; especially if they meet with a straggler, of what nation soever.

This made me not very sorry when we decamped, and we soon after received orders to march and invest Charleroy; before which place we staid somewhat above a week, and then drew off. I remember very well, that I was not the only person then in the camp that was at a loss to dive into the reason of this investiture and decampment: but since I at that time, among the politicians of the army, never heard a good one, I shall not venture to offer my sentiments at so great a distance.

We, after this, marched towards Mons; and, in our march, passed over the very grounds on which the battle of Seneff had been fought three years before. It was with no little pleasure that I re-surveyed a place, that had once been of so much danger to me; and where my memory and fancy now repeated back all those observations I had then made under some unavoidable confusion. Young as I was, both in years and experience, from my own reflections, and the sentiments of others, after the fight was over, methought I saw visibly before me the well-ordered disposition of the Prince of Condé; the inexpressible difficulties which the Prince of Orange had to encounter with; while at the same moment I could not omit to repay my debt to the memory of my first patron, Sir Walter Vane, who, there losing his life, left me a solitary wanderer to the wide world of fortune.

But these thoughts soon gave place to new objects, which every hour presented themselves in our continued march to Enghien, a place famous for the finest gardens in all Flanders, near which we encamped, on the very same ground which the French chose some years after at the battle of Steenkirk; of which I shall speak in its proper place. Here the Prince of Orange left our army, as we afterwards found, to pass into England; where he married the Princess Mary, daughter of the Duke of York. And after his departure, that campaign ended without any thing further material.

<small>Peace concluded.</small> Now began the year 1678, famous for the peace, and no less remarkable for an action previous to it, which has not failed to employ the talents of men, variously, as they stood affected. Our army, under the Prince of Orange, lay encamped at Soignies, where it was whispered that the peace was concluded. Notwithstanding which, two days after, being Sunday the 17th day of August, the army was drawn out, as most others as well as myself apprehended, in order to a *feux de joye*; but in lieu of

that, we found our march ordered towards St Dennis, where the Duke of Luxemburg lay, as he imagined, safe in inaccessible entrenchments.

About three of the clock our army arrived there, when we received orders to make the attack. It began with a most vigorous spirit, that promised no less than the success which ensued. The three English and three Scotch regiments, under the command of the ever-renowned Earl of Ossory, together with the Prince of Orange's guards, made their attack at a place called the Château, where the French took their refuge among a parcel of hop-poles; but their resource was as weak as their defence, and they were soon beaten out with a very great slaughter. *Prince of Orange arrives at St Dennis, and begins the attack.*

It was here that, a French officer having his pistol directed at the breast of the Prince, Monsieur D'Auverquerque interposed, and shot the officer dead upon the spot.

Duke of Luxemburg defeated, and peace proclaimed.

The fight lasted from three in the afternoon till nine at night; when, growing dark, the Duke of Luxemburg forsook his entrenchments, into which we marched next morning. And, to see the sudden change of things! that very spot of ground, where nothing but fire and fury appeared the day before, the next saw solaced with the proclamation of a peace.

About an hour before the attack began, the Duke of Monmouth arrived in the army, being kindly received by the Prince of Orange, bravely fighting by his side all that day. The woods, and the unevenness of the ground, rendered the cavalry almost useless; yet I saw a standard among some others, which was taken from the enemy, being richly embroidered with gold and silver, bearing the sun in the zodiac, with these haughty words, *Nihil obstabit eunte.* On the news of this unexpected victory, the States of Holland sent to congratulate the Prince; and to testify how much they valued his preservation, they presented

Monsieur D'Auverquerque, who had so bravely rescued him, with a sword, whose handle was of massy gold, set with diamonds. I forgot to mention, that this gentleman received a shot on his head at the battle of Seneff; and truly in all actions, which were many, he nobly distinguished himself by his bravery. He was father of this present Earl of Grantham.

The Names of the English Officers which I knew to be killed in this Action.

Lieut. Col. Archer,   Capt. Pemfield,
Capt. Charleton,   Lieut. Charleton,
Capt. Richardson,   Lieut. Barton,
Capt. Fisher,   Ensign Colvile.
With several others, whose names I have forgot.

Lieut. Col. Babington, who began the attack, by beating the French out of the hop garden, was taken prisoner. Col. Hales, who was a long time governor of Chelsea College, being then a captain, received a shot on his leg, of which he went lame to his dying day.

The war thus ended by the peace of Nimeguen, the regiment in which I served was appointed to lie in garrison at the Grave. We lay there near four years, our soldiers being mostly employed about the fortifications. It was here, and by that means, that I imbibed the rudiments of fortification, and the practical part of an engineer, which, in my more advanced years, was of no small service to me.

Nevertheless, in the year 1684, our regiment received orders to march to Haren, near Brussels; where, with other forces, we encamped, till we heard that Luxemburg, invaded by the French, in a time of the profoundest peace, had surrendered to them. Then we decamped, and marched to Mechlin, where we lay in the field till near November. Not that there was any war proclaimed; but as not knowing, whether those who had committed such acts of hostility in time of peace, might not take it in their heads to proceed yet further. In November we marched into that town, where Count Nivelle was governor: the Marquis de Grana at the same time governing the Netherlands in the jurisdiction of Spain.

Nothing of any moment happened after this, till the death of King Charles II. The summer after which, the three English and three Scotch regiments received orders to pass over into England, upon the occasion of Monmouth's rebellion; where, upon our arrival, we received orders to encamp on Hounslow-heath. But that rebellion being soon stifled, and King James having no farther need of us, those regiments were ordered to return again to Holland, into the proper service of those who paid them.

Though I am no stiff adherer to the doctrine of predestination, yet to the full assurance of a Providence I never could fail

English and Scotch regiments pass over into England.

to adhere. Thence came it, that my natural desire to serve my own native country, prevailed upon me to quit the service of another, though its neighbour and ally. Events are not always to direct the judgement; and therefore, whether I did best in following these fondling dictates of nature, I shall neither question, nor determine.

However, it was not long after my arrival in England, before I had a commission given me by King James, to be a lieutenant in a new-raised regiment under the command of Colonel Tufton, brother to the Earl of Thanet. Under this commission I sojourned out two peaceable campaigns on Hounslow-heath ; where I was an eye-witness of one mock siege of Buda : After which, our regiment was ordered to Berwick, where I remained till the Revolution.

<small>K. James abdicates the throne.</small> King James having abdicated the throne, and the Prince of Orange accepting the administration, all commissions were ordered to be renewed in his name. The officers of our regiment, as well as others,

severally took out theirs accordingly, a very few excepted, of which number was our colonel, who, refusing a compliance, his commission was given to Sir James Lesley.

The Prince of Orange presently after was declared and proclaimed king, and his princess queen, with a conjunctive power. Upon which our regiment was ordered into Scotland, where affairs appeared under a face of disquietude. We had our quarters at Leith, till the time the castle of Edinburgh, then under the command of the Duke of Gordon, had surrendered. After which, pursuant to fresh orders, we marched to Inverness, a place of no great strength, and as little beauty; though yet I think I may say, without the least danger of an hyperbole, that it is as pleasant as most places in that country. Here we lay two long winters, perpetually harassed upon parties, and hunting of somewhat wilder than their wildest game, namely,

Prince of Orange proclaimed king.

the Highlanders, who were, if not as nimble-footed, yet fully as hard to be found.

But General Mackay having received orders to build a fort at Inverlochy, our regiment, among others, was commanded to that service. The two regiments appointed on the same duty, with some few dragoons, were already on their march, which having joined, we marched together through Louquebar. This, sure, is the wildest country in the Highlands, if not in the world. I did not see one house in all our march; and their economy, if I may call it such, is much the same with that of the Arabs or Tartars. Huts, or cabins, of trees and trash, are their places of habitation; in which they dwell, till their half-horned cattle have devoured the grass, and then remove, staying no where longer than that convenience invites them.

In this march, or rather, if you please, most dismal peregrination, we could but very rarely go two on a breast; and oftner, like geese in a string, one after another.

So that our very little army had sometimes, or rather most commonly, an extent of many miles; our enemy, the Highlanders, firing down upon us from their summits all the way. Nor was it possible for our men, or very rarely at least, to return their favours with any prospect of success; for, as they popped upon us always on a sudden, they never staid long enough to allow any of our soldiers a mark, or even time enough to fire: and, for our men to march, or climb up those mountains, which to them were natural champain, would have been as dangerous, as it seemed to us impracticable. Nevertheless, under all these disheartening disadvantages, we arrived at Inverlochy, and there performed the task appointed, building a fort on the same spot where Cromwell had raised one before. And, which was not a little remarkable, we had with us one Hill, a colonel, who had been governor in Oliver's time, and who was now again appointed governor by General Mackay. Thus the work on which we were sent being effected, we marched back again by the way of Gillycrancky, where that memorable battle under Dundee had been fought the year before.

Some time after, Sir Thomas Levingston, afterwards Earl of Tiviot, having received intelligence, that the Highlanders intended to fall down into the lower countries, in a considerable body, got together a party of about five hundred, (the dragoons, called the Scotch Greys, inclusive,) with which he resolved, if possible, to give them a meeting. We left Inverness the last day of April, and encamped near a little town called Forrest, the place where, as tradition still confidently avers, the witches met Macbeth, and greeted him with their diabolical auspices. But this story is so naturally displayed in a play of the immortal Shakespear, that I need not descend here to any farther particulars.

Here Sir Thomas received intelligence, that the Highlanders designed to encamp upon the Spey, near the laird of Grant's castle. Whereupon we began our march about noon, and the next day, about the break thereof, we came to that river, where we soon discovered the Highlanders by their fires. Sir Thomas immediately, on sight of it, issued his orders for our fording the river, and falling upon them as soon after as possible. Both were accordingly performed, and with so good order, secrecy, and success, that Cannon and Balfour, their commanders, were obliged to make their escape naked. *Highlanders totally routed.*

They were about one thousand in number, of which were killed about three hundred; we pursued them, till they got up Cromdale-hill, where we lost them in a fog. And, indeed, so high is that hill, that they who perfectly knew it, assured me, that it never is without a little dark fog hanging over it. And to me, at that instant of time, they seemed rather to be people received up into clouds, than flying from an enemy.

Near this there was an old castle, called Lethendy, into which about fifty of them made their retreat, most of them gentlemen, resolving there to defend themselves to the last. Sir Thomas sent a messenger to them, with an offer of mercy, if they would surrender: but they refused the proferred quarter, and fired upon our men, killing two of our grenadiers, and wounding another. During my quarters at the Grave, having learnt to throw a grenado, I took three or four in a bag, and crept down by the side of a ditch or dyke, to an old thatched house near the castle, imagining, on my mounting the same, I might be near enough to throw them, so as to do execution. I found all things answer my expectation; and the castle wanting a cover, I threw in a grenado, which put the enemy immediately into confusion. The second had not so good success, falling short; and the third burst as soon as it was well out of my hand, though without damage to myself. But throwing the fourth in at a window, it so increased the confusion, which the first had put them into, that they immediately called out to me, upon their parole of safety, to come to them.

Accordingly I went up to the door, which they had barricaded, and made up with great stones; when they told me, they were ready to surrender, upon condition of obtaining mercy. I returned to Sir Thomas, and telling him what I had done, and the consequence of it, and the message they had desired me to deliver, (a great many of the Highland gentlemen, not of this party, being with him,) Sir Thomas, in a high voice, and broad Scotch, best to be heard and understood, ordered me back to tell them, " He would cut them all to pieces, for their murder of two of his grenadiers, after his proffer of quarter."

I was returning full of these melancholy tidings, when Sir Thomas, advancing after me a little distance from the rest of the company; " Hark ye, Sir," says he, " I believe there may be among them some of our old acquaintance, (for we had served together in the service of the States in

Flanders,) therefore, tell them, they shall have good quarter." I very willingly carried back a message so much changed to my mind; and, upon delivering of it, without the least hesitation, they threw down the barricado, opened the door, and out came one Brody, who, as he then told me, had had a piece of his nose taken off by one of my grenadoes. I carried him to Sir Thomas, who, confirming my message, they all came out, and surrendered themselves prisoners. This happened on May-day, in the morning; for which reason we returned to Inverness with our prisoners, and boughs in our hats; and the Highlanders never held up their heads so high after this defeat.

Upon this success, Sir Thomas wrote to court, giving a full account of the whole action. In which, being pleased to make mention of my behaviour, with some particularities, I had soon after a commission ordered me for a company in the regiment under the command of Brigadier Tiffin.

My commission being made out, signed, and sent to me, I repaired immediately to Portsmouth, where the regiment lay in garrison. A few days after I had been there, Admiral Russel arrived with the fleet, and anchored at St Helen's, where he remained about a week. On the 18th of May, the whole fleet set sail; and it being my turn the same day to mount the main guard, I was going the rounds very early, when I heard great shooting at sea. I went directly to acquaint the governor, and told him my sentiments, that the two contending fleets were actually engaged, which indeed proved true; for that very night a pinnace, which came from our fleet, brought news that Admiral Russel had engaged the French Admiral Turvile; and, after a long and sharp dispute, was making after them to their own coasts.

The next day, towards evening, several other expresses arrived, one after another, all agreeing in the defeat of the French fleet, and in the particulars of the burning their Rising Sun, together with many other of their men of war, at La Hogue. All which expresses were immediately forwarded to court, by Mr Gibson, our governor.

About two months after this, our regiment, among many others, was, according to order, shipped off on a secret expedition, under the command of the Duke of Leinster, no man knowing to what place we were going, or on what design; no, not the commander himself. However, when we were out at sea, the General, according to instructions, opening his commission, we were soon put out of our suspense, and informed, that our orders were to attack Dunkirk. But what was so grand a secret to those concerned in the expedition, having been intrusted to a female politician on land, it was soon discovered to the enemy; for which reason, our orders were countermanded, before we reached the place of action, and our forces received directions to land at Ostend.

Soon after this, happened that memorable battle at Steenkirk, which, as very few at that time could dive into the reason of, and mistaken accounts of it have passed for authentic, I will mention somewhat more particularly: The undertaking was bold, and, as many thought, bolder than was consistent with the character of the wise undertaker. Nevertheless, the French having taken Namur, and, as the malecontents alleged, in the very sight of a superior army, and nothing having been done by land of any moment, things were blown into such a dangerous fermentation, by a malicious and lying spirit, that King William found himself under a necessity of attempting something that might appease the murmurs of the people. He knew very well, though spoke in the senate, that it was not true, that his forces at the siege of Namur exceeded those of the enemy; no man could be more afflicted than he at the overflowing of the Mehaigne, from the continual rains, which obstructed the relief

Battle at Steenkirk.

he had designed for that important place; yet, since his maligners made an ill use of these false topics, to insinuate that he had no mind to put an end to the war, he was resolved to evince the contrary, by shewing them that he was not afraid to venture his life for the better obtaining what was so much desired.

To that purpose, receiving intelligence that the Duke of Luxemburg lay strongly encamped at Steenkirk, near Enghien, (though he was sensible he must pass through many defiles to engage him; and that the many thickets between the two armies would frequently afford him new difficulties,) he resolved there to attack him. Our troops at first were forced to hew out their passage for the horse; and there was no one difficulty that his imagination had drawn, that was lessened by experience; and yet so prosperous were his arms at the beginning, that our troops had made themselves masters of several pieces of the enemy's cannon. But the farther he advanced, the ground growing straiter, so strait as not to admit his armies being drawn up in battalia, the troops behind could not give timely succour to those engaged, and the cannon we had taken was forcibly left behind, in order to make a good retreat. The French had lost all their courage in the onset; for though they had too fair an opportunity, they did not think fit to pursue it; or, at least, did it very languidly. However, the malecontents at home, I remember, grew very well pleased after this; for, so long as they had but a battle for their money, like true Englishmen, lost or won, they were contented.

Several causes, I remember, were assigned for this miscarriage, as they called it: some there were who were willing to lay it upon the Dutch; and allege a saying of one of their generals, who, receiving orders to relieve some English and Scotch that were overpowered, was heard to say, " Damn them, since they love fighting, let them have their bellies full." But I should rather impute the disappointment to the great loss of so many of our bravest officers at the very first onset. General Mackay, Colonel Lanier, the Earl of Angus, with both his field-officers, Sir Robert Douglas, Colonel Hodges, and many others, falling, it was enough to put a very considerable army into confusion. I remember one particular action of Sir Robert Douglas, that I should think myself to blame should I omit: seeing his colours on the other side the hedge, in the hands of the enemy, he leaped over, slew the officer that had them, and then threw them over the hedge to his company; redeeming his colours at the expence of his life. Thus, the Scotch commander improved upon the Roman General; for the brave Posthumius cast his standard in the middle of the enemy, for his soldiers to retrieve'; but Douglas retrieved his from the middle of the enemy, without any assistance, and cast it back to his soldiers to retain, after he had so bravely rescued it out of the hands of the enemy.

From hence our regiment received orders to march to Dixmuyd, where we lay some time employed in fortifying that place. While we were there, I had one morning stedfastly fixed my eyes upon some ducks, that were swimming in a large water before me; when all on a sudden, in the midst of a perfect calm, I observed such a strange and strong agitation in the waters, that prodigiously surprised me. I was at the same moment seized with such a giddiness in my head, that, for a minute or two, I was scarce sensible, and had much ado to keep on my legs. I had never felt any thing of an earthquake before, which, as I soon after understood from others, this was; and it left, indeed, very apparent marks of its force, in a great rent in the body of the great church, which remains to this day.

Having brought the intended fortifications into some tolerable order, we received a command out of hand to reimbark for England. And, upon our landing, directions met us to march for Ipswich, where we had our quarters all that winter. From thence we were ordered up to London, to do duty in the Tower. I had not been there long, before an accident happened, as little to be accounted for, without a divine Providence, as some would make that Providence to be, that only can account for it.

<small>A dangerous accident at the Tower of London.</small> There was at that time, as I was assured by my Lord Lucas, constable of it, upwards of twenty thousand barrels of gunpowder, in that they call the White Tower, when all at once the middle flooring did not only give way, or shrink, but fell flat down upon other barrels of powder, together with many of the same combustible matter which had been placed upon it. It was a Providence strangely neglected at that time, and hardly thought of since: but let any considerate man consult the consequences, if it had taken fire; perhaps to the destruction of the whole city, or, at least, as far as the bridge and parts adjacent. Let his thoughts proceed to ex-

amine, why or how, in that precipitate fall, not one nail, nor one piece of iron, in that large fabric, should afford one little spark to enflame that mass of sulphurous matter it was loaded with; and if he is at a loss to find a Providence, I fear his friends will be more at a loss to find his understanding. But the battle of Landen happening while our regiment was here on duty, we were soon removed, to our satisfaction, from that pacific station, to one more active in Flanders.

Notwithstanding that fatal battle the year preceding, namely, A.D. 1694, the confederate army under King William lay encamped at Mont St André, an open place, and much exposed; while the French were entrenched up to their very teeth, at Vignamont, a little distance from us. This afforded matter of great reflection to the politicians of those times, who could hardly allow, that, if the confederate army suffered so much, as it really did in the battle of Landen, it could consist with right conduct to tempt, or rather dare a new engagement. But those sage objectors had forgot the well-known courage of that brave prince, and were as little capable of fathoming his designs. The enemy, who, to their sorrow, had by experience been made better judges, was resolved to traverse both; for which purpose they kept close within their entrenchments; so that after all his efforts, King William finding he could no way draw them to a battle, suddenly decamped, and marched directly to Pont Espiers, by long marches, with a design to pass the French lines at that place.

But, notwithstanding our army marched in a direct line, to our great surprise, we found the enemy had first taken possession of it. They gave this the name of the Long March, and very deservedly; for though our army marched upon the string, and the enemy upon the bow, sensible of the importance of the post, and the necessity of securing it, by double horseing with their foot, and by leaving their weary and

CAPTAIN CARLETON. 69

weak in their garrisons, and supplying their places with fresh men out of them, they gained their point in disappointing us. Though certain it is, that march cost them as many men and horses as a battle. However, their master, the French king, was so pleased with their indefatigable and auspicious diligence, that he wrote, with his own hand, a letter of thanks to the officers, for the great zeal and care they had taken to prevent the confederate army from entering into French Flanders.

King William, thus disappointed in that noble design, gave immediate orders for his whole army to march through Oudenard, and then encamped at Rosendale; after some little stay at that camp, we were removed to the Camerlins, between Newport and Ostend, once more to take our winter quarters there among the boors.

We were now in the year 1695, when the strong fortress of Namur, taken by the French in 1692, and since made by them much stronger, was invested by the Earl of

<small>Namur invested by the Earl of Athlone.</small>

Athlone. After very many vigorous attacks, with the loss of many men, the town was taken, the garrison retiring into the castle. Into which, soon after, notwithstanding all the circumspection of the besiegers, Mareschal Bouflers found means, with some dragoons, to throw himself.

<small>Prince Vaudemont's glorious retreat.</small> While King William was thus engaged in that glorious and important siege, Prince Vaudemont being posted at Watergaem, with about fifty battalions, and as many squadrons, the Mareschal Villeroy laid a design to attack him with the whole French army. The Prince imagined no less, therefore he prepared accordingly, giving us orders to fortify our camp, as well as the little time we had for it would permit. Those orders were pursued; nevertheless, I must confess, it was beyond the reach of my little reason to account for our so long stay in the sight of an army so much superior to ours. The Prince, in the whole, could hardly muster thirty thousand; and Villeroy was known to value himself upon ha-

ving one hundred thousand effective men. However, the Prince provisionally sent away all our baggage that very morning to Ghent, and still made shew as if he resolved to defend himself to the last extremity, in our little entrenchments. The enemy on their side began to surround us; and in their motions for that purpose, blew up little bags of gun-powder, to give the readier notice how far they had accomplished it. Another captain, with myself, being placed on the right, with one hundred men, (where I found Monsieur Montal endeavouring, if possible, to get behind us,) I could easily observe, they had so far attained their aim of encompassing us, as to the very fashion of a horses shoe. This made me fix my eyes so intently upon the advancing enemy, that I never minded what my friends were doing behind me; though I afterwards found that they had been fileing off so very artfully and privately, by that narrow opening of the horse shoe, that when the enemy imagined us past a possibility of escape, our little army at once, and of a sudden, was ready to disappear. There was a large wood on the right of our army, through which lay the road to Ghent, not broader than to admit of more than four to march a-breast. Down this the Prince had slid his forces, except to that very small party which the captain and myself commanded, and which was designedly left to bring up the rear. Nor did we stir till Captain Collier, then aid-de-camp to his brother, now Earl of Portmore, came with the word of command for us to draw off.

When Villeroy was told of our retreat, he was much surprised, as thinking it a thing utterly impossible. However, at last, being sensible of the truth of it, he gave orders for our rear to be attacked; but we kept firing from ditch to ditch, and hedge to hedge, till night came upon us ; and so our little army got clear of its gigantic enemy with very inconsiderable loss. However, the French failed not, in their customary way, to express the sense of their vexation at this disappointment, with fire and sword in the neighbourhood round. Thus Prince Vaudemont acquired more glory by that retreat than an entire victory could have given him; and it was not, I confess, the least part of satisfaction in life, that myself had a share of honour under him, to bring off the rear at that his glorious retreat at Arseel.

However, in further revenge of this political chicane of the Prince of Vaudemont, and to oblige, if possible, King William to raise the siege from before Namur, Villeroy entered into the resolution of bombarding Brussels. In order to which, he encamped at Anderleck, and then made his approaches as near as was convenient to the town. There he caused to be planted thirty mortars, and raised a battery of ten guns to shoot hot bullets into the place.

But before they fired from either, Villeroy, in compliment to the Duke of Bavaria, sent a messenger to know in what part

Villeroy bombards Brussels.

of the town his Duchess chose to reside, that they might, as much as possible, avoid incommoding her, by directing their fire to other parts. Answer was returned, that she was at her usual place of residence, the palace; and accordingly their firing from battery or mortars little incommoded them that way.

Five days the bombardment continued; and with such fury, that the centre of that noble city was quite laid in rubbish. Most of the time of bombarding, I was upon the counterscarp, where I could best see and distinguish; and I have often counted in the air, at one time, more than twenty bombs; for they shot whole vollies out of their mortars all together. This, as it must needs be terrible, threw the inhabitants into the utmost confusion. Cartloads of nuns, that for many years before had never been out of the cloister, were now hurried about from place to place, to find retreats of some security. In short, the groves, and parts remote, were all crowded;

and the most spacious streets had hardly a spectator left to view their ruins. Nothing was to be seen like that dexterity of our people in extinguishing the fires; for where the red-hot bullets fell, and raised new conflagrations, not burghers only, but the vulgar sort, stood staring, and with their hands impocketed, beheld their houses gradually consume; and without offering prudent or charitable hand to stop the growing flames.

But after they had almost thus destroyed that late fair city, Villeroy, finding he could not raise the siege of Namur by that vigorous attack upon Brussels, decamped at last from before it, and put his army on the march towards Namur, to try if he could have better success by exposing to show his pageant of one hundred thousand men. Prince Vaudemont had timely intelligence of the Duke's resolution and motion; and resolved, if possible, to get there before him. Nor was the attempt fruitless: he fortunately succeeded, though with much fatigue, and no little difficulty, after he had

Villeroy decamps.

put a trick upon the spies of the enemy, by pretending to encamp, and so soon as they were gone ordering a full march.

The castle of Namur had been all this time under the fire of the besieger's cannon; and soon after our little army under the Prince was arrived, a breach, that was imagined practicable, being made in the Terra Nova, (which, as the name imports, was a new work, raised by the French, and added to the fortifications, since it fell into their hands in 1692, and which very much increased the strength of the whole,) a breach, as I have said, being made in this Terra Nova, a storm, in a council of war, was resolved upon. Four entire regiments, in conjunction with some draughts made out of several others, were ordered for that work, myself commanding that part of them, which had been drawn out of Colonel Tiffin's. We were all to rendezvous at the abbey of Salsines, under the command of the Lord Cutts; the signal, when the attack was to be made, being agreed to be the blowing up of a bag of gun-powder upon the bridge of boats that lay over the Sambre.

So soon as the signal was made, we marched up to the breach with a decent intrepidity, receiving, all the way we advanced, the full fire of the Cohorn fort. But as soon as we came near enough to mount, we found it vastly steep and rugged. Notwithstanding all which, several did get up, and entered the breach; but not being supported as they ought to have been, they were all made prisoners. Which, together with a wound my Lord Cutts received, after we had done all that was possible for us, necessitated us to retire with the loss of many of our men.

Lord Cutts storms the castle of Namur; but obliged to retire.

Villeroy all this while lay in sight, with his army of one hundred thousand men, without making the least offer to incommode the besiegers; or even without doing any thing more than make his appearance in favour of the besieged, and reconnoitring our encampment: and, at last, seeing, or imagining that he saw, the attempt would be to little purpose, with all the good manners in the world, in the night, he withdrew that terrible meteor, and relieved our poor horses from feeding on leaves, the only inconvenience he had put us to.

<small>The castle capitulates.</small> This retreat leaving the garrison without all hope of relief, they in the castle immediately capitulated. But after one of the gates had been, according to articles, delivered up, and Count Guiscard was marching out at the head of the garrison, and Bouflers at the head of the dragoons; the latter was, by order of King William, arrested, in reprize of the garrison of Dixmuyd, who, contrary to the cartel, had been detained prisoners, and remained under arrest till they were set free.

<small>Assassination plot.</small> At the very beginning of the year 1696, was discovered a plot, fit only to have had its origin from hell, or Rome; a plot which would have put Hottentots and Barbarians out of countenance. This was called the assassination plot, from the design of it,

which was to have assassinated King William, a little before the time of his usual leaving England to head the army of the confederates in Flanders. And as nothing could give a nobler idea of the great character of that prince, than such a nefarious combination against him; so, with all considerate men, nothing could more depreciate the cause of his inconsiderate enemies. If I remember what I have read, the sons of ancient Rome, though heathens, behaved themselves against an enemy in a quite different manner. Their historians afford us more instances than a few of their generous intimations to kings and generals, under actual hostilities, of barbarous designs upon their lives. I proceed to this of our own countrymen.

Soon after the discovery had been made, by persons actually engaged in that inhuman design, the regiment, in which I served, with some others then in Flanders, received orders, with all expedition, to embark for England; though, on our arrival at Gravesend, fresh orders met us to remain on board the transports, till we had further directions.

On my going to London, a few days after, I was told, that two regiments only were now designed to come ashore; and that the rest would be remanded to Flanders, the danger apprehended being pretty well over. I was at Whitehall when I received this notice; where, meeting my Lord Cutts, (who had, ever since the storming of the Terra Nova at Namur, allowed me a share in his favour) he expressed himself in the most obliging manner; and at parting desired he might not fail of seeing me next morning at his house; for he had somewhat of an extraordinary nature to communicate to me.

At the time appointed, I waited on his lordship, where I met Mr Steel, (now Sir Richard, and at that time his secretary,) who immediately introduced me. I found in company with him three gentlemen; and after common salutations, his lordship delivered into my hands, an order from the King in council to go along with Captain Porter, Mr de la Rue, and Mr George Harris, (who proved to be those three with him,) to search all the transports at Gravesend, in order to prevent any of the conspirators getting out of England that way. After answering, that I was ready to pay obedience, and receiving, in private, the further necessary instructions, we took our leave, and oars soon after for Gravesend. It was in our passage down, that I understood that they had all been of the conspiracy, but now reluctant, were become witnesses.

When we came to Gravesend, I produced my authority to the commanding officer, who very readily paid obedience, and gave assistance: But after our most diligent search, finding nothing of what we looked for, we returned that very night to London.

Next day a proclamation was to come out for the apprehending three of four troopers, who were sent over by King James, with a thousand pounds reward for each: Mr George Harris, who was the fourth, being the only evidence against the other three. No sooner were we returned from Gravesend, but Harris had intelligence brought him, that Cassells, one of the three, was at Mr Allen's in the Savoy, under the name of Green. Upon which we went directly to the place, and enquiring for Mr Green, we were told he lodged there, and was in his room.

I was obliged by my order to go along with them, and assist them; and very well was it that I was so : for, in consideration of the reward in the proclamation, which, as I have said, was to come out the next day, Harris and the rest were for deferring his seizure, till the coming out of that proclamation ; but making answer, that, in case of his escape that night, I must be responsible to my superiors, who, under the most favourable aspect, would construe it a neglect of duty, they were forced to comply; and so he was taken up, and his name that night struck out of the proclamation. It is very true, by this faithful discharge of my trust, I did save the government one thousand pounds; but it is equally so, that I never had of my governors one farthing consideration for what others termed an over-officious piece of service; though, in justice, it must be owned, a piece of exact and disinterested duty.

Some few days after, attending by direction at the secretary's office, with Mr Harris, there came in a Dutchman, spluttering and making a great noise, that he was sure he could discover one of the conspirators; but the mien and the behaviour of the man would not give any body leave to give him any credit or regard. However, the man persisting in his assertions, I spoke to Mr Harris to take him aside, and ask him what sort of a person he was: Harris did so; and the Dutchman describing him, says Harris, returning to me, I'll be hanged if it be not Blackburn. Upon which we had him questioned somewhat more narrowly; when having no room to doubt, and understanding where he was, Colonel Rivet of the guards was sent for, and ordered to go along with us to seize him. We went accordingly; and it proving to be Blackburn, the Dutchman had five hundred pounds, and the colonel and others the remainder. Cassels and Blackburn, if still alive, are in Newgate, confined by act of parliament, one only witness, which was Harris, being producible against them.

When Blackburn was seized, I found in the chamber with him, one Davison, a watch-maker, living in Holbourn. I carried him along with me to the secretary of state; but nothing on his examination appearing against him, he was immediately discharged. He offered afterwards to present me with a fine watch of his own making, which I refused; and he long after owned the obligation.

So soon as the depth of this plot was fathomed, and the intended evil provided against, as well as prevented, King William went over into Flanders, and our regiment thereupon received orders for their immediate return. Nothing of any moment occurred till our arrival at our old quarters, the Camerlins, where we lay dispersed amongst the country boors, or farmers, as heretofore. However, for our better security in those quarters, and to preserve us from the excursions of the neighbouring garrison of Furnes, we were obliged to keep an out-guard at a little place called Shoerbeck. This guard was every forty-eight hours changed, and remounted with a captain, a lieutenant, an ensign, and threescore men.

When it came to my turn to relieve that guard, and for that purpose I was arrived at my post, it appeared to me with the face of a place of debauch, rather than business; there being too visible tokens, that the hard duty of both officers and soldiers had been that of hard drinking, the foulest error that a soldier can commit, especially when on his guard.

To confirm my apprehensions, a little after I had taken possession of my guard, the man of the house related to me such passages, and so many of them, that satisfied me, that if ten sober men had made the attack, they might have fairly knocked all my predecessors of the last guard on the head, without much difficulty. However, his account administered matter of caution to me, and put me upon taking a narrower view of our situation. In consequence whereof, at night I placed a centinel a quarter of a mile in the rear, and such other centinels as I thought necessary and convenient in other places; with orders, that upon sight of an enemy the centinel near should fire; and that upon hearing that, all the other centinels, as well as he, should hasten in to strengthen our main guard.

What my jealousy, on my landlord's relation, had suggested, happened accordingly; for, about one in the morning, I was alarmed with the cry of one of my centinels, *Turn out, for God's sake!* which he repeated, with vehemence, three or four times over. I took the alarm, got up suddenly, and with no little difficulty got my men into the ranks, when the person who made the outcry came running in, almost spent, and out of breath. It was the centinel, that I had luckily placed about a quarter of a mile off, who gave the alarm; and his musket flashing in the pan, without going off, he endeavoured to supply with his voice the defect of his piece. I had just got my men into their ranks, in order to receive the enemy, when by the moon-light, I discovered a party advancing upon us. My out-centinel challenged them, and, as I had precautioned, they answered, Hispanioli; though I knew them to be French.

However, on my survey of our situation by day-light, having marked in my mind a proper place for drawing up my men in case of an attack, which was too narrow to admit of more than two on a breast, and which would secure between us and the enemy a ditch of water, I resolved to put in practice what had entertained me so well in the theory. To that purpose I ordered my first rank to keep their post, stand still and face the enemy, while the other two ranks stooping, should follow me to gain the intended station; which done, the first rank had orders to file off, and fall behind. All was performed in excellent order; and I confess it was with no little pleasure, that I beheld the enemy, for the best part of an hour, in consultation, whether they should attack us or no. The result, nevertheless, of that consultation ended in this; that, seeing us so well upon our guard, it was most advisable to draw off. They soon put their resolution into practice, which I was very glad to see; on examination a little before, having found that my predecessor, as in other things, had failed of conduct in leaving me a garrison without ammunition.—Next morning I was very pleasingly surprised with a handsome present of wine, and some other necessary refreshments. At first I made a little scruple and hesitation whether or no to receive them; till the bearer assured me, that they were sent me from the officers of the next garrison, who had made me a visit the night before, as a candid acknowledgment of my conduct and good behaviour. I returned their compliment, that I hoped I should never receive men of honour otherwise than like a man of honour; which mightily pleased them. Every of which particulars the Ghent Gazetteer the week after published.

We had little to do except marching and counter-marching all the campaign after; till it was resolved, in a council of war, for the better preserving of Brussels from such insults, as it had before sustained from the French during the siege of Namur, to fortify Anderlech; upon which our regiment, as well as others, were commanded from our more pacific posts to attend that work. Our whole army was under movement to cover that resolution; and the train fell to my care and command in the march. There accompanied the train a fellow, seemingly ordinary, yet very officious and courteous, being ready to do any thing for any person, from the officer to the common soldier. He travelled along, and moved with the train, sometimes on foot, and sometimes getting a ride in some one or other of the waggons; but ever full of his chit-chat and stories of humour. By these insinuating ways he had screwed himself into the general good opinion; but the waggoners especially grew particularly fond of him. At the end of our march, all our powder-waggons were placed breast-abreast, and so close, that one miscarrying would leave little doubt of the fate of all the rest. This, in the camp, we commonly call the Park; and here it was that our new guest, like another Phæton, though under pretence of weariness, not ambition, got leave of the very last carter to the train, to take a nap in his waggon. One who had entertained a jealousy of him, and had watched him, gave information against him; upon which he was seized and brought to me as captain of the guard. I caused him to be searched; and, upon search, finding match, touchwood, and other dangerous materials upon him, I sent him and them away to the provoe. Upon the whole, a council of war was called, at which, upon a strict examination, he confessed himself a hired incendiary; and as such received his sentence to be burnt in the face of the army. The execution was a day or two after: when, on the very spot, he further acknowledged, that on sight or noise of the blow, it had been concerted that the French army should fall upon the confederates under those lamentable circumstances.

An incendiary taken and burnt in the face of the army.

The peace of Riswick soon after taking place, put an end to all incendiarisms of either sort. So that nothing of a military kind, which was now become my province, happened of some years after. Our regiment was first ordered into England, and

Peace of Riswick.

presently after into Ireland: but as these memoirs are not designed for the low amusement of a tea-table, but rather of the cabinet, a series of inglorious inactivity can furnish but very little towards them.

Yet, as little as I admired a life of inactivity, there are some sorts of activity to which a wise man might almost give supineness the preference: Such is that of barely encountering elements, and waging war with nature; and such, in my opinion, would have been the spending my commission, and very probably my life with it, in the West Indies. For though the climate (as some would urge) may afford a chance for a very speedy advance in honour, yet, upon revolving in my mind, that those rotations of the wheel of fortune are often so very quick, as well as uncertain, that I myself might as well be the first as the last; the whole of the debate ended in somewhat like that couplet of the excellent Hudibras:

Then he, that ran away and fled,
Must lie in honour's truckle-bed.

However, my better planets soon disannulled those melancholy ideas, which a rumour of our being sent into the West Indies had crowded my head and heart with: For, being called over into England, upon the very affairs of the regiment, I arrived there just after the orders for their transportation went over; by which means the choice of going was put out of my power, and the danger of refusing, which was the case of many, was very luckily avoided.

It being judged, therefore, impossible for me to return soon enough to gain my passage, one in power proposed to me, that I should resign to an officer then going over; and with some other contingent advantages, to my great satisfaction, I was put upon the half-pay list. This was more agreeable; for I knew, or at least imagined myself wise enough to foretel, from the over hot debate of the House of Commons upon the Partition Treaty, that it could not be long before the present peace would, at least, require patching.

Under this sort of uncertain settlement I remained with the patience of a Jew, though not with judaical absurdity, a faithful adherer to my expectation. Nor did the consequence fail of answering; a war was apparent, and soon after proclaimed. Thus, waiting for an opportunity, which I flattered myself would soon present, the little diversions of Dublin, and the moderate conversation of that people, were not of temptation enough to make my stay in England look like a burden.

<small>War proclaimed.</small>

But though the war was proclaimed, and preparations accordingly made for it, the expectations from all received a sudden damp, by the as sudden death of King William. That Prince, who had stared death in the face, in many sieges and battles, met with his fate in the midst of his diversions, who seized his prize in an hour, to human thought, the least adapted to it.

<small>K. William dies.</small>

He was a-hunting, (his customary diversion,) when, by an unhappy trip of his horse, he fell to the ground; and in the fall displaced his collar-bone. The news of it immediately alarmed the court, and all around; and the sad effects of it soon after gave all Europe the like alarm. France only, who had not disdained to seek it sooner by ungenerous means, received new hope, from what gave others motives for despair. He flattered himself, that that long-lived obstacle to his ambition thus removed, his successor would never fall into those measures, which he had wisely concerted for the liberties of Europe; but he, as well as others of his adherents, was gloriously deceived; that god-like queen, with a heart entirely English, prosecuted her royal predecessor's counsels; and, to remove all the very faces of jealousy, immediately on her accession dispatched to every court of the great confederacy, persons adequate to the importance of the message, to give assurances thereof.

This gave new spirit to a cause, that at first seemed to languish in its founder, as it struck its great opposers with a no less mortifying terror: and well did the great successes of her arms answer the prayers and efforts of that royal soul of the confederacies; together with the wishes of all, that, like her, had the good, as well as the honour of their country at heart, in which the liberties of Europe were included. The first campaign gave a noble earnest of the future. Bon, Keyserwaert, Venlo, and Ruremond, were found forerunners only of Donawert, Hochstet, and Blenheim. Such a march of English forces to the support of the tottering empire, as it gloriously manifested the ancient genius of a warlike people, so was it happily celebrated with a success answerable to the glory of the undertaking, which concluded in statues and princely donatives to an English subject, from the then only emperor in Europe. A small tribute, it is true, for ransomed nations and captive armies, which justly enough inverted the exclamations of a Roman emperor to the French monarch, who deprecated his legions lost pretty near the same spot: but to a much superior number, and on a much less glorious occasion.

But my good fortune not allowing me to participate in those glorious appendages of the English arms in Flanders, nor on the Rhine, I was resolved to make a push for it the first opportunity, and waste my minutes no longer on court attendances. And my Lord Cutts returning with his full share of laurels, for his never to be forgotten services at Venlo, Ruremond, and Hochstet, found his active genius now to be reposed, under the less agreeable burden of unhazardous honour, where quiet must provide a tomb for one already past any danger of oblivion; deep wounds and glorious actions having anticipated all that could be said in epitaphs or literal inscriptions. Soon after his arrival from Germany, he was appointed general of all her Majesty's forces in Ireland; upon which, going to congratulate him, he was pleased to enquire of me several things relating to that country; and, particularly, in what part of Dublin I would recommend his residence; offering at the same time, if I would go over with him, all the services that should fall in his way.

But inactivity was a thing I had too long lamented; therefore, after I had, as decently as I could, declined the latter part, I told his lordship, that as to a place of residence, I was master of a house in Dublin, large enough, and suitable to his great quality, which should be at his service, on any terms he thought fit; adding withal, that I had a mind to see Spain, where my Lord Peterborow was now going; and that if his lordship would favour me with a recommendation, it would suit my present inclinations much better than any further tedious recess. His lordship was so good to close with both my overtures; and spoke so effectually in my favour, that the Earl of Peterborow, then general of all the forces ordered on that expedition, bade me speedily prepare myself; and so when all things were ready, I embarked with that noble lord for Spain, to pursue his well-concerted undertaking; which, in the event, will demonstrate to the world, that little armies, under the conduct of auspicious generals, may sometimes produce prodigious effects.

The Jews, in whatever part of the world, are a people industrious in the increasing of Mammon; and, being accustomed to the universal methods of gain, are always esteemed best qualified for any undertaking, where that bears a probability of being a perquisite. Providing bread, and other requisites for an army, was ever allowed to carry along with it a profit answerable; and Spain was not the first country where that people had engaged in such an undertaking. Besides, on any likely appearance of great advantage, it is in the nature, as well as practice of that race, strenuously to assist one another; and that with the utmost confidence and prodigious alacrity. One of that number, both competent and willing enough to carry on an undertaking of that kind, fortunately came at that juncture to solicit the Earl of Peterborow to be employed as proveditor to the army and troops, which were, or should be, sent into Spain.

It will easily be admitted, that the Earl, under his present exigencies, did not decline to listen. And a very considerable sum being offered, by way of advance, the method common in like cases was pursued, and the sum proposed accepted; by which means the Earl of Peterborow found himself put into the happy capacity of proceeding upon his first concerted project. The name of the Jew, who signed the contract, was Curtisos; and he and his friends, with great punctuality, advanced the expected sum of one hundred thousand pounds sterling, or very near it; which was immediately ordered into the hands of the paymaster of the forces. For though the Earl took money of the Jews, it was not for his own, but public use. According to agreement, bills were drawn for the value from Lisbon, upon the Lord Godolphin, (then Lord-treasurer,) all which were, on that occasion, punctually complied with.

The Earl of Peterborow having thus fortunately found means to supply himself with money, and by that with some horse, after he had obtained leave of the Lord Galoway to make an exchange of two regiments of foot, received the Archduke, and all those who would follow him, aboard the fleet; and, at his own expence, transported him and his whole retinue to Barcelona: for all which prodigious charge, as I have been very lately informed, from very good hands, that noble Earl never to this day received any consideration from the government, or any person whatsoever.

We sailed from Lisbon, in order to join the squadron under Sir Cloudsley Shovel: meeting with which at the appointed station off Tangier, the men of war and transports thus united, made the best of their way for Gibraltar. There we staid no longer than to take aboard two regiments out of that garrison, in lieu of two out of our fleet. Here we found the Prince of Hesse, who immediately took a resolution to follow the Archduke in this expedition. He was a person of great gallantry, and having been viceroy of Catalonia, was received on board the fleet with the utmost satisfaction, as being a person capable of doing great service in a country where he was well known, and as well beloved.

Speaking Latin then pretty fluently, it gave me frequent opportunities of conversing with the two father confessors of the Duke of Austria; and upon that account I found myself honoured with some share in the favour of the Archduke himself. I mention this, not to gratify any vain humour, but as a corroborating circumstance, that my opportunities of information, in matters of consequence, could not thereby be supposed to be lessened; but that I might more reasonably be imagined to arrive at intelligence, that not very often, or at least not so soon, came to the knowledge of others.

From Gibraltar we sailed to the bay of Altea, not far distant from the city of Valencia, in the road of which we continued for some days. While we were there, as I was very credibly informed, the Earl of Peterborow met with some fresh disappointment; but what it was, neither I nor any body else, as far as I could perceive, could ever dive into: neither did it appear by any outward tokens in that noble general, that it lay so much at his heart, as those about him seemed to assure me it did.

However, while we lay in Altea Bay, two bomb vessels, and a small squadron, were ordered against Denia, which had a small castle, but rather fine than strong. And accordingly, upon our offer to bring to bear with our cannon, and preparing to fix our bomb vessels, in order to bombard the

Denia surrenders, and proclaims the Archduke King of Spain.

place, it surrendered, and acknowledged the Archduke as lawful king of Spain, and so proclaimed him. From this time, therefore, speaking of that prince, it shall be under that title. General Ramos was left commander here; a person who afterwards acted a very extraordinary part in the war carried on in the kingdom of Valencia.

But notwithstanding no positive resolutions had been taken for the operations of the campaign, before the Archduke's departure from Lisbon, the Earl of Peterborow, ever solicitous of the honour of his country, had premeditated another enterprize, which, had it been embraced, would, in all probability, have brought that war to a much more speedy conclusion; and at the same time have obviated all those difficulties, which were but too apparent in the siege of Barcelona. He had justly and judiciously weighed, that there were no forces in the middle parts of Spain, all their troops being in the extreme parts of the kingdom, either on the frontiers of Portugal, or in the city of Barcelona; that with King Philip, and the royal family at Madrid, there were only some few horse, and those in a bad condition, and which only served for guards; if, therefore, as he rightly projected within himself, by the taking of Valencia, or any sea-port town, that might have secured his landing, he had marched directly for Madrid, what could have opposed him? But I shall have occasion to dilate more upon this head a few pages hence; and therefore shall here only say, that though that project of his might have brought about a speedy and wonderful revolution, what he was by his orders afterwards obliged to, against his inclinations, to pursue, contributed much more to his great reputation, as it put him under a frequent necessity of overcoming difficulties, which, to any other general, would have appeared unsurmountable.

Valencia is a city towards the centre of Spain, to the seaward, seated in a rich and most populous country, just fifty leagues

Valencia described.

from Madrid; it abounds in horses and mules; by reason of the great fertility of its lands, which they can, to great advantage, water when and as they please. This city and kingdom was as much inclined to the interest of King Charles as Catalonia itself; for, even on our first appearance, great numbers of people came down to the bay of Altea, with not only a bare offer of their services, but loaded with all manner of provisions, and loud acclamations of *Viva Carlos, tercero, Viva.* There were no regular troops in any of the places round about it, or in the city itself. The nearest were those few horse in Madrid, one hundred and fifty miles distant; nor any foot nearer than Barcelona, or the frontiers of Portugal.

Description of Barcelona.

On the contrary, Barcelona is one of the largest and most populous cities in all Spain, fortified with bastions; one side thereof is secured by the sea, and the other by a strong fortification, called Monjouick. The place is of so large a circumference, that thirty thousand men would scarce suffice to form the lines of circumvallation. It once resisted for many months an army of that force; and is almost at the greatest distance from England of any place belonging to that monarchy.

This short description of these two places will appear highly necessary, if it be considered, that no person without it would be able to judge of the design which the Earl of Peterborow intended to pursue, when he first took the Archduke aboard the fleet. Nevertheless, the Earl now found himself under a necessity of quitting that noble design, upon his receipt of orders from England, while he lay in the bay of Altea, to proceed directly to Catalonia; to which the Archduke, as well as many sea and land officers, were most inclined; and the Prince of Hesse more than all the rest.

On receiving those orders, the Earl of Peterborow seemed to be of opinion, that from an attempt, which he thought under a probability of success, he was condemned to undertake what was next to an impossibility of effecting; since nothing appeared to him so injudicious as an attempt upon Barcelona. A place at such a distance from receiving any reinforcement or relief; the only place in which the Spaniards had a garrison of regular forces; and those in number rather exceeding the army he was to undertake the siege with; was enough to cool the ardour of a person of less penetration and zeal than what the Earl had on all occasions demonstrated. Whereas, if the General, as he intended, had made an immediate march to Madrid, after he had secured Valencia, and the towns adjacent, which were all ready to submit and declare for King Charles; or if otherwise inclined, had it not in their power to make any considerable resistance; to which, if it be added, that he could have had mules and horses immediately provided for him, in what number he pleased, together with carriages necessary for artillery, baggage, and ammunition; in few days he could have forced King Philip out of Madrid, where he had so little force to oppose him. And as there was nothing in his way to prevent or obstruct his marching thither, it is hard to conceive any other part King Philip could have acted in such an extremity, than to retire either towards Portugal or Catalonia. In either of which cases, he must have left all the middle part of Spain open to the pleasure of the enemy; who, in the mean time, would have had it in their power to prevent any communication of those bodies at such opposite extremes of the country, as were the frontiers of Portugal and Barcelona, where only, as I said before, were any regular troops.

And on the other side, as the forces of the Earl of Peterborow were more than sufficient for an attempt where there was so little danger of opposition; so if their army on the frontiers of Portugal should have marched back upon him into the country, either the Portuguese army could have entered into Spain without opposition, or, at worst, supposing the General had been forced to retire, his retreat would have been easy and safe into those parts of Valencia and Andeluzia, which he previously had secured. Besides Gibraltar, the strongest place in Spain, if not in the whole world, was already in our possession, and a great fleet at hand ready to give assistance in all places near the sea. From all which it is pretty apparent, that in a little time the war on our side might have been supported without entering the Mediterranean; by which means all reinforcements would have been much nearer at hand, and the expences of transporting troops and ammunition very considerably diminished.

But none of these arguments, though every one of them is founded on solid reason, were of force enough against the prevailing opinion for an attempt upon Catalonia. Mr Crow, agent for the queen in those parts, had sent into England most positive assurances, that nothing would be wanting, if once our fleet made an invasion amongst the Catalans: The Prince of Hesse likewise abounded in mighty offers, and prodigious assurances; all which enforced our army to that part of Spain, and that gallant prince to those attempts in which he lost his life. Very much against the inclination of our general, who foresaw all those difficulties, which were no less evident afterwards to every one; and the sense of which occasioned those delays, and that opposition to any effort upon Barcelona, which ran through so many successive councils of war.

However, pursuant to his instructions from England, the repeated desires of the Archduke, and the importunities of the Prince of Hesse, our general gave orders to sail from Altea towards the bay of Barcelona, the chief city of Catalonia. Nevertheless, when we arrived there, he was very unwilling to land any of the forces, till he saw some probability of that assistance and

Earl of Peterborow arrives in Barcelona bay, and after some time lands the forces.

succour so much boasted of, and so often promised. But as nothing appeared but some small numbers of men, very indifferently armed, and without either gentlemen or officers at the head of them; the Earl of Peterborow was of opinion, this could not be deemed sufficient encouragement for him to engage in an enterprize, which carried so poor a face of probability of success along with it. In answer to this it was urged, that till a descent was made, and the affair thoroughly engaged in, it was not to be expected that any great numbers would appear, or that persons of condition would discover themselves. Upon all which it was resolved the troops should be landed.

Accordingly, our forces were disembarked, and immediately encamped; notwithstanding which, the number of succours increased very slowly, and that after the first straggling manner. Nor were those that did appear any way to be depended on; coming when they thought fit, and going away when they pleased, and not to be brought under any regular discipline. It was then pretended, that until they saw the artillery landed as well as forces, they would not believe any siege actually intended. This brought the General under a sort of necessity of complying in that also. Though certainly so to do must be allowed a little unreasonable, while the majority in all councils of war declared the design to be impracticable; and the Earl of Peterborow had positive orders to proceed according to such majorities.

At last the Prince of Hesse was pleased to demand pay for those stragglers, as officers and soldiers, endeavouring to maintain, that it could not be expected, that men should venture their lives for nothing. Thus, we came to Catalonia upon assurances of universal assistance; but found, when we came there, that we were to have none unless we paid for it. And as we were sent thither without money to pay for any thing, it had certainly been for us more tolerable to have been in a country where we might have taken by force what we could not obtain any other way.

However, to do the Miquelets all possible justice, I must say, that, notwithstanding the number of them, which hovered about the place, never much exceeded fifteen hundred men; if sometimes more, oftener less; and though they never came under any command, but planted themselves where and as they pleased, yet did they considerable service in taking possession of all the country houses and convents, that lay between the hills and the plain of Barcelona; by means whereof they rendered it impossible for the enemy to make any sorties or sallies at any distance from the town.

And now began all those difficulties to bear, which long before, by the General, had been apprehended. The troops had continued under a state of inactivity for the space of three weeks, all which was spent in perpetual contrivances and disputes amongst ourselves, not with the enemy. In six several councils of war the siege of Barcelona, under the circumstances we then lay, was rejected as a madness and impossibility. And though the General and Brigadier Stanhope (afterward Earl Stanhope) consented to some effort, yet it was rather that some effort should be made to satisfy the expectation of the world, than with any hopes of success. However, no consent at all could be obtained from any council of war; and the Dutch General in particular declared, that he would not obey even the commands of the Earl of Peterborow, if he should order the sacrifice of the troops under him in so unjustifiable a manner, without the consent of a council of war.

And yet all those officers, who refused their consent to the siege of Barcelona, offered to march into the country, and attempt any other place, that was not provided with so strong and numerous a garrison; taking it for granted, that no town in Catalonia, Barcelona excepted, could make long resistance; and in case the troops in that garrison should pursue them, they then might have an opportunity of fighting them at less disadvantage in the open field, than behind the walls of a place of such strength. And, indeed, should they have issued out on any such design, a defeat of those troops would have put the province of Catalonia, together with the kingdoms of Arragon and Valencia, into the hands of King Charles, more effectually than the taking of Barcelona itself.

Let it be observed, *en passant*, that by those offers of the land officers in a council of war, it is easy to imagine what would have been the success of our troops, had they marched directly from Valencia to Madrid. For, if after two months alarm, it was thought reasonable, as well as practicable, to march into the open country rather than attempt the siege of Barcelona, where forces equal, if not superior in number, were ready to follow us at the heels, what might not have been expected from an invasion by our troops when and where they could meet with little opposition? But, leaving the consideration of what might have been, I shall now endeavour, at least with great exactness, to set down some of the most remarkable events, from our taking to the relief of Barcelona.

The repeated refusals of the councils of war for undertaking the siege of so strong a place, with a garrison so numerous, and those refusals grounded upon such solid reasons, against a design so rash, reduced the General to the utmost perplexity. The court of King Charles was immerged in complaint; all belonging to him lamenting the hard fate of that Prince, to be brought into Catalonia only to return again, without the offer of any one effort in his favour. On the other hand, our own officers and soldiers were highly dissatisfied, that they were reproached, because not disposed to enter upon, and engage themselves in impossibilities. And, indeed, in the manner that the siege was proposed and insisted upon by the Prince of Hesse, in every of the several councils of war, after the loss of many men, thrown away to no other purpose, but to avoid the shame (as the expression ran) of coming like fools and going away like cowards, it could have ended in nothing but a retreat at last.

It afforded but small comfort to the Earl to have foreseen all these difficulties, and to have it in his power to say, that he would never have taken the Archduke on board, nor have proposed to him the hopes of a recovery of the Spanish monarchy from King Philip, if he could have imagined it probable, that he should not have been at liberty to pursue his own design, according to his own judgment. It must be allowed very hard for him, who had undertaken so great a work, and that without any orders from the government; and by so doing, could have had no justification but by success; I say, it must be allowed to be very hard, (after the undertaking had been approved in England,) that he should find himself to be directed in this manner by those at a distance, upon ill grounded and confident reports from Mr Crow; and compelled, as it were, though General, to follow the sentiments of strangers, who either had private views of ambition, or had no immediate care or concern for the troops employed in this expedition.

Such were the present unhappy circumstances of the Earl of Peterborow in the camp before Barcelona: Impossibilities proposed; no expedients to be accepted; a court reproaching; councils of war rejecting; and the Dutch General refusing the assistance of the troops under his command; and, what surmounted all, a despair of bringing such animosities and differing opinions to any tolerable agreement. Yet all these difficulties, instead of discouraging the Earl, set every faculty of his more afloat; and, at last, produced a lucky thought, which was happily attended with events extraordinary, and scenes of success much beyond his expectation; such as the General himself was heard to confess, it had been next to folly to have looked for; as certainly, *in prima facie*, it would hardly have borne proposing, to take by surprise a place much stronger than Barcelona itself. True it is, that his only hope of succeeding consisted in this: That no person could suppose such an enterprize could enter into the imagination of man; and, without doubt, the General's chief dependence lay upon what he found true in the sequel; that the governor and garrison of Monjouick, by reason of their own security, would be very negligent, and very little upon their guard.

However, to make the experiment, he took an opportunity, unknown to any person but an aid-de-camp that attended him, and went out to view the fortifications; and there being no horse in that strong fortress, and the Miquelets being possessed of all the houses and gardens in the plain, it was not difficult to give himself that satisfaction, taking his way by the foot of the hill. The observation he made of the place itself, the negligence and supineness of the garrison, together with his own uneasy circumstances, soon brought the Earl to a resolution of putting his first conceptions in execution; satisfied as he was, from the situation of the ground between Monjouick and the town, that if the first was in our possession, the siege of the latter might be undertaken with some prospect of success.

From what has been said, some may be apt to conclude, that the siege afterward succeeding, when the attack was made from the side of Monjouick, it had not been impossible to have prevailed, if the effort had been made on the east side of the town, where our forces were at first encamped, and where only we could have made our approaches, if Monjouick had not been in our power. But a few words will convince any of common experience of the utter impossibility of success upon the east part of the town, although many almost miraculous accidents made us succeed, when we brought our batteries to bear upon that part of Barcelona towards the west. The ground to the east was a perfect level for many miles, which would have necessitated our making our approaches in a regular way; and consequently our men must have been exposed to the full fire of their whole artillery. Besides, the town is on that side much stronger than any other; there is an out-work just under the walls of the town, flanked by the courtin and the faces of two bastions, which might have cost us half our troops to possess, before we could have raised a battery against the walls. Or supposing, after all, a competent breach had been made, what a wise piece of work must it have been to have attempted a storm, against double the number of regular troops within?

On the contrary, we were so favoured by the situation, when we made the attack from the side of Monjouick, that the breach was made, and the town taken, without opening of trenches, or without our being at all incommoded by any sallies of the enemy; as, in truth, they made not one during the whole siege. Our great battery, which consisted of upwards of fifty heavy cannon, supplied from the ships, and managed by the seamen, were placed upon a spot of rising ground, just large enough to contain our guns, with two deep hollow ways on each side the field, at each end whereof we had raised a little redoubt, which served to preserve our men from the shot of the town. Those little redoubts, in which we had some field-pieces, flanked the battery, and rendered it entirely secure from any surprise of the enemy. There were several other smaller batteries raised upon the hills adjacent, in places not to be approached, which, in a manner, rendered all the artillery of the enemy useless, by reason their men could not ply them, but with the utmost danger; whereas, ours were secure, very few being killed, and those mostly by random shot.

But, to return to the General: forced as he was to take this extraordinary resolution, he concluded, the readiest way to surprise his enemies, was to elude his friends. He therefore called a council of war ashore, of the land-officers; and aboard, of the admirals and sea-officers: In both which it was resolved, that in case the siege of Barcelona was judged impracticable, and that the troops should be reimbarked by a day appointed, an effort should be made upon the kingdom of Naples. Accordingly, the day affixed being come, the heavy artillery, landed for the siege, was returned aboard the ships, and every thing in appearance prepared for a reimbarkment. During which, the General was obliged to undergo all the reproaches of a dissatisfied court; and what was more uneasy to him, the murmurings of the sea-officers, who, not so competent judges in what related to sieges, were one and all inclined to a design upon Barcelona; and the rather, because, as the season was so far spent, it was thought altogether improper to engage the fleet in any new undertaking. However, all things were so well disguised by our seeming preparations for a retreat, that the very night our troops were in march towards the attack of Monjouick, there were public entertainments and rejoicings in the town for the raising of the siege.

The Prince of Hesse had taken large liberties in complaining against all the proceedings in the camp before Barcelona; even to insinuations, that though the Earl gave his opinion for some effort in public, yet used he not sufficient authority over the other general officers to incline them to comply; throwing out withal some hints, that the General, from the beginning, had declared himself in favour of other operations, and against coming to Catalonia; the latter part whereof was nothing but fact. On the other side, the Earl of Peterborow complained, that the boasted assistance was no way made good; and that in failure thereof, his troops were to be sacrificed to the humours of a stranger; one who had no command, and whose conduct might bear a question whether equal to his courage. These reproaches of one another had bred so much ill blood between those two great men, that for above a fortnight they had no correspondence, nor ever exchanged one word.

The Earl marches to Monjouick.
The Earl, however, having made his proper dispositions, and delivered out his orders, began his march in the evening, with twelve hundred foot and two hundred horse, which, of necessity, were to pass by the quarters of the Prince of Hesse. That Prince, on their appearance, was told, that the General was come to speak with him; and, being brought into his apartment, the Earl acquainted him, that he had at last resolved upon an attempt against the enemy; adding, that now, if he pleased, he might be a judge of their behaviour, and see whether his officers and soldiers had

deserved that character which he had so liberally given them. The Prince made answer, that he had always been ready to take his share; but could hardly believe, that troops marching that way could make any attempt against the enemy to satisfaction. However, without further discourse, he called for his horse.

By this we may see what share fortune has in the greatest events. In all probability the Earl of Peterborow had never engaged in such a dangerous affair, in cold blood, and unprovoked; and if such an enterprize had been resolved on in a regular way, it is very likely he might have given the command to some of the general officers; since it is not usual, nor hardly allowable, for one, that commands in chief, to go in person on such kind of services. But here we see the General and Prince, notwithstanding their late indifferent harmony, engaged together in this most desperate undertaking.

Brigadier Stanhope and Mr Methuen,

(now Sir Paul,) were the General's particular friends, and those he most consulted, and most confided in; yet he never imparted this resolution of his to either of them; for he was not willing to engage them in a design so dangerous, and where there was so little hope of success; rather choosing to reserve them as persons most capable of giving advice and assistance in the confusion, great enough already, which yet must have been greater, if any accident had happened to himself. And I have very good reason to believe, that the motive, which mainly engaged the Earl of Peterborow in this enterprize, was to satisfy the Prince of Hesse and the world, that his diffidence proceeded from his concern for the troops committed to his charge, and not for his own person. On the other hand, the great characters of the two gentlemen just mentioned are so well known, that it will easily gain credit, that the only way the General could take to prevent their being of the party, was to conceal it from them, as he did from all mankind, even from the Archduke himself. And certainly there never was a more universal surprise, than when the firing was heard next morning from Monjouick.

But I now proceed to give an exact account of this great action; of which no person, that I have heard of, ever yet took upon him to deliver to posterity the glorious particulars; and yet the consequences and events, by what follows, will appear so great, and so very extraordinary, that few, if any, had they had it in their power, would have denied themselves the pleasure, or the world the satisfaction, of knowing it.

The troops, which marched all night along the foot of the mountains, arrived two hours before day under the hill of Monjouick, not a quarter of a mile from the outward works: For this reason, it was taken for granted, whatever the design was which the General had proposed to himself, that it would be put in execution before day-light; but the Earl of Peterborow was now pleased to inform the officers of the reasons why he chose to stay till the light appeared. He was of opinion that any success would be impossible, unless the enemy came into the outward ditch under the bastions of the second inclosure; but that if they had time allowed them to come thither, there being no palisadoes, our men, by leaping in upon them, after receipt of their first fire, might drive them into the upper works; and following them close, with some probability, might force them, under that confusion, into the inward fortifications.

Such were the General's reasons then and there given; after which, having promised ample rewards to such as discharged their duty well, a lieutenant, with thirty men, was ordered to advance towards the bastion nearest the town; and a captain, with fifty men, to support him. After the enemy's fire, they were to leap into the ditch; and their orders were to follow them close, if they retired into the upper works: Nevertheless, not to pursue them farther, if they made into the inner fort; but to endeavour to cover themselves within the gorge of the bastion.

A lieutenant and a captain, with the like number of men, and the same orders, were commanded to a demi-bastion, at the extremity of the fort towards the west, which was above musket-shot from the inward fortification. Towards this place the wall, which was cut into the rock, was not faced for about twenty yards; and here our own men got up, where they found three pieces of cannon upon a platform, without any men to defend them.

Those appointed to the bastion towards the town, were sustained by two hundred men; with which the General and Prince went in person. The like number, under the directions of Colonel Southwell, were to sustain the attack towards the west; and about five hundred men were left under the command of a Dutch colonel, whose orders were to assist, where, in his own judgment, he should think most proper; and these were drawn up between the two parties appointed to begin the assault. My lot was on the side where the Prince and Earl were in person; and where we sustained the only loss from the first fire of the enemy.

Our men, though quite exposed, and though the glacis was all escarped upon the live rock, went on with an undaunted courage; and, immediately after the first fire of the enemy, all, that were not killed or wounded, leaped in, *pel-mel*, amongst the enemy; who, being thus boldly attacked, and seeing others pouring in upon them, retired in great confusion; and some one way, some another, ran into the inward works.

Confederate army attack Monjouick.

There was a large port in the flank of the principal bastion, towards the northeast, and a covered way, through which the General and the Prince of Hesse followed the flying forces; and by that means became possessed of it. Luckily enough, here lay a number of great stones in the gorge of the bastion, for the use of the fortification; with which we made a sort of breast-work, before the enemy recovered of their amaze, or made any considerable fire upon us from their inward fort, which commanded the upper part of that bastion.

We were afterwards informed, that the commander of the citadel, expecting but one attack, had called off the men from the most distant and western part of the fort, to that side which was next the town; upon which our men got into a demi-bastion in the most extreme part of the fortification. Here they got possession of three pieces of cannon, with hardly any opposition; and had leisure to cast up a little entrenchment, and to make use of the guns they had taken to defend it. Under this situation, the enemy, when drove into the inward fort, were exposed to our fire from those places we were possessed of, in case they offered to make any sally, or other attempt against us. Thus, we every moment became better and better prepared against any effort of the garrison. And, as they could not pretend to assail us without evident hazard, so nothing remained for us to do till we could bring up our artillery and mortars. Now it was that the General sent for the thousand men under Brigadier Stanhope's command, which he had posted at a convent, half way between the town and Monjouick.

There was almost a total cessation of fire, the men on both sides being under cover. The General was in the upper part of the bastion; the Prince of Hesse below, behind a little work at the point of the bastion, whence he could only see the heads of the enemy over the parapet of the inward fort. Soon after an accident happened, which cost that gallant Prince his life.

The enemy had lines of communication between Barcelona and Monjouick. The governor of the former, upon hearing the firing from the latter, immediately sent four hundred dragoons on horseback, under orders, that two hundred dismounting should reinforce the garrison, and the other two hundred should return with their horses back to the town.

When those two hundred dragoons were accordingly got into the inward fort, unseen by any of our men, the Spaniards, waving their hats over their heads, repeated over and over, *Viva el Rey, Viva.* This the Prince of Hesse unfortunately took for a signal of their desire to surrender. Upon which, with too much warmth and precipitancy, calling to the soldiers following, " They surrender, they surrender !" he advanced with near three hundred men, (who followed him without any orders from their General,) along the curtain which led to the ditch of the inward fort. The enemy suffered them to come into the ditch, and there surrounding them, took two hundred of them prisoners, at the same time making a discharge upon the rest, who were running back the way they came. This firing brought the Earl of Peterborow

Two hundred men taken by the Spaniards.

down from the upper part of the bastion, to see what was doing below. When he had just turned the point of the bastion, he saw the Prince of Hesse retiring, with the men that had so rashly advanced. The Earl had exchanged a very few words with him, when, from a second fire, that Prince received a shot in the great artery of the thigh, of which he died immediately, falling down at the General's feet, who instantly gave orders to carry off the body to the next convent.

<small>The Prince of Hesse killed.</small>

Almost the same moment, an officer came to acquaint the Earl of Peterborow, that a great body of horse and foot, at least three thousand, were on their march from Barcelona towards the fort. The distance is near a mile, all uneven ground; so that the enemy was either discoverable, or not to be seen, just as they were marching on the hills, or in the vallies. However, the General directly got on horseback, to take a view of those forces from the rising ground without the fort, having left all the posts, which were already taken, well secured with the allotted numbers of officers and soldiers.

But the event will demonstrate of what consequence the absence or presence of one man may prove on great occasions: No sooner was the Earl out of the fort, the care of which he had left under the command of the Lord Charlemont, (a person of known merit and undoubted courage, but somewhat too flexible in his temper,) when a panic fear (though the Earl, as I have said, was only gone to take a view of the enemy) seized upon the soldiery, which was a little too easily complied with by the Lord Charlemont, then commanding officer. True it is; for I heard an officer, ready enough to take such advantages, urge to him, that none of all those posts we were become masters of, were tenable; that to offer at it would be no better than wilfully sacrificing human lives to caprice and humour ; and just like a man's knocking his head against stone walls, to try which was hardest. Having overheard this piece of lip-oratory, and finding by the answer that it was too likely to prevail, and that all I was like to say would avail nothing, I slipped away as fast as I could, to acquaint the General with the danger impending.

As I passed along, I took notice, that the panic was upon the increase; the general rumour affirming, that we should be all cut off by the troops that were come out of Barcelona, if we did not immediately gain the hills, or the houses possessed by the Miquelets. Officers and soldiers, under this prevailing terror, quitted their posts; and in one united body (the Lord Charlemont at the head of them) marched, or rather hurried out of the fort; and were come half-way down the hill before the Earl of Peterborow came up to them; though, on my acquainting him with the shameful and surprising accident, he made no stay; but answering, with a good deal of vehemence, " Good God, is it possible!" hastened back as fast as he could.

I never thought myself happier than in this piece of service to my country. I confess I could not but value it, as having been therein more than a little instrumental in the glorious successes which succeeded; since immediately upon this notice from me, the Earl galloped up the hill, and lighting when he came to Lord Charlemont, he took his half pike out of his hand; and turning to the officers and soldiers, told them, if they would not face about and follow him, they should have the scandal and eternal infamy upon them, of having deserted their posts, and abandoned their general.

It was surprising to see with what alacrity and new courage they faced about, and followed the Earl of Peterborow. In a moment they had forgot their apprehensions; and, without doubt, had they met with any opposition, they would have behaved themselves with the greatest bravery. But as these motions were unperceived by the enemy, all the posts were regained, and anew possessed in less than half an hour, without any loss; though, had our forces marched half musket-shot further, their retreat would have been perceived, and all the success attendant on this glorious attempt must have been entirely blasted.

Another incident which attended this happy enterprize was this: The two hundred men which fell into the hands of the enemy, by the unhappy mistake of the Prince of Hesse, were carried directly into the town. The Marquis of Risburg, a lieutenant-general, who commanded the three thousand men which were marching from the town to the relief of the fort, examined the prisoners as they passed by; and they all agreeing that the General and the Prince of Hesse were in person with the troops that made the attack on Monjouick, the Marquis gave immediate orders to retire to the town; taking it for granted, that the main body of the troops attended the Prince and General; and that some design therefore was on foot to intercept his return, in case he should venture too far. Thus, the unfortunate loss of our two hundred men turned to our advantage, in preventing the advance of the enemy, which must have put the Earl of Peterborow to inconceivable difficulties.

The body of one thousand, under Brigadier Stanhope, being come up to Monjouick, and no interruption given us by the enemy, our affairs were put into very good order on this side; while the camp on the other side was so fortified, that the enemy, during the siege, never made one effort against it. In the mean time, the communication between the two camps was secure enough; although our troops were obliged to a tedious march along the foot of the hills, whenever the General thought fit to relieve those on duty on the side of the attack, from those regiments encamped on the west side of Barcelona.

The next day, after the Earl of Peterborow had taken care to secure the first camp to the eastward of the town, he gave orders to the officers of the fleet to land the artillery and ammunition behind the fortress to the westward. Immediately upon the landing whereof, two mortars were fixed; from both which we plied the fort of Monjouick furiously with our bombs. But the third or fourth day, one of our shells fortunately lighting on their magazine of powder, blew it up; and with it the governor, and many principal officers who were at dinner with him. The blast, at the same instant, threw down a face of one of the smaller bastions; which the vigilant Miquelets, ready enough to take all advantages, no sooner saw, (for they were under the hill, very near the place,) but they readily entered, while the enemy were under the utmost confusion. If the Earl, no less watchful than they, had not at the same moment thrown himself in with some regular troops, and appeased the general disorder, in all probability the garrison had been put to the sword. However, the General's presence not only allayed the fury of the Miquelets,

Magazine of Monjouick blown up, and the fortress taken.

but kept his own troops under strictest discipline : so that, in a happy hour for the frighted garrison, the General gave officers and soldiers quarters, making them prisoners of war.

How critical was that minute wherein the General met his retreating commander! A very few steps farther had excluded us our own conquests, to the utter loss of all those greater glories which ensued. Nor would that have been the worst; for, besides the shame attending such an ill concerted retreat from our acquests on Monjouick, we must have felt the accumulative disgrace of infamously retiring aboard the ships that brought us ; but heaven reserved for our General amazing scenes, both of glory and mortification.

I cannot here omit one singularity of life, which will demonstrate men's different way of thinking, if not somewhat worse ; when, many years after, to one in office, who seemed a little too deaf to my complaints, and by that means irritating my human passions, in justice to myself, as well as cause, I urged this piece of service, by which I not only preserved the place, but the honour of my country; that *minister petite*, to mortify my expectations, and baffle my plea, with a grimace as odd as his logic, returned, that, in his opinion, the service pretended was a disservice to the nation; since perseverance had cost the government more money than all our conquests were worth, could we have kept them. So irregular are the conceptions of man, when even great actions thwart the bent of an interested will.

The fort of Monjouick being thus surprisingly reduced, furnished a strange vivacity to men's expectations, and as extravagantly flattered their hopes; for, as success never fails to excite weaker minds to pursue their good fortune, though many times to their own loss; so is it often too apt to push on more elevated spirits, to renew the encounter for atchieving new conquests, by hazarding too rashly all their former glory. Accordingly, every body now began to make his utmost efforts; and looked upon himself as a drone, if he was not employed in doing something or other towards pushing forward the siege of Barcelona itself, and raising proper batteries for that purpose. But, after all, it must, in justice, be acknowledged, that, notwithstanding this prodigious success that attended this bold enterprise, the land forces, of themselves, without the assistance of the sailors, could never have reduced the town. The commanders and officers of the fleet had always evinced themselves favourers of this project upon Barcelona. A new undertaking so late in the year, as I have said before, was their utter aversion, and what they hated to hear of. Elated, therefore, with a beginning so auspicious, they gave a more willing assistance than could have been asked, or judiciously expected. The admirals forgot their element, and acted as general officers at land: They came every day from their ships, with a body of men formed into companies, and regularly marshalled, and commanded by captains and lieutenants of their own. Captain Littleton, in particular, one of the most advanced captains in the whole fleet, offered, of himself, to take care of the landing and conveyance of the artillery to the camp. And answerable to that his first zeal, was his vigour all along; for, finding it next to an impossibility to draw the cannon and mortars up such vast precipices by horses, if the country had afforded them, he caused harnesses to be made for two hundred men; and by that means, after a prodigious fatigue and labour, brought the cannon and mortars, necessary for the siege, up to the very batteries.

Barcelona beseiged. In this manner was the siege begun; nor was it carried on with any less application; the approaches being made by an army of besiegers, that very little, if at all, exceeded the number of the besieged; not altogether in a regular manner, our few forces would not admit it; but yet with regularity enough to secure our two little camps, and preserve a communication between both, not to be interrupted or incommoded by the enemy. We had soon erected three several batteries against the place, all on the west side of the town, viz. one of nine guns, another of twelve, and the last of upwards of thirty. From all which we plied the town incessantly, and with all imaginable fury; and very often in whole vollies.

Nevertheless, it was thought not only advisable, but necessary, to erect another battery, upon a lower piece of ground, under a small hill; which, lying more within reach, and opposite to those places where the walls were imagined weakest, would annoy the town the more; and being designed for six guns only, might soon be perfected. A French engineer had the direction; and, indeed, very quickly perfected it. But, when it came to be considered which way to get the cannon to it, most were of opinion that it would be absolutely impracticable, by reason of the vast descent; though, I believe, they might have added a stronger reason, and perhaps more intrinsic, that it was extremely exposed to the fire of the enemy.

Having gained some little reputation in the attack of Monjouick, this difficulty was at last to be put upon me; and as some, not my enemies, supposed, more out of envy than good will. However, when I came to the place, and had carefully taken a view of it, though I was sensible enough of the difficulty, I made my main objection as to the time for accomplishing it; for it was then between nine and ten, and the guns were to be mounted by day-light. Neither could I at present see any other way to answer their expectations, than by casting the cannon down the precipice, at all hazards, to the place below, where that fourth battery was erected.

This wanted not objections to; and therefore, to answer my purpose, as to point of time, sixty men more were ordered me as much as possible to facilitate the work by numbers; and, accordingly, I set about it. Just as I was setting all hands to work, and had given orders to my men to begin some paces back, to make the descent more gradual, and thereby render the task a little more feasible, Major Collier, who commanded the train, came to me; and perceiving the difficulties of the undertaking, in a fret, told me, I was imposed upon; and vowed he would go and find out Brigadier Petit, and let him know the impossibility, as well as the unreasonableness, of the task I was put upon. He had scarce uttered those words, and turned himself round to perform his promise, when an unlucky shot with a musket ball wounded him through the shoulder; upon which he was carried off, and I saw him not till some considerable time after.

By the painful diligence, and the additional complement of men, however, I so well succeeded, (such was my great good fortune,) that the way was made, and the guns, by the help of fascines, and other lesser preparations below, safely let down and mounted ; so that that fourth battery began to play upon the town before break of day ; and with all the success that was proposed.

In short, the breach, in a very few days after, was found wholly practicable; and all things were got ready for a general storm.

<small>Governor of Barcelona beats a parley, and agrees to surrender in three days.</small> Which Don Valasco, the governor, being sensible of, immediately beat a parley; upon which it was, among other articles, concluded, that the town should be surrendered in three days; and the better to ensure it, the bastion, which commanded the Port St Angelo, was directly put into our possession.

But before the expiration of the limited three days, a very unexpected accident fell out, which hastened the surrender. Don Valasco, during his government, had behaved himself very arbitrarily, and thereby procured, as the consequence of it, a large proportion of ill will, not only among the townsmen, but among the Miquelets, who had, in their zeal to King Charles, flocked from all parts of Catalonia to the siege of their capital; and who, on the signing of the articles of surrender, had found various ways, being well acquainted with the most private avenues, to get by night into the town; so that early in the morning they began to plunder all that they knew enemies to King Charles, or thought friends to the Prince, his competitor.

Their main design was upon Valasco, the governor, whom, if they could have got into their hands, it was not to be questioned, but as far as his life and limbs would have served, they would have sufficiently satiated their vengeance upon. He expected no less; and therefore concealed himself, till the Earl of Peterborow could give orders for his more safe and private conveyance by sea to Alicant.

Nevertheless, in the town all was in the utmost confusion; which the Earl of Peterborow, at the very first hearing, hastened to appease; with his usual alacrity he rode all alone to Port St Angelo, where, at that time, myself happened to be; and demanding to be admitted, the officer of the guard, under fear and surprise, opened the wicket, through which the Earl entered, and I after him.

Scarce had we gone a hundred paces, when we saw a lady of apparent quality, and indisputable beauty, in a strange, but most affecting agony, flying from the apprehended fury of the Miquelets; her lovely hair was all flowing about her shoulders, which, and the consternation she was in, rather added to, than any thing diminished from the charms of an excess of beauty. She, as is very natural to people in distress, made up directly to the Earl, her eyes satisfying her he was a person likely to give her all the protection she wanted. And, as soon as ever she came near enough, in a manner that declared her quality before she spoke, she craved that protection, telling him, the better to secure it, who it was that asked it. But the generous Earl presently convinced her, he wanted no intreaties, having, before he knew her to be the Duchess of Popoli, taken her by the hand, in order to convey her through the wicket, which he entered at, to a place of safety without the town.

I staid behind, while the Earl conveyed the distressed Duchess to her requested asylum; and I believe it was much the longest part of an hour before he returned. But as soon as ever he came back, he, and myself, at his command, repaired to the place of most confusion, which the extraordinary noise full readily directed us to; and which happened to be on the parade before the palace. There it was that the Miquelets were making their utmost efforts to get into their hands the almost sole occasion of the tumult, and the object of their raging fury, the person of Don Valasco, the late governor.

It was here that the Earl preserved that governor from the violent, but perhaps too just resentments of the Miquelets; and, as I said before, conveyed him by sea to Alicant. And, indeed, I could little doubt the effect, or be any thing surprised at the easiness of the task, when I saw, that wherever he appeared, the popular fury was in a moment allayed, and that every dictate of that General was assented to with the utmost chearfulness and deference. Valasco, before his embarkment, had given orders, in gratitude to his preserver, for all the gates to be delivered up, though short of the stipulated term; and they were accordingly so delivered, and our troops took possession so soon as ever that governor was aboard the ship that was to convey him to Alicant.

During the siege of Barcelona, Brigadier Stanhope ordered a tent to be pitched as near the trenches as possibly could be with safety; where he not only entertained the chief officers who were upon duty, but likewise the Catalonian gentlemen, who brought Miquelets to our assistance. I remember I saw an old cavalier, having his only son with him, who appeared a fine young gentleman, about twenty years of age, go into the tent, in order to dine with the Brigadier. But whilst they were at dinner, an unfortunate shot came from the bastion of St Antonio, and entirely struck off the head of the son. The father immediately rose up, first looking down upon his headless child, and then lifting up his eyes to heaven, whilst the tears ran down his cheeks, he crossed himself, and only said, *Fiat voluntas tua !* and bore it with a wonderful patience. It was a sad spectacle, and truly it affects me now whilst I am writing.

The Earl of Peterborow, though for some time after the revolution he had been employed in civil affairs, returned to the military life with great satisfaction, which was ever his inclination. Brigadier Stanhope, who was justly afterwards created an earl, did well deserve this motto, " *Tam Marte quam Mercurio;*" for truly he behaved, all the time he continued in Spain, as if he had been inspired with conduct; for the victory at Almanar was entirely owing to him; and likewise at the battle of Saragosa he distinguished himself with great bravery. That he had not success at Bruhega was not his fault; for no man can resist fate; for it was decreed by heaven, that Philip should remain King of Spain, and Charles to be emperor of Germany. Yet each of these monarchs have been ungrateful to the instruments which the Almighty made use of to preserve them upon their thrones; for one had not been king of Spain but for France; and the other had not been emperor but for England.

Barcelona, the chief place in Catalonia, being thus in our hands, as soon as the garrison, little inferior to our army, had marched out with drums beating, colours flying, &c. according to the articles, Charles the Third made his public entry, and was proclaimed king, and received with the general acclamations, and all other demonstrations of joy suitable to that great occasion.

Some days after which, the citizens, far from being satiated with their former demonstrations of their duty, sent a petition to the king, by proper deputies for that purpose appointed, desiring leave to give more ample instances of their affections in a public cavalcade. The King granted their request, and the citizens, pursuant thereto, made their preparations. *Public rejoicings.*

On the day appointed, the king, placed in a balcony belonging to the house of the Earl of Peterborow, appeared ready to honour the show. The ceremonial, to speak nothing figuratively, was very fine and grand: Those of the first rank made their appearance in decent order, and upon fine horses; and others under arms, and in companies, marched with native gravity and grandeur, all saluting his Majesty as they passed by, after the Spanish manner, which that Prince returned with the movement of his hand to his mouth; for the kings of Spain are not allowed to salute, or return a salute, by any motion to, or of, the hat.

After these followed several pageants; the first of which was drawn by mules, set off to the height with stateliest feathers, and adorned with little bells. Upon the top of this pageant appeared a man dressed all in green, but in the likeness of a dragon. The pageant making a stop just over against the balcony where the king sat, the dragonical representative diverted him with great variety of dancings; the Earl of Peterborow all the time throwing out dollars by handfuls among the populace, which they as constantly received with the loud acclamation, and repeated cries of *Viva, Viva, Carlos Terceros! Viva la Casa d'Austria!*

When that had played its part, another pageant, drawn as before, made a like full stop before the same balcony. On this was placed a very large cage, or aviary, the cover of which, by springs contrived for that purpose, immediately flew open, and out of it a surprising flight of birds of various colours. These, all amazed at their sudden liberty, which I took to be the emblem intended, hovered a considerable space of time over and about their place of freedom, chirping, singing, and otherwise testifying their mighty joy for their so unexpected enlargement.

There were many other pageants; but having little in them very remarkable, I have forgot the particulars. Nevertheless, every one of them was dismissed with the like acclamations of *Viva, Viva*; the whole concluding with bonfires and illuminations, common on all such occasions.

I cannot here omit one very remarkable instance of the catholic zeal of that Prince, which I was soon after an eye-witness of. I was at that time in the fruit-market, when the King passing by in his coach, the host, (whether by accident, or contrivance, I cannot say,) was brought, at that very juncture, out of the great church, in order, as I after understood, to a poor sick woman's receiving the sacrament. On sight of the host, the King came out of his coach, kneeled down in the street, which at that time proved to be very dirty, till the host passed by; then rose up, and taking the lighted flambeau from him who bore it, he followed the priest up a strait nasty alley, and there up a dark ordinary pair of stairs, where the poor sick woman lay. There he staid till the whole ceremony was over, when, returning to the door of the church, he very faithfully restored the lighted flambeau to the fellow he had taken it from, the people all the while crying out, *Viva, Viva!* an acclamation, we may imagine, intended to his zeal, as well as his person.

Another remarkable accident, of a much more moral nature, I must, in justice to the temperance of that, in this truly inimitable people, recite. I was one day walking in one of the most populous streets of that city, where I found an uncommon concourse of people, of all sorts, got together; and imagining so great a crowd could not be assembled on a small occasion, I prest in among the rest; and, after a good deal of struggling and difficulty, reached into the ring and centre of that mixed multitude. But how did I blush, with what confusion did I appear, when I found one of my own countrymen, a drunken grenadier, the attractive loadstone of all the high and low mob, and the butt of all their merriment! It will be easily imagined to be a thing not a little surprising to one of our country, to find that a drunken man should be such a wonderful sight: However, the witty sarcasms that were then by high and low thrown upon that senseless creature, and, as I interpreted matters, me in him, were so pungent, that if I did not curse my curiosity, I thought it best to withdraw myself as fast as legs could carry me away.

Barcelona being now under King Charles, the towns of Gironne, Tarragona, Tortosa, and Lerida, immediately declared for him. To every one of which engineers being ordered, it was my lot to be sent to Tortosa.

This town is situated on the side of the river Ebro, over which there is a fair and famous bridge of boats. The waters of this river are always of a dirty red colour, somewhat fouler than our moorish waters; yet it is the only water the inhabitants drink, or covet to drink; and every house providing for its own convenience, cisterns to preserve it in, by a few hours standing it becomes as clear as the clearest rock water, but as soft as milk. In short, for softness, brightness, and pleasantness of taste, the natives prefer it to all the waters in the world. And I must declare in favour of their opinion, that none ever pleased me like it.

This town was of the greater moment to our army, as opening a passage into the kingdom of Valencia on one side, and the kingdom of Arragon on the other: And being of itself tolerably defensible, in human appearance might probably repay a little care and charge in its repair and improvement. Upon this employ was I appointed, and thus was I busied, till the arrival of the Earl of Peterborow with his little army, in order to march to Valencia, the capital of that province. Here he left in garrison Colonel Hans Hamilton's regiment; the place, nevertheless, was under the command of a Spanish governor, appointed by King Charles.

While the Earl staid a few days at this place, under expectation of the promised succours from Barcelona, he received a *proprio* (or express) from the king of Spain, full of excuses, instead of forces. And yet the very same letter, in a paradoxical manner, commanded him, at all events, to attempt the relief of Santo Mattheo, where Colonel Jones commanded, and which was then under siege by the Conde de los Torres, (as was the report,) with upwards of three thousand men. The Earl of Peterborow could not muster above one thousand foot, and about two hundred horse; a small force to make an attempt of that nature upon such a superior power: Yet the Earl's vivacity, (as will be occasionally further observed in the course of these Memoirs,) never much regarded numbers, so there was but room, by any stratagem, to hope for success. True it is, for his greater encouragement and consolation, the same letter intimated, that a great concourse of the country people being up in arms, to the number of many thousands, in favour of King Charles, and wanting only officers, the enterprize would be easy, and unattended with much danger. But, upon mature enquiry, the Earl found that great body of men all *in nubibus*; and that the Conde, in the plain truth of the matter, was much stronger than the letter at first represented.

Santo Mattheo was a place of known importance; and that from its situation, which cut off all communication between Catalonia and Valencia; and, consequently, should it fall into the hands of the enemy, the Earl's design upon the latter must inevitably have been postponed. It must be granted, the commands for attempting the relief of it were pressing and peremptory; nevertheless, the Earl was very conscious to himself, that as the promised reinforcements were suspended, his officers would not approve of the attempt upon the foot of such vast inequalities; and their own declared sentiments soon confirmed the dictates of the Earl's reason. He therefore addresses himself to those officers in a different manner: He told them, he only desired they would be passive, and leave it to him to work his own way. Accordingly, the Earl found out, and hired two Spanish spies, for whose fidelity, (as his great precaution always led him to do,) he took sufficient security; and dispatched them with a letter to Colonel Jones, governor of the place, intimating his readiness, as well as ability, to relieve him; and, above all, exhorting him to have the Miquelets in the town ready, on sight of his troops, to issue out, pursue, and plunder; since that would be all they would have to do, and all he would expect at their hands. The spies were dispatched accordingly; and, pursuant to instructions, one betrayed and discovered the other, who had the letter in charge to deliver to Colonel Jones. The Earl, to carry on the feint, having in the mean time, by dividing his troops, and marching secretly over the mountains, drawn his men together, so as to make their appearance on the height of a neighbouring mountain, little more than cannon-shot from the enemy's camp. The tale of the spies was fully confirmed, and the Conde, (though an able general,) marched off with some precipitation with his army; and by that means the Earl's smaller number of twelve hundred, had liberty to march into the town without interruption. I must not let slip an action of Colonel Jones's just before the Earl's delivery of them. The Conde, for want of artillery, had set his miners to work; and the Colonel, finding they had made some dangerous advances, turned the course of a rivulet, that ran through the middle of the town, in upon

Santo Mattheo relieved by the Earl of Peterborow.

them, and made them quit a work they thought was brought to perfection.

Santo Mattheo being relieved, as I have said, the Earl, though he had so far gained his ends, left not the flying enemy without a feint of pursuit; with such caution, nevertheless, that in case they should happen to be better informed of his weakness, he might have a resource either back again to Santo Mattheo, or to Vinaros on the seaside; or some other place, as occasion might require. But having just before received fresh advice, that the reinforcements he expected were anew countermanded; and that the Duke of Anjou had increased his troops to twelve thousand men; the officers, not enough elated with the last success to adventure upon new experiments, resolved, in a council of war, to advise the Earl, who had just before received a discretionary commission in lieu of troops, so to post the forces under him, as not to be cut off from being able to assist the king in person; or to march to the defence of Catalonia, in case of necessity.

Pursuant to this resolution of the council of war, the Earl of Peterborow, though still intent upon his expedition into Valencia, (which had been afresh commanded, even while his supplies were countermanded,) orders his foot, in a truly bad condition, by tedious marches day and night over the mountains, to Vinaros; and with his two hundred horse, set out to prosecute his pretended design of pursuing the flying enemy; resolved, if possible, notwithstanding all seemingly desperate circumstances, to perfect the security of that capital.

To that purpose, the Earl, with his small body of patrolers, went on frightening the enemy, till they came under the walls of Nules, a town fortified with the best walls, regular towers, and in the best repair of any in that kingdom. But even here, upon the appearance of the Earl's forlorn, (if they might not properly at that time all have passed under that character,) under the same panic they left that fencible town, with only one thousand of the town's people, well armed, for the defence of it. Yet was it scarce to be imagined, that the Earl, with his small body of two hundred horse, should be able to gain admission; or, indeed, under such circumstances, to attempt it. But, bold as the undertaking was, his good genius went along with him; and so good a genius was it, that it rarely left him without a good effect. He had been told the day before, that the enemy, on leaving Nules, had got possession of Villa Real, where they put all to the sword. What would have furnished another with terror, inspired his lordship with a thought as fortunate as it was successful. The Earl rides up to the very gates of the town, at the head of his party, and peremptorily demands the chief magistrate, or a priest, immediately to be sent out to him; and that under penalty of being all put to the sword, and used as the enemy had used those at Villa Real the day or two before. The troops, that had so lately left the place, had left behind them more terror than men; which, together with the peremptory demand of the Earl, soon produced some priests to wait upon the General. By their readiness to obey, the Earl very justly imagined fear to be the motive; wherefore, to improve their terror, he only allowed them six minutes time to resolve upon a surrender, telling them, that otherwise, so soon as his artillery was come up, he would lay them under the utmost extremities. The priests returned with this melancholy message into the place; and in a very short time after the gates were thrown open. Upon the Earl's entrance, he found two hundred horse, which were the original of his lordship's forming that body of horse, which afterwards proved the saving of Valencia.

Nules surrendered to the Earl of Peterborow.

The news of the taking of Nules soon overtook the flying enemy; and so increased the apprehensions of their danger, that they renewed their march the same day; though what they had taken before would have satisfied them much better without it. On the other hand, the Earl was so well pleased with his success, that, leaving the enemy to fly before their fears, he made a short turn towards Castillon de la Plana, a considerable, but open town, where his lordship furnished himself with four hundred horses more; and all this under the assurance that his troops were driving the enemy before them out of the kingdom. Hence he sent orders to Colonel Pierce's regiment at Vinaros to meet him at Oropesa, a place at no great distance; where, when they came, they were very pleasingly surprised at their being well mounted, and furnished with all accoutrements necessary. After which, leaving them cantoned in walled towns, where they could not be disturbed without artillery, that indefatigable General, leaving them full orders, went on his way towards Tortosa.

At Vinaros the Earl met with advice, that the Spanish militia of the kingdom of Valencia were assembled, and had already advanced a day's march at least into that country. Upon which, collecting, as fast as he could, the whole corps together, the Earl resolved to penetrate into Valencia directly; notwithstanding this whole collected body would amount to no more than six hundred horse and two thousand foot.

But there was a strong pass over a river, just under the walls of Molviedro, which must be first disputed and taken. This, Brigadier Mahoni, by the orders of the Duke of Arcos, who commanded the troops of the Duke of Anjou in the kingdom of Valencia, had taken care to secure. Molviedro, though not very strong, is a walled town, very populous of itself; and had in it, besides a garrison of eight hundred men, most of Mahoni's dragoons. It lies at the very bottom of a high hill; on the upper part whereof they show the ruins of the once famous Saguntum; famous sure to eternity, if letters shall last so long, for an inviolable fidelity to a negligent confederate, against an implacable enemy. Here yet appear the visible vestigia of awful antiquity, in half standing arches, and the yet unlevelled walls and towers of that once celebrated city. I could not but look upon all these with the eyes of despite, in regard to their enemy Hannibal ; with those of disdain, in respect to the uncommon and unaccountable supineness of its confederates, the Romans ; but with those of veneration, as to the memory of a glorious people, who, rather than stand reproached with a breach of faith, or the brand of cowardice, chose to sacrifice themselves, their wives, children, and all that was dear to them, in the flames of their expiring city.

In Molviedro, as I said before, Mahoni commanded, with eight hundred men, besides inhabitants; which, together with our having but little artillery, induced the officers, under the Earl of Peterborow, reasonably enough to imagine and declare, that there could be no visible appearance of surmounting such difficulties. The Earl, nevertheless, instead of indulging such despondencies, gave them hope, that what strength served not to accomplish, art might possibly obtain. To that purpose, he proposed an interview between himself and Mahoni; and accordingly sent an officer with a trumpet to intimate his desire. The motion was agreed to; and the Earl having previously stationed his troops to advantage, and his little artillery at a convenient distance, with orders they should appear on a slow march on the side of a rising hill, during the time of conference, went to the place appointed; only, as had been stipulated, attended with a small party of horse. When they were met, the Earl first offered all he could to engage Mahoni to the interest of King Charles; proposing some things extravagant enough, (as Mahoni himself some time after told me,) to stagger the faith of a catholic; but all to little purpose; Mahoni was inflexible, which obliged the Earl to new measures.

Whereupon the Earl frankly told him,

that he could not, however, but esteem the confidence he had put in him; and therefore, to make some retaliation, he was ready to put it in his power to avoid the barbarities lately executed at Villa Real. " My relation to you," continued the General, " inclines me to spare a town under your command. You see how near my forces are; and can hardly doubt our soon being masters of the place: What I would therefore offer you," said the Earl, "is a capitulation, that my inclination may be held in countenance by my honour. Barbarities, however justified by example, are my utter aversion, and against my nature; and to testify so much, together with my good will to your person, was the main intent of this interview."

This frankness so far prevailed on Mahoni, that he agreed to return an answer in half an hour. Accordingly, an answer was returned by a Spanish officer, and a capitulation agreed upon; the Earl at the same time endeavouring to bring over that officer to King Charles, on much the same topics he used with Mahoni. But finding this equally fruitless, whether it was that he tacitly reproached the officer with a want of consideration in neglecting to follow the example of his commander, or what else, he created in that officer such a jealousy of Mahoni, that was afterward very serviceable to him in his further design.

To forward which to a good issue, the Earl immediately made choice of two dragoons, who, upon promise of promotion, undertook to go as spies to the Duke of Arcos, whose forces lay not far off, on the other side a large plain, which the Earl must unavoidably pass, and which would inevitably be attended with almost insuperable dangers, if there attacked by a force so much superior. Those spies, according to instructions, were to discover to the Duke, that they overheard the conference between the Earl and Mahoni; and at the same time saw a considerable number of pistoles delivered into Mahoni's hands, large promises passing at that instant reciprocally : but above all, that the Earl had recommended to him the procuring the march of the Duke over the plain between them. The spies went and delivered all according to concert; concluding, before the Duke, that they would ask no reward, but undergo any punishment, if Mahoni did not very soon send to the Duke a request to march over the plain, in order to put the concerted plot in execution. It was not long after this pretended discovery, before Mahoni did send indeed an officer to the Duke, desiring the march of his forces over the plain ; but, in reality, to obstruct the Earl's passage, which he knew very well must be that and no other way. However, the Duke being prepossessed by the spies, and what those Spanish officers that at first escaped had before infused, took things in their sense ; and as soon as Mahoni, who was forced to make the best of his way over the plain before the Earl of Peterborow, arrived at his camp, he was

178   MEMOIRS OF

put under arrest, and sent to Madrid. The Duke having thus imbibed the venom, and taken the alarm, immediately decamped in confusion, and took a different route than at first he intended; leaving that once formidable plain open to the Earl, without an enemy to obstruct him. In some little time after he arrived at Madrid, Mahoni made his innocence appear, and was created a general; while the Duke of Arcos was recalled from his post of honour.

The Earl's entry into the city of Valencia.

The day after, we arrived at Valencia; the gates of which fine city were set open to us with the highest demonstrations of joy. I called it a fine city; but sure it richly deserves a brighter epithet; since it is a common saying among the Spaniards, that " the pleasures of Valencia would make a Jew forget Jerusalem." It is most sweetly situated in a very beautiful plain, and within half a league of the Mediterranean sea. It never wants any of the fragrancies of nature, and always has something to delight the most curious eye. It is famous to a proverb for fine women ; but as infamous, and only in that so, for the race of bravoes, the common companions of the ladies of pleasure in this country. These wretches are so case-hardened, they will commit a murder for a dollar, though they run their country for it when they have done. Not that other parts of this nation are uninfested with this sort of animals; but here their numbers are so great, that if a catalogue was to be taken of those in other parts of that country, perhaps nine in ten would be found by birth to be of this province.

But to proceed: though the citizens, and all sorts of people, were redundant in their various expressions of joy, for an entry so surprising, and utterly lost to their expectation, whatever it was to their wishes, the Earl had a secret concern for the public, which lay gnawing at his heart, and which yet he was forced to conceal. He knew, that he had not four thousand soldiers in the place, and not powder or ammunition for those; nor any provisions laid in for any thing like a siege. On the other hand, the enemy without were upwards of seven thousand, with a body of four thousand more, not fifteen leagues off, on their march to join them. Add to this, the Mareschal de Thesse was no farther off than Madrid, a very few days march from Valencia; a short way indeed for the Earl, (who, as was said before, was wholly unprovided for a siege, which was reported to be the sole end of the Mareschal's moving that way.) But the Earl's never-failing genius resolved again to attempt that by art, which the strength of his forces utterly disallowed him. And in the first place, his intelligence telling him that sixteen twenty-four pounders, with stores and ammunition answerable for a siege, were shipped off for the enemy's service at Alicant, the Earl forthwith lays a design, and with his usual success intercepts them all, supplying that way his own necessities at the expence of the enemy.

The four thousand men ready to reinforce the troops nearer Valencia, were the next point to be undertaken; but *hic labor, hoc opus;* since the greater body under the Conde de las Torres, (who, with Mahoni, was now reinstated in his post,) lay between the Earl and those troops intended to be dispersed. And what enhanced the difficulty, the river Xucar must be passed in almost the face of the enemy. Great disadvantages as these were, they did not discourage the Earl. He detached by night four hundred horse and eight hundred foot, who marched with such hasty silence, that they surprised that great body, routed them, and brought into Valencia, six hundred prisoners very safely, notwithstanding they were obliged, under the same night-covert, to pass very near a body of three thousand of the enemy's horse. Such a prodigious victory would hardly have gained credit in that city, if the prisoners brought in had not been living witnesses of the action, as well as the triumph. The Conde

A small party of the Earl's routs a body of four thousand.

de las Torres, upon these two military rebuffs, drew off to a more convenient distance, and left the Earl a little more at ease in his new quarters.

Here the Earl of Peterborow made his residence for some time. He was extremely well beloved; his affable behaviour exacted as much from all; and he preserved such a good correspondence with the priests and the ladies, that he never failed of the most early and best intelligence; a thing by no means to be slighted in the common course of life; but much more commendable and necessary in a General, with so small an army, at open war, and in the heart of his enemy's country.

The Earl, by this means, some small time after, receiving early intelligence that King Philip was actually on his march to Barcelona, with an army of upwards of twenty-five thousand men, under the command of a Mareschal of France, began his march towards Catalonia, with all the troops that he could gather together, leaving in Valencia a small body of foot, such as in that exigence could best be spared. The whole body thus collected made very little more than two thousand foot and six hundred horse; yet resolutely with these he sets out for Barcelona : In the neighbourhood of which, as soon as he arrived, he took care to post himself and his diminutive army in the mountains which environ that city; where he not only secured them against the enemy, but found himself in a capacity of putting himself under perpetual alarms. Nor was the Mareschal, with his great army, capable of returning the Earl's compliment of disturbance; since he himself, every six or eight hours, put his troops into such a varying situation, that always when most arduously sought, he was farthest off from being found. In this manner the General bitterly harassed the troops of the enemy; and by these means struck a perpetual terror into the besiegers. Nor did he only this way annoy the enemy; the precautions he had used, and the measures he had taken in other places, with a view to prevent their return to Madrid, though the invidious endeavoured to bury them in oblivion, having equally contributed to the driving of the Mareschal of France, and his catholic king, out of the Spanish dominions.

But to go on with the siege: the breaches in the walls of that city, during its siege by the Earl, had been put into tolerable repair; but those of Monjouick, on the contrary, had been as much neglected. However, the garrison made shift to hold out a battery of twenty-three days, with no less than fifty pieces of cannon; when, after a loss of the enemy of upwards of three thousand men, (a moiety of the army employed against it when the Earl took it,) they were forced to surrender at discretion. And this cannot but merit our observation, that a place which the English general took in little more than an hour, and with very inconsiderable loss, afforded the Mareschal

Monjouick taken by the Mareschal of France.

of France a resistance of twenty-three days.

Upon the taking of Fort Monjouick, the Mareschal de Thess gave immediate orders for batteries to be raised against the town. Those orders were put in execution with all expedition; and at the same time his army fortified themselves with such entrenchments, as would have ruined the Earl's former little army to have raised, or his present much lesser army to have attempted the forcing them. However, they sufficiently demonstrated their apprehensions of that watchful General, who lay hovering over their heads upon the mountains. Their main effort was to make a breach between Port St Antonio and that breach which our forces had made the year before; to effect which, they took care to ply them very diligently both from cannon and mortars; and in some few days their application was answered with a practicable breach for a storm. Which, however, was prudently deferred for some time, and that

Barcelona besieged.

through fear of the Earl's falling on the back of them whenever they should attempt it; which, consequently, they were sensible, might put them into some dangerous disorder.

And now it was that the Earl of Peterborow resolved to put in practice the resolution he had some time before concerted within himself. About nine or ten days before the raising of the siege, he had received an express from Brigadier Stanhope, (who was aboard Sir John Leake's fleet appointed for the relief of the place, with the reinforcements from England,) acquainting the Earl, that he had used all possible endeavours to prevail on the Admiral to make the best of his way to Barcelona; but that the Admiral, however, persisted in a positive resolution not to attempt the French fleet before that place under the Count de Tholouse, till the ships were joined him which were expected from Ireland, under the command of Sir George Bing. True it was, the fleet under Admiral Leake was of equal strength with that under the French admiral; but, jealous of the informations he had received, and too ready to conclude that people in distress were apt to make representations too much in their own favour; he held himself, in point of discretion, obliged not to hazard the queen's ships, when a reinforcement of both cleaner and larger were under daily expectation.

This unhappy circumstance, (notwithstanding all former glorious deliverances,) had almost brought the Earl to the brink of despair; and to increase it, the Earl every day received such commands from the King within the place, as must have sacrificed his few forces, without the least probability of succeeding. Those all tended to his forcing his way into the town; when, in all human appearance, not one man of all that should make the attempt could have done it, with any hope or prospect of surviving. The French were strongly encamped at the foot of the mountains, distant two miles from Barcelona: towards the bottom of those hills, the avenues into the plain were possessed and fortified by great detachments from the enemy's army. From all which it will be evident, that no attempt could be made without giving the enemy time to draw together what body of foot they pleased. Or, supposing it feasible, under all these difficult circumstances, for some of them to have forced their passage, the remainder, that should have been so lucky to have escaped their foot, would have found themselves exposed in open field to a pursuit of four thousand horse and dragoons; and that for two miles together; when, in case of their inclosing them, the bravest troops in the world, under such a situation, would have found it their best way to have surrendered themselves prisoners of war.

Nevertheless, when Brigadier Stanhope sent that express to the Earl, which I just now mentioned, he assured him in the same, that he would use his utmost diligence, both by sea and land, to let him have timely notice of the conjunction of the fleets, which was now all they had to depend upon. Adding withal, that if the Earl should at any time receive a letter, or paper, though directed to nobody, and with nothing in it, but a half sheet of paper, cut in the middle, he, the Earl, might certainly depend upon it, that the two fleets were joined, and making the best of their way for Barcelona. It will easily be imagined, the express was to be well paid ; and being made sensible that he ran little or no hazard in carrying a piece of blank paper, he undertook it, and as fortunately arrived with it to the Earl, at a moment when chagrin and despair might have hurried him to some resolution that might have proved fatal. The messenger himself, however, knew nothing of the joining of the fleets, or the meaning of his message.

As soon as the Earl of Peterborow received this welcome message from Brigadier Stanhope, he marched the very same night, with his whole little body of forces, to a town on the sea-shore, called Sigeth. No person guessed the reason of his march, or knew any thing of what the intent of it was. The officers, as formerly, obeyed without enquiry; for they were led to it by so many unaccountable varieties of success, that affiance became a second nature, both in officer and soldier.

The town of Sigeth was about seven leagues to the westward of Barcelona; where, as soon as the Earl with his forces arrived, he took care to secure all the small fishing-boats, feluccas, and sattées; nay, in a word, every machine in which he could transport any of his men; so that in two days time he had got together a number sufficient for the conveyance of all his foot.

But a day or two before the arrival of the English fleet off Sigeth, the officers of his troops were under a strange consternation at a resolution their General had taken. Impatient of delay, and fearful of the fleets passing by without his knowledge, the Earl summoned them together a little before night, at which time he discovered to the whole assembly, that he himself was obliged to endeavour to get aboard the English fleet; and that, if possible, before the French scouts should be able to make any discovery of their strength: that, finding himself of no further use on shore, having already taken the necessary precautions for their transportation and security, they had nothing to do but to pursue his orders, and make the best of their way to Barcelona, in the vessels which he had provided for them: that they might do this in perfect security when they saw the English fleet pass by; or if they should pass by in the night, an engagement with the French, which would be an inevitable consequence, would give them sufficient notice what they had to do further.

This declaration, instead of satisfying, made the officers ten times more curious: But when they saw their General going, with a resolution to lie out all night at sea, in an open boat, attended with only one officer; and understood that he intended to row out in his felucca five or six leagues distance from the shore; it is hardly to be expressed what amazement and concern surprised them all. Mr Crow, the Queen's minister, and others, expressed a particular dislike and uneasiness; but all to no purpose, the Earl had resolved upon it. Accordingly, at night he put out to sea in his open felucca, all which he spent five leagues from shore, with no other company than one captain and his rowers.

In the morning, to the great satisfaction of all, officers and others, the Earl came again to land; and immediately began to put his men into the several vessels which lay ready in port for that purpose. But at night their amaze was renewed, when they found their General ready to put in execution his old resolution, in the same equipage, and with the same attendance. Accordingly, he again felucca'd himself; and they saw him no more till they were landed on the Mole in Barcelona.

When the Earl of Peterborow first engaged himself in the expedition to Spain, he proposed to the Queen and her ministry, that Admiral Shovel might be joined in commission with him in the command of the fleet. But this year, when the fleet came through the Straits, under Vice-Admiral Leake, the Queen had sent a commission to the Earl of Peterborow for the full command, whenever he thought fit to come aboard in person. This it was that made the General endeavour, at all hazards, to get aboard the fleet by night; for he was apprehensive, and the sequel proved his apprehensions too well grounded, that Admiral Leake would make his appearance with the whole body of the fleet, which made near twice the number of the ships of the enemy; in which case it was natural to suppose, that the Count de Tholouse, as soon as ever the French scouts should give notice of our strength, would cut his cables, and put out to sea, to avoid an engagement. On the other hand, the Earl was very sensible, that if a part of his ships had kept astern, that the superiority might have appeared on the French side; or rather if they had bore away in the night, towards the coast of Africa, and fallen to the eastward of Barcelona the next day, a battle had been inevitable, and a victory equally certain ; since the enemy, by this means, had been tempted into an engagement, and their retreat being cut off, and their whole fleet surrounded with almost double their number, there had hardly been left for any of them a probability of escaping.

Therefore, when the Earl of Peterborow put to sea again the second evening, fearful of losing such a glorious opportunity, and impatient to be aboard to give the necessary orders, he ordered his rowers to obtain the same station, in order to discover the English fleet. And according to his wishes he did fall in with it; but unfortunately the night was so far advanced, that it was impossible for him then to put his project into practice. Captain Price, a gentleman of Wales, who commanded a third rate, was the person he first came aboard of; but how amazed was he to find, in an open boat, at open sea, the person who had commission to command the fleet! So soon as he was entered the ship, the Earl sent the ship's pinnace with letters to Admiral Leake, to acquaint him with his orders and intentions; and to Brigadier Stanhope, with a notification of his safe arrival; but the darkness of the night proved so great an obstacle, that it was a long time before the pinnace could reach the Admiral. When day appeared, it was astonishing to the whole fleet, to see the union flag waving at the main-top-mast head. No body could trust his own eyes, or guess at the meaning, till better certified by the account of an event so singular and extraordinary.

When we were about six leagues distance

Earl of Peterborow arrives on board the English fleet.

from Barcelona, the port we aimed at, one of the French scouts gave the alarm, who making the signal to another, he communicated it to a third, and so on, as we afterward sorrowfully found, and as the Earl had before apprehended. The French Admiral being thus made acquainted with the force of our fleet, hoisted sail, and made the best of his way from us, either pursuant to orders, or under the plausible excuse of a retreat.

This favourable opportunity thus lost, there remained nothing to do but to land the troops with all expedition; which was executed accordingly: The regiments, which the Earl of Peterborrow embarked the night before, being the first that got into the town. Let the reader imagine how pleasing such a sight must be to those in Barcelona, reduced as they were to the last extremity. In this condition, to see an enemy's fleet give way to another with reinforcements from England, the sea at the same instant covered with little vessels crowded with greater succours; what was there wanting to complete the glorious scene, but what the General had projected, a fight at sea, under the very walls of the invested city, and the ships of the enemy sinking, or towed in by the victorious English! But night, and a few hours, defeated the latter part of that well-intended landscape.

King Philip, and the Mareschal of France, had not failed to push on the siege with all imaginable vigour; but this retreat of the Count de Tholouse, and the news of those reinforcements, soon changed the scene. Their courage without was abated proportionably, as theirs within was elated. In these circumstances, a council of war being called, it was unanimously resolved to raise the siege. Accordingly, next morning, the first of May, 1706, while the sun was under a total eclipse, in a suitable hurry and confusion, they broke up, leaving behind them most of their cannon and mortars, together with vast quantities of all sorts of ammunition and provisions, scarce stopping to look back till they had left all but the very verge of the disputed dominion behind them.

King Charles looked with new pleasure upon this lucky effort of his old deliverers. Captivity is a state no way desirable to persons however brave, of the most private station in life; but for a king, within two days of falling into the hands of his rival, to receive so seasonable and unexpected a deliverance, must be supposed, as it really did, to open a scene to universal rejoicing among us, too high for any words to express, or any thoughts to imagine, to those that were not present, and partakers of it. He forthwith gave orders for a medal to be struck suitable to the occasion; one of which, set round with diamonds, he presented to Sir John Leake, the English Admiral. The next orders were for re-casting all the damaged brass cannon which the enemy had left; upon every one of which was, by order, a sun eclipsed, with this motto under it: "*Magna parvis obscurantur.*"

I have often wondered that I never heard any body curious enough to enquire what could be the motives to the King of Spain's quitting his dominions upon the raising of this siege; very certain it is, that he had a fine army, under the command of a Mareschal of France, not very considerably decreased, either by action or desertion: but all this would rather increase the curiosity, than abate it. In my opinion, then, though men might have curiosity enough, the question was purposely evaded, under an apprehension, that an honest answer must inevitably give a higher idea of the General, than their inclinations led them to. At first view, this may carry the face of a paradox; yet, if the reader will consider, that in every age virtue has had its shaders or maligners, he will himself easily solve it, at the same time that he finds himself compelled to allow, that those who found themselves unable to prevent his great services, were willing, in a more subtile manner, to endeavour at the annulling of them by silence and concealment.

This will appear more than bare supposition, if we compare the present situation, as to strength, of the two contending powers: The French, at the birth of the siege, consisted of five thousand horse and dragoons, and twenty-five thousand foot, effective men. Now, grant that their killed and wounded, together with their sick in the hospitals, might amount to five thousand, yet as their body of horse was entire, and in the best condition, the remaining will appear to be an army of twenty-five thousand at least. On the other side, all the forces in Barcelona, even with their reinforcements, amounted to no more than seven thousand foot, and four hundred horse. Why then, when they raised their siege, did not they march back into the heart of Spain, with their so much superior army? or, at least, towards their capital? The answer can be this, and this only; because the Earl of

Peterborow had taken such provident care to render all secure, that it was thereby rendered next to an impossibility for them so to do. That General was satisfied, that the capital of Catalonia must, in course, fall into the hands of the enemy, unless a superior fleet removed the Count de Tholouse, and threw in timely succours into the town: And as that could not depend upon him, but others, he made it his chief care and assiduous employment to provide against those strokes of fortune to which he found himself again likely to be exposed, as he often had been; and, therefore, had he recourse to that vigilance and precaution which had often retrieved him, when to others his circumstances seemed to be most desperate.

The generality of mankind, and the French in particular, were of opinion, that the taking Barcelona would prove a decisive stroke, and put a period to the war in Spain; and yet at that very instant, I was inclined to believe, that the General flattered himself it would be in his power to give the enemy sufficient mortification, even though the town should be obliged to submit to King Philip. The wise measures taken induced me so to believe, and the sequel approved it; for the Earl had so well expended his caution, that the enemy, on the disappointment, found himself under a necessity of quitting Spain; and the same would have put him under equal difficulties, had he carried the place. The French could never have undertaken that siege without depending on their fleet, for their artillery, ammunition, and provisions; since they must be inevitably forced to leave behind them the strong towns of Tortosa, Lerida, and Taragona. The Earl, therefore, whose perpetual difficulties seemed rather to render him more sprightly and vigorous, took care himself to examine the whole country between the Ebro and Barcelona; and, upon his doing so, was pleasingly, as well as sensibly, satisfied, that it was practicable to render their return into the heart of Spain impossible, whether they did or did not succeed in the siege they were so intent to undertake.

There were but three ways they could attempt it : The first of which was by the sea-side, from Taragona towards Tortosa ; the most barren, and consequently the most improper, country in the universe to sustain an army ; and yet to the natural, the Earl had added such artificial difficulties, as rendered it absolutely impossible for an army to subsist, or march that way.

The middle way lay through a better country indeed, yet only practicable by the care which had been taken to make the road so. And even here, there was a necessity of marching along the side of a mountain, where, by vast labour and industry, a high way had been cut for two miles, at least, out of the main rock. The Earl, therefore, by somewhat of the same labour, soon made it impassable. He employed to that end many thousands of the country people, under a few of his own officers and troops, who, cutting up twenty several places, made so many precipices, perpendicular almost as a wall, which rendered it neither safe, or even to be attempted by any single man in his wits, much less by an army. Besides, a very few men, from the higher cliffs of the mountain, might have destroyed an army with the arms of nature only, by rolling down large stones, and pieces of the rock, upon the enemy passing below.

The last and uppermost way, lay through the hilly part of Catalonia, and led to Lerida, towards the head of the Ebro, the strongest place we had in all Spain, and which was as well furnished with a very good garrison. Along this road there lay many old castles and little towns in the mountains, naturally strong; all which would not only have afforded opposition, but at the same time have entertained an enemy with variety of difficulties; and especially as the Earl had given orders, and taken care that all cattle, and every thing necessary to sustain an army, should be conveyed into places of security, either in the mountains, or thereabouts. These three ways thus precautiously secured, what had the Earl to apprehend but the safety of the Archduke; which yet was through no default of his, if in any danger from the siege?

For I well remember, on receipt of an express from the Duke of Savoy, (as he frequently sent such to enquire after the proceedings in Spain,) I was shewed a letter, wrote about this time by the Earl of Peterborow to that Prince, which raised my spirits, though then at a very low ebb. It was too remarkable to be forgot; and the substance of it was, that his highness might depend upon it, that he (the Earl) was in much better circumstances than he was thought to be: That the French officers knowing nothing of the situation of the country, would find themselves extremely disappointed, since, in case the siege was raised, their army should be obliged to abandon Spain: Or, in case the town was taken, they should find themselves shut up in that corner of Catalonia, and under an impossibility of forcing their way back, either through Arragon or Valencia: That by this means, all Spain, to the Ebro, would be open to the Lord Galoway, who might march to Madrid, or any where else, without opposition. That he had no other uneasiness or concern upon him, but for the person of the Archduke, whom he had nevertheless earnestly solicited not to remain in the town on the very first appearance of the intended siege.

Barcelona being thus relieved, and King Philip forced out of Spain, by these cautious steps taken by the Earl of Peterborow, before we bring him to Valencia, it will be necessary to intimate, that, as it always was the custom of that General to settle, by a council of war, all the measures to be taken, whenever he was obliged for the service to leave the Archduke; a council of war was now accordingly held, where all the general officers, and those in greatest employments at court, assisted. Here every thing was in the most solemn manner concerted and resolved upon; here garrisons were settled for all the strong places, and governors appointed: but the main article then agreed upon was, that King Charles should immediately begin his journey to Madrid, and that by the way of Valencia. The reason assigned for it was, because that kingdom being in his possession, no difficulties could arise which might occasion delay, if his Majesty took that route. It was likewise agreed in the same council, that the Earl of Peterborow should embark all the foot, not in garrisons, for their more speedy, as well as more easy conveyance to Valencia. The same council of war agreed, that all the horse in that kingdom should be drawn together; the better to insure the measures to be taken for the opening and facilitating his Majesty's progress to Madrid.

Accordingly, after these resolutions were taken, the Earl of Peterborow embarks his forces, and sails for Valencia, where he was doubly welcomed by all sorts of people, upon account of his safe arrival, and the news he brought along with it. By the joy they expressed, one would have imagined that the General had escaped the same danger with the King; and, in truth, had their King arrived with him in person, the most loyal and zealous would have found themselves at a loss how to have expressed their satisfaction in a more sensible manner.

Soon after his landing, with his customary vivacity, he applied himself to put in execution the resolutions taken in the councils of war at Barcelona; and, a little to improve upon them, he raised an entire regiment of dragoons, bought them horses, provided them clothes, arms, and accoutrements; and in six weeks time had them ready to take the field; a thing, though hardly to be paralleled, is yet scarce worthy to be mentioned among so many nobler actions of his; yet, in regard to another General, it may merit notice, since, while he had Madrid in possession near four months, he neither augmented his troops, nor laid up any magazines; neither sent he all that time any one express to concert any measures with the Earl of Peterborow; but lay under a perfect inactivity, or which was worse, negotiating that unfortunate project of carrying King Charles to Madrid, by the round about and ill-concerted way of Arragon; a project not only contrary to the solemn resolutions of the council of war, but which, in reality, was the root of all our succeeding misfortunes; and that only for the wretched vanity of appearing to have had some share in bringing the King to his capital; but how minute a share it was, will be manifest, if it be considered that another General had first made the way easy, by driving the enemy out of Spain; and that the French General only staid at Madrid till the return of those troops, which were, in a manner, driven out of Spain.

And yet that transaction, doughty as it was, took up four most precious months, which most certainly might have been much better employed in rendering it impossible for the enemy to re-enter Spain; nor had there been any great difficulty in so doing, but the contrary, if the General at Madrid had thought convenient to have joined the troops under the Earl of Peterborow, and then to have marched directly towards Pampelona, or the frontiers of France. To this the Earl of Peterborow solicited the King, and those about him; he advised, desired, and intreated him to lose no time, but to put in execution those measures resolved on at Barcelona. A council of war in Valencia renewed the same application; but all to no purpose, his route was ordered him, and that to meet his Majesty on the frontiers of Arragon. There, indeed, the Earl did meet the King; and the French General an army, which, by virtue of a decrepid intelligence, he never saw or heard of till he fled from it to his camp at Guadalira. Inexpressible was the confusion in this fatal camp: The King from Arragon, the Earl of Peterborow from Valencia, arriving in it the same day, almost the same hour, that the Earl of Galway entered, under a hasty retreat before the French army.

But to return to order, which a zeal of justice has made me somewhat anticipate; the Earl had not been long at Valencia before he gave orders to Major-General Windham, to march with all the forces he had, which were not above two thousand men, and lay siege to Requina, a town ten leagues distant from Valencia, and in the way to Madrid. The town was not very strong, nor very large; but sure the oddliest fortified that ever was. The houses in a circle connectively composed the wall; and the people, who defended the town, instead of firing from hornworks, counter-

Requina besieged.

scarps, and bastions, fired out of the windows of their houses.

Notwithstanding all which, General Windham found much greater opposition than he at first imagined; and therefore, finding he should want ammunition, he sent to the Earl of Peterborow for a supply; at the same time assigning, as a reason for it, the unexpected obstinacy of the town. So soon as the Earl received the letter, he sent for me; and told me I must repair to Requina, where they would want an engineer; and that I must be ready next morning, when he should order a lieutenant, with thirty soldiers, and two matrosses, to guard some powder for that service. Accordingly, the next morning, we set out, the lieutenant, who was a Dutchman, and commander of the convoy, being of my acquaintance.

We had reached Saint Jago, a small village about midway between Valencia and Requina, when the officer, just as he was got without the town, resolving to take up his quarters on the spot, ordered the mules to be unloaded. The powder, which consisted of forty-five barrels, was piled up in a circle, and covered with oil-cloth to preserve it from the weather; and though we had agreed to sup together at my quarters within the village, yet, being weary and fatigued, he ordered his field-bed to be put up near the powder, and so lay down to take a short nap. I had scarce been at my quarters an hour, when a sudden shock attacked the house so violently, that it threw down tiles, windows, chimneys, and all. It presently came into my head what was the occasion; and, as my fears suggested, so it proved: For, running to the door, I saw a cloud ascending from the spot I left the powder pitched upon. In haste making up to which, nothing was to be seen but the bare circle upon which it had stood. The bed was blown quite away, and the poor lieutenant all to pieces, several of his limbs being found separate, and at a vast distance each from the other; and particu-

Forty-five barrels of powder blown up by an accident.

larly an arm, with a ring on one of the fingers. The matrosses were, if possible, in a yet worse condition, that is, as to manglement and laceration. All the soldiers who were standing, and any thing near, were struck dead. Only such as lay sleeping on the ground escaped; and of those one assured me, that the blast removed him several feet from his place of repose. In short, enquiring into this deplorable disaster, I had this account: That a pig running out of the town, the soldiers endeavoured to intercept its return; but driving it upon the matrosses, one of them, who was jealous of its getting back into the hands of the soldiers, drew his pistol to shoot it, which was the source of this miserable catastrophe. The lieutenant carried along with him a bag of dollars to pay the soldiers' quarters; of which the people, and the soldiers that were saved, found many, but blown to an inconceivable distance.

With those few soldiers that remained alive, I proceeded, according to my orders, to Requina; where, when I arrived, I gave General Windham an account of the disaster at St Jago. As such it troubled him, and not a little on account of the disappointment. However, to make the best of a bad market, he gave orders for the forming of a mine, under an old castle, which was part of the wall. As it was ordered, so it was begun, more *in terrorem*, than with any expectation of success from it as a mine. Nevertheless, I had scarce began to frame the oven of the mine, when those within the town desired to capitulate. This being all we could aim at, under the miscarriage of our powder at St Jago, (none being yet arrived to supply that defect,) articles were readily granted them; pursuant to which, that part of the garrison, which was composed of Castilian gentry, had liberty to go wherever they thought best, and the rest were made prisoners of war. Requina being thus reduced to the obedience of Charles III. a new raised regiment of Spaniards was left in garrison, the

Requina surrenders.

colonel of which was appointed governor; and our supply of powder having at last got safe to us, General Windham marched his little army to Cuenca.

<small>Cuenca besieged.</small> Cuenca is a considerable city, and a bishopric; therefore, to pretend to sit down before it with such a company of foragers, rather than an army, must be placed among the hardy influences of the Earl of Peterborow's auspicious administration. On the out part of Cuenca there stood an old castle, from which, upon our approach, they played upon us furiously: But as soon as we could bring two pieces of our cannon to bear, we answered their fire with so good success, that we soon obliged them to retire into the town. We had raised a battery of twelve guns against the city, on their rejection of the summons sent them to come under the obedience of King Charles; going to which, from the old castle last reduced, I received a shot on the toe of one of my shoes, which carried that

part of the shoe entirely away, without any further damage.

When I came to that battery, we plied them warmly, (as well as from three mortars,) for the space of three days, their nights included; but observing, that in one particular house, they were remarkably busy, people thronging in and out below, and those above firing perpetually out of the windows, I was resolved to have one shot at that window, and made those officers about me take notice of it. True it was, the distance would hardly allow me to hope for success; yet, as the experiment could only be attended with the expence of a single ball, I made it. So soon as the smoke of my own cannon would permit it, we could see clouds of dust issuing from out of the window, which, together with the people's crowding out of doors, convinced the officers, whom I had desired to take notice of it, that I had been no bad marksman.

Upon this, two priests were sent out of

the place with proposals ; but they were so triflingly extravagant, that as soon as ever the General heard them, he ordered their answer in a fresh renewal of the fire of both cannon and mortars. And it happened to be with so much havoc and execution, that they were soon taught reason: and sent back their divines, with much more moderate demands. After the General had a little modelled these last, they were accepted ; and according to the articles of capitulation, the city was that very day surrendered into our possession. The Earl of Duncannon's regiment took guard of all the gates; and King Charles was proclaimed in due form.

Cuenca surrenders.

The Earl of Peterborow, during this expedition, had left Valencia, and was arrived at my Lord Galway's camp at Guadalaxara; who, for the confederates, and King Charles in particular, unfortunately was ordered from Portugal, to take the command from a General, who had all along been almost miraculously successful, and by his own great actions paved the way for a safe passage to that his supplanter.

Yet, even in this fatal place, the Earl of Peterborow made some proposals, which, had they been embraced, might, in all probability, have secured Madrid from falling into the hands of the enemy: But, in opposition thereto, the Lord Galway, and all his Portuguese officers, were for forcing the next day the enemy to battle. The almost only person against it was the Earl of Peterborow; who then and there took the liberty to evince the impossibility of coming to an engagement. This the next morning too evidently made apparent, when, upon the first motion of our troops towards the river, which they pretended to pass, and must pass, before they could engage, they were so warmly saluted from the batteries of the enemy, and their small shot, that our regiments were forced to retire in confusion to their camp. By which rebuff, all heroical imaginations were at present laid aside, to consider how they might make their retreat to Valencia.

The retreat being at last resolved on, and a multiplicity of generals rendering our bad circumstances much worse, the Earl of Peterborow met with a fortunate reprieve, by solicitations from the queen, and desires tantamount to orders, that he would go with the troops left in Catalonia, to the relief of the Duke of Savoy. It is hardly to be doubted that that General was glad to withdraw from those scenes of confusion, which were but too visible to eyes even less discerning than his. However, he forbore to prepare himself to put her majesty's desires in execution, as they were not peremptory, till it had been resolved by the unanimous consent of a council of war, where the king, all the generals, and ministers, were present, that it was expedient for the service that the Earl of Peterborow, during the winter season, should comply with her majesty's desires, and go for Italy; since he might return before the opening of the campaign, if it should be necessary. And return indeed he did, before the campaign opened, and brought along with him one hundred thousand pounds from Genoa, to the great comfort and support of our troops, which had neither money nor credit. But, on his return, that noble Earl found the Lord Galway had been near as successful against him, as he had been unsuccessful against the enemy. Thence was the Earl of Peterborow recalled to make room for an unfortunate general, who, the next year, suffered himself to be decoyed into that fatal battle of Almanza.

The Earl of Peterborow, on his leaving Valencia, had ordered his baggage to follow him to the camp at Guadalaxara; and it arrived in our little camp, so far safe in its way to the greater at Guadalaxara. I think it consisted of seven loaded waggons; and General Windham gave orders for a small guard to escort it; under which they proceeded on their journey: But, about eight leagues from Cuenca, at a pretty town called Huette, a party from the Duke of Berwick's army, with boughs in their hats, the better to appear what they were not, (for the bough in the hat is the badge of the English, as white paper is the badge of the French,) came into the town, crying all the way, " *Viva Carlos Tercero Viva !*" With these acclamations in their mouths, they advanced up to the very waggons; when attacking the guards who had too much deluded themselves with appearances, they routed them, and immediately plundered the waggons of all that was valuable, and then marched off.

The noise of this soon reached the ears of the Earl of Peterborow at Guadalaxara. When, leaving my Lord Galway's camp, pursuant to the resolutions of the council of war, with a party only of fourscore of Killegrew's dragoons, he met General Windham's little army within a league of Huette, the place where his baggage had been plundered. The Earl had strong motives of suspicion, that the inhabitants had given intelligence to the enemy; and, as is very natural, giving way to the first dictates of resentment, he resolved to have laid the town in ashes; But when he came near it, the clergy and magistrates, upon their knees, disavowing the charge, and asserting their innocence, prevailed on the good nature of that generous Earl, without any great difficulty, to spare the town, at least not to burn it.

We marched, however, into the town, and that night took up our quarters there; and the magistrates, under the dread of our avenging ourselves, on their part took care that we were well supplied. But, when they were made sensible of the value of the loss, which the Earl had sustained; and that on a moderate computation it amounted to at least eight thousand pistoles; they voluntarily presented themselves next morning, and, of their own accord, offered to make his lordship full satisfaction, and, that, in their own phrase, *de contado*, in ready money. The Earl was not displeased at their offer; but generously made answer, That he was just come from my Lord Galway's camp at Chincon, where he found they were in a likelihood of wanting bread; and, as he imagined it might be easier to them to raise the value in corn, than in ready money; if they would send to that value in corn to the Lord Galway's camp, he would be satisfied. This they with joy embraced, and immediately complied with.

I am apt to think the last century, (and I very much fear the current will be as deficient,) can hardly produce a parallel instance of generosity, and true public spiritedness: And the world will be of my opinion, when I have corroborated this with another passage some years after. The commissioners for stating the debts due to the army, meeting daily for that purpose, at their house in Darby Court in Channel Row, I there mentioned to Mr Read, gentleman to his lordship, this very just and honourable claim upon the government, as monies advanced for the use of the army. Who told me in a little time after, that he had mentioned it to his Lordship; but with no other effect than to have it rejected with a generous disdain.

While we staid at Huette, there was a little incident in life, which gave me great diversion. The Earl, who had always maintained a good correspondence with the fair sex, hearing from one of the priests of the place, that, on the alarm of burning the town, one of the finest ladies in all Spain had taken refuge in the nunnery, was desirous to speak with her.

The nunnery stood upon a small rising hill within the town, and, to obtain the view, the Earl had presently in his head this stratagem; he sends for me, as engineer, to have my advice, how to raise a proper fortification upon that hill, out of the nunnery. I waited upon his Lordship to the place, where, declaring the intent of our coming, and giving plausible reasons for it, the train

P

took, and immediately the lady abbess, and the fair lady, came out to make intercession, that his Lordship would be pleased to lay aside that design. The divine oratory of one, and the beautiful charms of the other, prevailed; so his Lordship left the fortification to be the work of some future generation.

From Huette the Earl of Peterborow marched forwards for Valencia; with only those fourscore dragoons, which came with him from Chincon, leaving General Windham pursuing his own orders to join his forces to the army, then under the command of the Lord Galway. But stopping at Campilio, a little town in our way, his Lordship had information of a most barbarous fact committed that very morning by the Spaniards, at a small villa, about a league distant, upon some English soldiers.

A captain of the English Guards, (whose name has slipped my memory, though I well knew the man) marching in order to join the battalion of the Guards, then under the command of General Windham, with some of his soldiers, that had been in the hospital, took up his quarters in that little villa. But on his marching out of it, next morning, a shot in the back laid that officer dead upon the spot: and as it had been before concerted, the Spaniards of the place at the same time fell upon the poor weak soldiers, killing several; not even sparing their wives. This was but a prelude to their barbarity; their savage cruelty was only whetted, not glutted. They took the surviving few, hurried and dragged them up a hill, a little without the villa. On the top of this hill there was a hole, or opening, somewhat like the mouth of one of our coal-pits; down this they cast several, who, with hideous shrieks and cries, made more hideous by the echoes of the chasm, there lost their lives.

This relation was thus made to the Earl of Peterborow, at his quarters at Campilio, who immediately gave orders for to sound to horse. At first we were all surprised;

but were soon satisfied, that it was to revenge, or rather do justice, on this barbarous action.

As soon as we entered the villa, we found that most of the inhabitants, but especially the most guilty, had withdrawn themselves on our approach. We found, however, many of the dead soldiers' clothes, which had been conveyed into the church, and there hid. And a strong accusation being laid against a person belonging to the church, and full proof made, that he had been singularly industrious in the execution of that horrid piece of barbarity on the hill, his Lordship commanded him to be hanged up at the knocker of the door.

After this piece of military justice, we were led up to the fatal pit, or hole, down which many had been cast headlong. There we found one poor soldier alive, who, upon his throwing in, had catched fast hold of some impending bushes, and saved himself on a little jutty within the concavity. On hearing us talk English, he cried out;

and ropes being let down, in a little time he was drawn up; when he gave us an ample detail of the whole villany. Among other particulars, I remember he told me of a very narrow escape he had in that obscure recess. A poor woman, one of the wives of the soldiers, who was thrown down after him, struggled, and roared so much, that they could not, with all their force, throw her cleverly in the middle; by which means falling near the side, in her fall she almost beat him from his place of security.

Upon the conclusion of this tragical relation of the soldier thus saved, his Lordship gave immediate orders for the firing of the villa, which was executed with due severity: after which his Lordship marched back to his quarters at Campilio; from whence, two days after, we arrived at Valencia; where, the first thing presented to that noble Lord, was all the papers taken in the plunder of his baggage, which the Duke of Berwick had generously ordered to be returned him, without waste or opening.

It was too manifest, after the Earl's arrival at this city, that the alteration in the command of the English forces, which before was only received as a rumour, had deeper grounds for belief than many of his friends in that city could have wished. His Lordship had gained the love of all by a thousand engaging condescensions; even his gallantries, being no way prejudicial, were not offensive; and though his Lordship did his utmost to conceal his chagrin, the sympathy of those around him made such discoveries upon him, as would have disappointed a double portion of his caution. They had seen him unelated under successes, that were so near being unaccountable, that in a country of less superstition than Spain, they might almost have passed for miraculous; they knew full well, that nothing but that series of successes had paved a passage for the General that was to supersede him; those only having removed all the difficulties of his march from Portugal to Madrid ; they knew him the older General; and therefore, not knowing, that, in the court he came from, intrigue was too often the soul of merit, they could not but be amazed at a change, which his Lordship was unwilling any body should perceive by himself.

It was upon this account, that, as formerly, he treated the ladies with balls, and, to pursue the Dons in their own humour, ordered a Tawridore, or Bull-feast. In Spain, no sort of public diversions are esteemed equal with this. But the bulls provided at Valencia, not being of the right breed, nor ever initiated in the mysteries, did not acquit themselves at all masterly ; and consequently, did not give the diversion or satisfaction expected. For which reason I shall omit giving a description of this bull-feast ; and desire my reader to suspend his curiosity till I come to some, which, in the Spanish sense, were much more entertaining; that is, attended with much greater hazards and danger.

But though I have said the gallantries of the General were mostly political, at least very inoffensive; yet there happened about this time, and in this place, a piece of gallantry, that gave the Earl a vast deal of offence and vexation; as a matter, that in its consequences might have been fatal to the interest of King Charles, if not to the English nation in general; and which I the rather relate, in that it may be of use to young officers and others; pointing out to them the danger, not to say folly, of inadvertent and precipitate engagements, under unruly passions.

I have said before, that Valencia is famous for fine women. It indeed abounds in them; and among those, are great numbers of courtezans, not inferior in beauty to any. Nevertheless, two of our English officers, not caring for the common road, however safe, resolved to launch into the deeper seas, though attended with much greater danger. Amours, the common failing of that fair city, was the occasion of this accident, and two nuns the objects. It is customary in that country for young people in an evening to resort to the grates of the nunneries, there to divert themselves, and the nuns, with a little pleasant and inoffensive chit-chat. For, though I have heard some relate a world of nauseous passages at such conversations, I must declare, that I never saw, or heard any thing unseemly; and therefore, whenever I have heard any such from such fabulists, I never so much wronged my judgment as to afford them credit.

Our two officers were very assiduous at the grates of a nunnery in this place; and having there pitched upon two nuns, prosecuted their amours with such vigour, that, in a little time, they had made a very great progress in their affections, without in the least considering the dangers that must attend themselves and the fair; they had exchanged vows, and prevailed upon the weaker vessels to endeavour to get out to their lovers. To effect which, soon after, a plot was laid ; the means, the hour, and every thing agreed upon.

It is the custom of that nunnery, as of many others, for the nuns to take their weekly courses in keeping the keys of all the doors. The two love-sick ladies giving notice to their lovers at the grate, that one of their turns was come, the night and hour was appointed, which the officers punctually observing, carried off their prey without either difficulty or interruption.

But next morning when the nuns were missing, what an uproar was there over all the city ! The ladies were both of quality ; and therefore the tidings were first carried to their relations. They received the news with vows of utmost vengeance ; and, as is usual in that country, put themselves in arms for that purpose. There needed no great canvassing for discovering who were the aggressors : the officers had been too frequent and too public in their addresses, to leave any room for question. Accordingly, they were complained of and sought for; but sensible at last of their past temerity, they endeavoured, and with a great deal of difficulty perfected, their escape.

Less fortunate were the two fair nuns; their lovers, in their utmost exigency, had forsaken them; and they, poor creatures, knew not where to fly. Under this sad dilemma they were taken; and, as in like offences, condemned directly to the punishment of immuring. And what greater punishment is there on earth, than to be confined between four narrow walls, only open at the top; and thence to be half supported with bread and water, till the offenders gradually starve to death?

The Earl of Peterborow, though highly exasperated at the proceedings of his officers, in compassion to the unhappy fair, resolved to interpose by all the moderate means possible. He knew very well, that no one thing could so much prejudice the Spaniard against him, as the countenancing such an action; wherefore, he inveighed against the officers, at the same time that he endeavoured to mitigate in favour of the ladies: but all was in vain; it was urged against those charitable intercessions, that they had broke their vows; and, in that, had broke in upon the laws of the nunnery and religion; the consequence of all which could be nothing less than the punishment appointed to be inflicted. And which was the hardest of all, the nearest of their relations most opposed all his generous mediations; and those, who, according to the common course of nature, should have thanked him for his endeavours to be instrumental in rescuing them from the impending danger, grew more and more enraged, because he opposed them in their design of a cruel revenge.

Notwithstanding all which, the Earl persevered; and after a deal of labour, first got the penalty suspended; and, soon after, by the dint of a very considerable sum of money, (a most powerful argument, which prevails in every country,) saved the poor nuns from immuring; and at last, though with great reluctance, he got them received again into the nunnery. As to the warlike lovers, one of them was the year after slain at the battle of Almanza ; the other is yet living, being a brigadier in the army.

While the Earl of Peterborow was here with his little army of great heretics, neither priests nor people were so open in their superstitious fopperies, as I at other times found them. For which reason I will make bold, and, by an antichronism in this place, a little anticipate some observations that I made some time after the Earl left it. And as I have not often committed such a transgression, I hope it may be the more excusable now, and no way blemish my Memoirs, that I break in upon the series of my Journal.

Valencia is a handsome city, and a bishoprick ; and is considerable, not only for the pleasantness of its situation and beauti ful ladies, but (which at some certain times, and on some occasions, to them is more valuable than both those put together) for being the birth-place of Saint Vincent, the patron of the place; and next, for its being the place where Santo Domingo, the first institutor of the Dominican order, had his education. Here, in honour of the last, is a spacious and very splendid convent of the Dominicans. Walking by which, I one day observed over the gate, a figure of a man in stone; and near it, a dog, with a lighted torch in his mouth. The image I rightly enough took to intend that of the saint; but inquiring of one of the order at the gate the meaning of the figures near it, he very courteously asked me to walk in, and then entertained me with the following relation:

When the mother of Santo Domingo, said that religious, was with child of that future saint, she had a dream which very much afflicted her. She dreamt that she heard a dog bark in her belly; and inquiring (at what oracle is not said) the meaning of her dream, she was told, " that that child should bark out the Gospel,"(excuse the bareness of the expression, it may run better in Spanish; though, if I remember right, Erasmus gives it in Latin much the same turn,) " which should thence shine out like that lighted torch." And this is the reason, that whereever you see the image of that saint, a dog and a lighted torch is in the group.

He told me at the same time, that there had been more popes and cardinals of that order than of any, if not all the other. To confirm which, he led me into a large gallery, on each side whereof he shewed me the pictures of all the popes and cardinals that had been of that order; among which, I particularly took notice of that of Cardinal Howard, great uncle to the present Duke of Norfolk. But after many encomiums of their society, with which he interspersed his discourse, he added one that I least valued it for, that the sole care and conduct of the inquisition was intrusted with them.

Finding me attentive, or not so contradictory as the English humour generally is, he next brought me into a fair and large cloister, round which I took several turns with him; and, indeed, the place was too delicious to tire, under a conversation less pertinent or courteous than that he entertained me with. In the middle of the cloister, was a small, but pretty and sweet grove of orange and lemon trees; these bore fruit ripe and green, and flowers, altogether on one tree; and their fruit was so very large and beautiful, and their flowers so transcendently odoriferous, that all I had ever seen of the like kind in England, could comparatively pass only for beauty in epitome, or nature imitated in wax-work. Many flocks also of pretty little birds, with their cheerful notes, added not a little to my delight. In short, in life, I never knew or found three of my senses at once so exquisitely gratified.

Not far from this, Saint Vincent, the patron, as I said before, of this city, has a chapel dedicated to him. Once a year they do him honour in a sumptuous procession. Then are their streets all strewed with flowers, and their houses set off with their richest tapestries; every one strives to excel his neighbour in distinguishing himself by the honour he pays to that saint; and he is the best catholic, as well as the best citizen, in the eye of the religious, who most exerts himself on this occasion.

The procession begins with a cavalcade of all the friars of all the convents in and about the city. These walk two and two with folded arms, and eyes cast down to the very ground, and with the greatest outward appearance of humility imaginable; nor, though the temptation from the fine women that filled their windows, or the rich tapestries that adorned the balconies, might be allowed sufficient to attract, could I observe that any one of them all ever moved them upwards.

After the friars is borne, upon the shoulders of twenty men at least, an image of that saint, of solid silver, large as the life: It is placed in a great chair of silver likewise; the staves that bear him up, and upon which they bear him, being of the same metal. The whole is a most costly and curious piece of workmanship, such as my eyes never before or since beheld.

The magistrates follow the image and its supporters, dressed in their richest apparel, which is always on this day, and on this occasion, particularly sumptuous and distinguishing. Thus is the image, in the greatest splendour, borne and accompanied round that fine city; and at last conveyed to the place from whence it came: and so concludes that annual ceremony.

The Valencians, as to the exteriors of religion, are the most devout of any in Spain, though in common life you find them amorous, gallant, and gay, like other people; yet on solemn occasions, there shines outright such a spirit, as proves them the very bigots of bigotry: as a proof of which assertion, I will now give some account of such observations, as I had time to make upon them, during two Lent seasons while I resided there.

CAPTAIN CARLETON. 243

The week before the Lent commences, commonly known by the name of Carnival Time, the whole city appears a perfect Bartholomew fair; the streets are crowded, and the houses empty; nor is it possible to pass along without some gambol or jack-pudding trick offered to you. Ink, water, and sometimes ordure, are sure to be hurled at your face or clothes; and if you appear concerned or angry, they rejoice at it, pleased the more, the more they displease; for all other resentment is at that time out of season, though at other times few in the world are fuller of resentment, or more captious.

The younger gentry, or Dons, to express their gallantry, carry about them egg-shells, filled with orange or other sweet water, which they cast at ladies in their coaches, or such other of the fair sex as they happen to meet in the streets.

But, after all, if you would think them extravagant to day, as much transgressing the rules of common civility, and neither regarding decency to one another, nor the duty they owe to Almighty God; yet when Ash-Wednesday comes, you will imagine them more unaccountable in their conduct, being then as much too excessive in all outward indications of humility and repentance. Here you shall meet one, bare-footed, with a cross on his shoulder, a burden rather fit for somewhat with four feet, and which his poor two are ready to sink under, yet the vain wretch bears and sweats, and sweats and bears, in hope of finding merit in an ass's labour.

Others you shall see naked to their waists, whipping themselves with scourges made for the purpose, till the blood follows every stroke; and no man need be at a loss to follow them by the very tracks of gore they shed in this frantic perambulation. Some who, from the thickness of their hides, or other impediments, have not power by their scourgings to fetch blood of themselves, are followed by surgeons with their lancets, who, at every turn, make use of them, to evince the extent of their patience and zeal by the smart of their folly. While others, mingling amour with devotion, take particular care to present themselves all macerated before the windows of their mistresses; and even in that condition, not satisfied with what they have barbarously done to themselves, they have their operators at hand, to evince their love by the number of their gashes and wounds; imagining the more blood they lose, the more love they shew, and the more they shall gain. These are generally devoto's of quality; though the tenet is universal, that he that is most bloody is most devout.

After these street-exercises, these ostentatious castigations, are over, these self-sacrificers repair to the great church, the bloodier the better; there they throw themselves in a condition too vile for the eye of a female, before the image of the Virgin Mary; though I defy all their race of Fathers, and their infallible Hóly Father into the bargain, to produce any authority to fit it for belief, that she ever delighted in such sanguinary holocausts.

During the whole time of Lent, you will see in every street some priest or friar, upon some stall or stool, preaching up repentance to the people; and with violent blows on his breast, crying aloud, " *Mia culpa, mia maxima culpa,*" till he extract reciprocal returns from the hands of his auditors on their own breasts.

When Good-Friday is come, they entertain it with the most profound show of reverence and religion, both in their streets and in their churches. In the last, particularly, they have contrived about twelve o'clock suddenly to darken them, so as to render them quite gloomy. This they do, to intimate the eclipse of the sun, which at that time happened. And to signify the rending of the vail of the temple, you are struck with a strange artificial noise at the very same instant.

But when Easter day appears, you find it in all respects with them a day of rejoicing; for, though abstinence from flesh with them, who at no time eat much, is not so great a mortification as with those of the same persuasion in other countries, who eat much more, yet there is a visible satisfaction darts out at their eyes, which demonstrates their inward pleasure in being set free from the confinement of mind to the dissatisfaction of the body. Every person you now meet greets you with a Resurrexit Jesus; a good imitation of the primitive Christians, were it the real effect of devotion. And all sorts of the best music (which here indeed is the best in all Spain) proclaim an auspicious valediction to the departed season of superficial sorrow and stupid superstition. But enough of this: I proceed to weightier matters.

While we lay at Valencia, under the vigilance and care of the indefatigable Earl, news was brought, that Alicant was besieged by General Gorge by land, while a squadron of men-of-war battered it from the sea; from both which the besiegers played their parts so well, and so warmly plyed them with their cannon, that an indifferent practicable breach was made in a little time.

Mahoni commanded in the place, being again received into favour; and cleared as he was of those political insinuations before intimated, he now seemed resolved to confirm his innocence by a resolute defence. However, perceiving that all preparations tended towards a storm, and knowing full well the weakness of the town, he withdrew his garrison into the castle, leaving the town to the defence of its own inhabitants.

Just as that was doing, the sailors, not much skilled in sieges, nor at all times capable of the coollest consideration, with a resolution natural to them, stormed the walls to the side of the sea; where, not meeting with much opposition, (for the people of the town apprehended the least danger there,) they soon got into the place; and, as soon as got in, began to plunder. This obliged the people, for the better security of themselves, to open their gates, and seek a refuge under one enemy, in opposition to the rage of another.

General Gorge, as soon as he entered the town, with a good deal of seeming lenity, put a stop to the ravages of the sailors; and ordered proclamation to be made throughout the place, that all the inhabitants should immediately bring in their best effects into the great church for their better security. This was by the mistaken populace as readily complied with; and neither friend nor foe at all disputing the command, or questioning the integrity of the intention, the church was presently crowded with riches of all sorts and sizes. Yet after some time remaining there, they were all taken out, and disposed of by those that had as little property in them as the sailors they were pretended to be preserved from.

The Earl of Peterborow, upon the very first news of the siege, had left Valencia, and taken shipping for Alicant, where he arrived soon after the surrender of the town, and that outcry of the goods of the townsmen. Upon his arrival, Mahoni, who was blocked up in the castle, and had experienced his indefatigable diligence, being in want of provisions, and without much hope of relief, desired to capitulate. The Earl granted him honourable conditions, upon which he delivered up the castle, and Gorge was made governor.

Upon his Lordship's taking ship at Valencia, I had an opportunity of marching with those dragoons which escorted him from Castile, who had received orders to march into Murcia. We quartered the first night at Alcira, a town that the river Segra almost surrounds, which renders it capable of being made a place of vast strength, though now of small importance.

The next night we lay at Xativa, a place famous for its steadiness to King Charles. General Basset, a Spaniard, being governor, it was besieged by the forces of King Philip; but, after a noble resistance, the enemy were beat off, and the siege raised;

for which effort, it is supposed, that on the retirement of King Charles out of this country, it was deprived of its old name Xativa, and is now called San Felippo; though to this day, the people thereabouts much disallow by their practice, that novel denomination.

We marched next morning by Monteza; which gives name to the famous title of Knights of Monteza. It was, at the time that Colonel O'Guaza, an Irishman, was governor, besieged by the people of the country, in favour of King Charles; but very ineffectually, so it never changed its sovereign. That night we quartered at Fonte da las Figuras, within one league of Almanza, where that fatal and unfortunate battle, which I shall give an account of in its place, was fought the year after, under the Lord Galway.

On our fourth day's march we were obliged to pass Villena, where the enemy had a garrison. A party of Mahoni's dragoons made a part of that garrison, and they were commanded by Major O'Roirk, an Irish officer, who always carried the reputation of a good soldier, and a brave gentleman.

I had all along made it my observation, that Captain Matthews, who commanded those dragoons that I marched with, was a person of much more courage than conduct; and he used as little precaution here, though just marching under the eye of the enemy, as he had done at other times. As I was become intimately acquainted with him, I rode up to him, and told him the danger, which, in my opinion, attended our present march. I pointed out to him just before Villena a jutting hill, under which we must unavoidably pass; at the turning whereof, I was apprehensive the enemy might lie, and either by ambuscade, or otherwise, surprise us; I therefore intreated we might either wait the coming of our rear guard, or at least march with a little more leisure and caution. But he, taking little notice of all I said, kept on his round march; seeing which, I pressed forward my mule, which was a very good one, and rid as fast as her legs could carry her, till I had got on the top of the hill. When I came there, I found both my expectation and my apprehensions answered: for I could very plainly discern three squadrons of the enemy ready drawn up, and waiting for us at the very winding of the hill.

Hereupon I hastened back to the captain with the like speed, and told him the discovery I had made; who nevertheless kept on his march, and it was with a good deal of difficulty that I at last prevailed on him to halt, till our rear guard of twenty men had got up to us. But those joining us, and a new troop of Spanish dragoons, who had marched towards us that morning, appearing in sight; our captain, as if he was afraid of their rivalling him in his glory, at the very turn of the hill, rode in a full gallop, with sword in hand, up to the enemy. They stood their ground till we were advanced within two hundred yards of them, and then in confusion endeavoured to retire into the town.

They were obliged to pass over a small bridge, too small to admit of such a company in so much haste; their crowding upon which obstructed their retreat, and left all that could not get over to the mercy of our swords, which spared none. However, narrow as the bridge was, Captain Matthews was resolved to venture over after the enemy; on doing which, the enemy made a halt, till the people of the town, and the very priests, came out to their relief with fire arms. On so large an appearance, Captain Matthews thought it not advisable to make any further advances; so, driving a very great flock of sheep from under the walls, he continued his march towards Elda. In this action we lost Captain Topham and three dragoons.

I remember we were not marched very far from the place where this rencounter happened, when an Irish dragoon overtook the captain, with a civil message from Major O'Roirk, desiring that he would not entertain a mean opinion of him for the defence that was made; since, could he have got the Spaniards to have stood their ground, he should have given him good reason for a better. The captain returned a complimental answer, and so marched on. This Major O'Roirk, or O'Roork, was the next year killed at Alkay, being much lamented; for he was esteemed both for his courage and conduct, one of the best of the Irish officers in the Spanish service. I was likewise informed, that he was descended from one of the ancient kings of Ireland; the mother of the honourable Colonel Paget, one of the grooms of the bedchamber to his present Majesty, was nearly related to this gallant gentleman.

One remarkable thing I saw in that action, which affected and surprised me: a Scotch dragoon, of but a moderate size, with his large basket-hilted sword, struck off a Spaniard's head at one stroke, with the same ease, in appearance, as a man would do that of a poppy.

When we came to Elda, (a town much in the interest of King Charles, and famous for its fine situation, and the largest grapes in Spain,) the inhabitants received us in a manner as handsome as it was peculiar; all standing at their doors with lighted torches; which, considering the time we entered, was far from an unwelcome or disagreeable sight.

The next day, several requested to be the messengers of the action at Villena to the Earl of Peterborow at Alicant; but the captain returned this answer to all, that in consideration of the share that I might justly claim in that day's transactions, he could not think of letting any other person be the bearer. So, giving me his letters to the Earl, I the next day delivered them to him at Alicant. At the delivery, Colonel Killegrew (whose dragoons they were) being present, he expressed a deal of satisfaction at the account, and his Lordship was pleassed at the same time to appoint me sole engineer of the castle of Alicant.

Soon after which, that successful General embarked for Genoa, according to the resolutions of the council of war at Guadalaxara, on a particular commission from the Queen of England, another from Charles King of Spain, and charged at the same time with a request of the Marquis das Minas, General of the Portugueze forces, to negociate bills for one hundred thousand pounds for the use of his troops. In all which, though he was (as ever) successful; yet may it be said without a figure, that his departure, in a good measure, determined the success of the confederate forces in that kingdom. True it is, the general returned again with the fortunate fruits of those negociations: but never to act in his old auspicious sphere: and therefore, as I am now to take leave of this fortunate General, let me do it with justice, in an appeal to the world, of the not to be paralleled usage (in these latter ages at least) that he met with for all his services; such a vast variety of enterprizes, all successful, and which had set all Europe in amaze; services that had given occasion to such solemn and public thanksgivings in our churches, and which had received such very remarkable approbations, both of sovereign and parliament, and which had been represented in so lively a manner, in a letter wrote by the King of Spain, under his own hand, to the Queen of England, and communicated to both Houses in the terms following:

" Madam, my Sister,

" I should not have been so long ere I did myself the honour to repeat the assurances of my sincere respects to you, had I not waited for the good occasion which I now acquaint you with, that the city of Barcelona is surrendered to me by capitulation. I doubt not but you will receive this great news with entire satisfaction, as well because this happy success is the effect of your arms, always glorious, as from the pure motives of that bounty and maternal affection you have for me, and for every thing which may contribute to the advancement of my interest.

"I must do this justice to all the officers and common soldiers, and particularly to my Lord Peterborow, that he has shewn in this whole expedition, a constancy, bravery, and conduct, worthy of the choice that your Majesty has made of him, and that he could no ways give me better satisfaction than he has, by the great zeal and application, which he has equally testified for my interest, and for the service of my person. I owe the same justice to Brigadier Stanhope, for his great zeal, vigilance, and very wise conduct, which he has given proofs of upon all occasions : as also to all your officers of the fleet, particularly to your worthy Admiral, Shovel, assuring your Majesty, that he has assisted me in this expedition, with an inconceivable readiness and application, and that no Admiral will be ever better able to render me greater satisfaction than he has done. During the siege of Barcelona, some of your Majesty's ships, with the assistance of the troops of the country, have reduced the town of Tarragona, and the officers are made prisoners of war. The town of Girone has been taken at the same time by surprise, by the troops of the country. The town of Lerida has submitted, as also that of Tortosa upon the Ebro; so that we have taken all the places of Catalonia, except Roses. Some places in Arragon, near Sarragosa, have declared for me, and the garrison of the castle of Denia in Valencia have maintained their post, and repulsed the enemy; 400 of the enemy's cavalry have entered into our service, and a great number of their infantry have deserted.

"This, madam, is the state that your arms, and the inclination of the people, have put my affairs in. It is unnecessary to tell you what stops the course of these conquests; it is not the season of the year, nor the enemy; these are no obstacles to your troops, who desire nothing more than to act under the conduct that your Majesty has appointed them. The taking of Barcelona, with so small a number of troops, is very remarkable; and what has been done in this siege is almost without example; that with seven or eight thousand men of your troops, and two hundred Miquelets, we should surround and invest a place, that thirty thousand French could not block up.

"After a march of thirteen hours, the troops climbed up the rocks and precipices, to attack a fortification stronger than the place, which the Earl of Peterborow has sent you a plan of; two generals, with the grenadiers, attacked it sword in hand. In which action the Prince of Hesse died gloriously, after so many brave actions; I hope his brother and his family will always have your Majesty's protection. With eight hundred men they forced the covered way, and all the entrenchments and works, one after another, till they came to the last work which surrounded it, against five hundred men of regular troops which defended the place, and a reinforcement they had received; and three days afterwards we became masters of the place. We afterwards attacked the town on the side of the castle. We landed again our cannon, and the other artillery, with inconceivable trouble, and formed two camps, distant from each other three leagues, against a garrison almost as numerous as our army, whose cavalry was double the strength of ours. The first camp was so well entrenched, that it was defended by two thousand men and the dragoons; whilst we attacked the town with the rest of our troops. The breach being made, we prepared to make a general assault with all the army. These are circumstances, Madam, which distinguish this action, perhaps, from all others.

" Here has happened an unforeseen accident. The cruelty of the pretended viceroy, and the report spread abroad, that he would take away the prisoners, contrary to the capitulation, provoked the burghers, and some of the country people, to take up arms against the garrison, whilst they were busy in packing up their baggage, which was to be sent away the next day; so that every thing tended to slaughter; but your Majesty's troops, entering into town with the Earl of Peterborow, instead of seeking pillage, a practice common upon such occasions, appeased the tumult, and have saved the town, and even the lives of their enemies, with a discipline and generosity without example.

"What remains is, that I return you my most hearty thanks for sending so great a fleet, and such good and valiant troops to my assistance. After so happy a beginning, I have thought it proper, according to the sentiments of your Generals and Admirals, to support, by my presence, the conquests that we have made; and to shew my subjects, so affectionate to my person, that I cannot abandon them. I receive such succours from your Majesty, and from your generous nation, that I am loaded with your bounties; and am not a little concerned to think, that the support of my interest should cause so great an expence. But, Madam, I sacrifice my person, and my subjects in Catalonia expose also their lives and fortunes, upon the assurances they have of your Majesty's generous protection. Your Majesty and your council knows better than we do, what is necessary for our conservation. We shall then expect your Majesty's succours, with an entire confidence in your bounty and wisdom. A further force is necessary: we give no small diversion to France, and without doubt they will make their utmost efforts against me as soon as possible; but I am satisfied, that the same efforts will be made by my allies to defend me. Your goodness, Madam, inclines you, and your power enables you, to support those that the tyranny of France would oppress. All that I can insinuate to your wisdom, and that of your allies, is, that the forces employed in this country will not be unprofitable to the public good, but will be under an obligation and necessity to act with the utmost vigour against the enemy. I am, with an inviolable affection, respect, and most sincere acknowledgment,

  Madam, my Sister,
   Your most affectionate Brother,
         CHARLES."

*From the Camp at Senia, before Barcelona,
the 22d of October, 1705.*

And yet, after all, was this noble General not only recalled, the command of the fleet taken from him, and that of the army given to my Lord Galway, without assignment of cause; but all manner of falsities were industriously spread abroad, not only to diminish, if they could, his reputation, but to bring him under accusations of a malevolent nature. I can hardly imagine it necessary here to take notice, that afterward he disproved all those idle calumnies and ill-invented rumours; or to mention what compliments he received, in the most solemn manner, from his country, upon a full examination and thorough canvassing of his actions in the House of Lords. But this is too notorious to be omitted, that all officers coming from Spain were purposely intercepted in their way to London, and craftily examined upon all the idle stories which had passed, tending to lessen his character: and when any officers had asserted the falsity of those inventions, (as they all did, except a military sweetner or two,) and that there was no possibility of laying any thing amiss to the charge of that General, they were told, that they ought to be careful, however, not to speak advantageously of that Lord's conduct, unless they were willing to fall martyrs in his cause; a thing scarce to be credited even in a popish country. But Scipio was accused, though (as my author finely observes) by wretches only known to posterity by that stupid accusation.

As a mournful valediction, before I enter upon any new scene, the reader will pardon this melancholy expostulation. How mortifying must it be to an Englishman, after he has found himself solaced with a relation of so many surprising successes of her Majesty's arms, under the Earl of Peterborow; successes, that have laid before our eyes provinces and kingdoms reduced, and towns and fortresses taken and relieved; where we have seen a continued series of happy events, the fruits of conduct and vigilance; and caution and foresight preventing dangers that were held, at first view, certain and unsurmountable: to change this glorious landscape, I say, for scenes every way different, even while our troops were as numerous as the enemy, and better provided, yet always baffled and beaten, and flying before the enemy, till fatally ruined in the battle of Almanza: how mortifying must this be to any lover of his country! But I proceed to my Memoirs.

Alicant is a town of the greatest trade of any in the kingdom of Valencia, having a strong castle, being situated on a high hill, which commands both town and harbour.

In this place I resided a whole year; but it was soon after my first arrival, that Major Collier (who was shot in the back at Barcelona, as I have related in the siege of that place) hearing of me, sought me out at my quarters; and, after a particular enquiry into the success of that difficult task that he left me upon, and my answering all his questions to satisfaction, (all which he received with evident pleasure,) he threw down a purse of pistoles upon the table; which I refusing, he told me, in a most handsome manner, his friendship was not to be preserved but by my accepting it.

After I had made some very necessary repairs, I pursued the orders I had received from the Earl of Peterborow, to go upon the erecting a new battery between the castle and the town. This was a task attended with difficulties, neither few in number, nor small in consequence; for it was to be raised upon a great declivity, which must render the work both laborious and precarious. However, I had the good fortune to effect it much sooner than was expected; and it was called Gorge's battery, from the name of the governor then commanding; who, out of an uncommon profusion of generosity, wetted that piece of gossiping with a distinguishing bowl of punch. Brigadier Bougard, when he saw this work some time after, was pleased to honour it with a singular admiration and approbation, for its completeness, notwithstanding its difficulties.

This work, and the siege of Carthagena, then in our possession, by the Duke of Berwick, brought the Lord Galway down to this place. Carthagena is of so little distance from Alicant, that we could easily hear the cannon playing against, and from it, in our castle, where I then was. And I remember my Lord Galway, on the fourth day of the siege, sending to know if I could make any useful observations as to the success of it; I returned, that I was of opinion the town was surrendered, from the sudden cessation of the cannon, which, by our news next day from the place, proved to be fact. Carthagena is a small sea-port town in Murcia; but has so good an harbour, that when the famous Admiral Doria was asked, which were the three best havens in the Mediterranean, he readily returned, June, July, and Carthagena.

Upon the surrender of this place, a detachment of foot was sent by the governor, with some dragoons, to Elsha; but it being a place of very little strength, they were soon made prisoners of war.

The siege of Carthagena being over, the Lord Galway returned to his camp; and the Lord Duncannon dying in Alicant, the first guns that were fired from Gorge's battery, were the minute-guns for his funeral. His regiment had been given to the Lord Montandre, who lost it before he had possession, by an action as odd as it was scandalous.

That regiment had received orders to march to the Lord Galway's camp, under the command of their Lieutenant-Colonel

Bateman, a person before reputed a good officer, though his conduct here gave people, not invidious, too much reason to call it in question. On his march, he was so very careless and negligent, (though he knew himself in a country surrounded with enemies, and that he was to march through a wood, where they every day made their appearance in great numbers,) that his soldiers marched with their muskets slung at their backs, and went one after another, (as necessity had forced us to do in Scotland,) himself at the head of them, in his chaise, riding a considerable way before.

It happened there was a captain, with threescore dragoons, detached from the Duke of Berwick's army, with a design to intercept some cash that was ordered to be sent to Lord Galway's army from Alicant. This detachment, missing of that intended prize, was returning very disconsolately, *re infecta*; when their captain, observing that careless and disorderly march of the English, resolved, boldly enough, to attack them in the wood. To that purpose he secreted his little party behind a great barn; and so soon as they were half passed by, he falls upon them in the centre with his dragoons, cutting and slashing at such a violent rate, that he soon dispersed the whole regiment, leaving many dead and wounded upon the spot. The three colours were taken; and the gallant Lieutenant-Colonel taken out of his chaise, and carried away prisoner with many others; only one officer, who was an ensign, and so bold as to do his duty, was killed.

The Lieutenant who commanded the grenadiers, received the alarm time enough to draw his men into a house in their way; where he bravely defended himself for a long time; but, being killed, the rest immediately surrendered. The account of this action I had from the commander of the enemy's party himself, some time after, while I was a prisoner. And Captain Mahoni, who was present when the news was brought, that a few Spanish dragoons had defeated an English regiment, which was this under Bateman, protested to me, that the Duke of Berwick turned pale at the relation; and when they offered to bring the colours before him, he would not so much as see them. A little before the Duke went to supper, Bateman himself was brought to him; but the Duke turned away from him without any further notice, than coldly saying, " that he thought he was very strangely taken." The wags of the army made a thorough jest of him, and said his military conduct was of a piece with his economy, having, two days before his march, sent his young handsome wife into England, under the guardianship of the young chaplain of the regiment.

April 15. In the year 1707, being Easter Monday, we had in the morning a flying report in Alicant, that there had been the day before a battle at Almanza, between the army under the command of the Duke of Berwick, and that of the English, under Lord Galway, in which the latter had suffered an entire defeat. We at first gave no great credit to it; but, alas, we were too soon woefully convinced of the truth of it, by numbers that came flying to us from the conquering enemy. Then indeed we were satisfied of truths, too difficult before to be credited. But as I was not present in that calamitous battle, I shall relate it, as I received it from an officer then in the Duke's army.

To bring the Lord Galway to a battle, in a place most commodious for his purpose, the Duke made use of this stratagem: he ordered two Irishmen, both officers, to make their way over to the enemy as deserters; putting this story in their mouths, that the Duke of Orleans was in full march to join the Duke of Berwick with twelve thousand men; that this would be done in two days, and that then they would find out the Lord Galway, and force him to fight, wherever they found him.

Battle of Almanza. Lord Galway, who at this time lay before Villena, receiving this intelligence from those well instructed deserters, immediately raised the siege ; with a resolution, by a hasty march, to force the enemy to battle, before the Duke of Orleans should be able to join the Duke of Berwick. To effect this, after a hard march of three long Spanish leagues in the heat of the day, he appears a little after noon in the face of the enemy with his fatigued forces. Glad and rejoiced at the sight, for he found his plot had taken, Berwick, the better to receive him, draws up his army in a half moon, placing at a pretty good advance three regiments to make up the centre, with express order, nevertheless, to retreat at the very first charge. All which was punctually observed, and had its desired effect: for the three regiments, at the first attack, gave way, and seemingly fled towards their camp ; the English, after their customary manner, pursuing them with shouts and hollowings. As soon as the Duke of Berwick perceived his trap had taken, he ordered his right and left wings to close ; by which means, he at once cut off from the rest of their army all those who had so eagerly pursued the imaginary runaways. In short, the rout was total, and the most fatal blow that ever the English received during the whole war with Spain. Nor, as it is thought, with a great probability of reason, had those troops that made their retreat to the top of the hills, under Major General Shrimpton, met with any better fate than those on the plain, had the Spaniards had any other General in the command than the Duke of Berwick; whose native sympathy gave a check to the ardour of a victorious enemy. And this was the sense of the Spaniards themselves after the battle; verifying herein that noble maxim, " that victory to generous minds is only an inducement to moderation."

The day after this fatal battle, (which gave occasion to a Spanish piece of wit, " that the English General had routed the French,") the Duke of Orleans did arrive indeed in the camp, but with an army of only fourteen attendants.

The fatal effects of this battle were soon made visible, and to none more than those in Alicant. The enemy grew every day more and more troublesome; visiting us in parties more boldly than before; and often hovering about us so very near, that with our cannon we could hardly teach them to keep a proper distance. Gorge, the governor of Alicant, being recalled into England, Major General Richards was by King Charles appointed governor in his place. He was a Roman Catholic, and very much beloved by the natives on that account; though, to give him his due, he behaved himself extremely well in all other respects. It was in his time, that a design was laid of surprising Guardamere, a small sea-port town in Murcia : But the military bishop, (for he was, in a literal sense, excellent *tam Marte, quam Mercurio,*) among his many other exploits, by a timely expedition, prevented that.

Governor Richards, my post being always in the castle, had sent to desire me to give notice whenever I saw any parties of the enemy moving. Pursuant to this order, discovering, one morning, a considerable body of horse towards Elsha, I went down into the town, and told the governor what I had seen; and without any delay he gave his orders, that a captain, with threescore men, should attend me to an old house about a mile distance. As soon as we had got into it, I set about barricading all the open places, and avenues, and put my men in a posture ready to receive an enemy, as soon as he should appear; upon which the captain, as a feint, ordered a few of his men to shew themselves on a rising ground just before the house. But we had like to have caught a Tartar: for, though the enemy took the train I had laid, and, on sight of our small body on the hill, sent a party from their greater body to intercept them, before they could reach the town; yet the sequel proved, we had mistaken their number, and it soon appeared to be much greater than we at first imagined. However, our

out-scouts, as I may call them, got safe into
the house; and, on the appearance of the
party, we let fly a full volley, which laid dead
on the spot three men and one horse. Hereupon the whole body made up to the house,
but stood aloof upon the hill without reach
of our shot. We soon saw our danger from
the number of the enemy: and well for us
it was, that the watchful governor had taken
notice of it, as well as we in the house. For
observing us surrounded with the enemy,
and by a power so much superior, he marched himself, with a good part of the garrison, to our relief. The enemy stood a little
time as if they would receive them; but
upon second thoughts they retired, and, to
our no little joy, left us at liberty to come
out of the house and join the garrison.

Scarce a day passed but we had some
visits of the like kind, attended sometimes
with rencounters of this nature; insomuch
that there was hardly any stirring out in
safety for small parties, though never so little a way. There was within a little mile of
the town, an old vineyard, environed with

a loose stone wall : an officer and I made an agreement to ride thither for an airing. We did so, and, after a little riding, it came into my head to put a fright upon the officer. And very lucky for us both was that unlucky thought of mine ; pretending to see a party of the enemy make up to us, I gave him the alarm, set spurs to my horse, and rid as fast as legs could carry me. The officer no way bated of his speed ; and we had scarce got out of the vineyard, but my jest proved earnest ; twelve of the enemy's horse pursuing us to the very gates of the town. Nor could I ever after prevail upon my fellow-traveller to believe, that he owed his escape to merriment more than speed.

Soon after my charge, as to the fortifications, was pretty well over, I obtained leave of the governor to be absent for a fortnight, upon some affairs of my own at Valencia. On my return from whence, at a town called Venissa, I met two officers of an English regiment, going to the place from whence I last came. They told me, after common

congratulations, that they had left Major
Boyd at a little place called Capel, hi-
ring another mule, that he rode on thither
having tired and failed him; desiring withal, that if I met him, I would let him know
that they would stay for him at that place.
I had another gentleman in my company,
and we had travelled on not above a league
further, whence, at a little distance, we were
both surprised with a sight that seemed to
have set all art at defiance, and was too odd
for any thing in nature. It appeared all in
red, and to move; but so very slowly, that
if we had not made more way to that than
it did to us, we should have made it a day's
journey before we met it. My companion
could as little tell what to make of it as I;
and, indeed, the nearer it came, the more
monstrous it seemed, having nothing of the
tokens of man, either walking, riding, or
in any posture whatever. At last, coming
up with this strange figure of a creature,
(for now we found it was certainly such,)
what, or rather who, should it prove to be,

but Major Boyd! He was a person of himself far from one of the least proportion; and, mounted on a poor little ass, with all his warlike accoutrements upon it, you will allow must make a figure almost as odd as one of the old Centaurs. The Morocco saddle that covered the ass, was of burden enough for the beast without its master; and the additional holsters and pistols made it much more weighty. Nevertheless, a curb bridle of the largest size covered his little head, and a long red cloak, hanging down to the ground, covered jack-boots, ass, master, and all. In short, my companion and I, after we could specifically declare it to be a man, agreed we never saw a figure so comical in all our lives. When we had merrily greeted our Major, (for a Cynick could not have forborn laughter,) he excused all as well as he could, by saying, he could get no other beast. After which, delivering our message, and condoling with him for his present mounting, and wishing him better at his next quarters, he settled into his old pace, and we into ours, and parted.

We lay that night at Altea, famous for its bay for ships to water at. It stands on a high hill; and is adorned, not defended, with an old fort.

Thence we came to Alicant, where having now been a whole year, and having effected what was held necessary, I once more prevailed upon the governor to permit me to take another journey. The Lord Galway lay at Tarraga, while Lerida lay under the siege of the Duke of Orleans; and having some grounds of expectation given me, while he was at Alicant, I resolved at least to demonstrate I was still living. The governor favoured me with letters, not at all to my disadvantage; so taking ship for Barcelona, just at our putting into the harbour, we met with the English fleet, on its return from the expedition to Toulon under Sir Cloudsly Shovel.

I staid but very few days at Barcelona, and then proceeded on my intended journey to Tarraga; arriving at which place, I delivered my packet to the Lord Galway, who received me with very great civility; and, to double it, acquainted me at the same time, that the governor of Alicant had wrote very much in my favour: but though it was a known part of that noble Lord's character, that the first impression was generally strongest, I had reason soon after to close with another saying, equally true, " that general rules always admit of some exception." While I was here, we had news of the taking of the town of Lerida; the prince of Hesse (brother to that brave prince who lost his life before Monjouick) retiring into the castle with the garrison, which he bravely defended a long time after.

When I was thus attending my Lord Galway at Tarraga, he received intelligence that the enemy had a design to lay siege to Denia; whereupon he gave me orders to repair there as engineer. After I had received my orders, and taken leave of his lordship, I set out, resolving, since it was left to my choice, to go by way of Barcelona, and there take shipping for the place of my station; by which I proposed to save more time than would allow me a full opportunity of visiting Montserat, a place I had heard much talk of, which had filled me with a longing desire to see it. To say truth, I had been told such extravagant things of the place, that I could hardly impute more than one half of it to any thing but Spanish rhodomontadoes, the vice of extravagant exaggeration being too natural to that nation.

Montserat is a rising lofty hill, in the very middle of a spacious plain, in the principality of Catalonia, about seven leagues distant from Barcelona to the westward, somewhat inclining to the north. At the very first sight, its oddness of figure promises something extraordinary; and even at that distance the prospect makes somewhat of a grand appearance: hundreds of aspiring pyramids presenting themselves all at once to the eye, look, if I may be allowed so

Description of Montserat.

to speak, like a little petrified forest ; or, rather, like the awful ruins of some capacious structure, the labour of venerable antiquity. The nearer you approach, the more it affects ; but till you are very near, you can hardly form in your mind any thing like what you find it when you come close to it. Till just upon it, you would imagine it a perfect hill of steeples ; but so intermingled with trees of magnitude, as well as beauty, that your admiration can never be tired, or your curiosity surfeited. Such I found it on my approach ; yet much less than what I found it was, so soon as I entered upon the very premises.

Now that stupendous cluster of pyramids affected me in a manner different to all before ; and I found it so finely grouped with verdant groves, and here and there interspersed with aspiring, but solitary trees, that it no way lessened my admiration, while it increased my delight. These trees, which I call solitary, as standing single, in opposition to the numerous groves, which are close and thick, (as I observed when I ascended to take a view of the several cells,) rise generally out of the very clifts of the main rock, with nothing, to appearance, but a soil or bed of stone for their nurture. But though some few naturalists may assert, that the nitre in the stone may afford a due proportion of nourishment to trees and vegetables; these, in my opinion, were all too beautiful, their bark, leaf, and flowers, carried too fair a face of health, to allow them even to be the foster-children of rock and stone only.

Upon this hill, or if you please, grove of rocks, are thirteen hermits cells, the last of which lies near the very summit. You gradually advance to every one, from bottom to top, by a winding ascent; which to do would otherwise be impossible, by reason of the steepness; but though there is a winding ascent to every cell, as I have said, I would yet set at defiance the most observant, if a stranger, to find it feasible to visit them in order, if not precautioned to follow the poor borigo, or old ass, that, with paniers hanging on each side of him, mounts regularly, and daily, up to every particular cell. The manner is as follows :

In the paniers there are thirteen partitions ; one for every cell. At the hour appointed, the servant having placed the paniers on his back, the ass, of himself, goes to the door of the convent at the very foot of the hill, where every partition is supplied with their several allowances of victuals and wine. Which, as soon as he has received, without any further attendance, or any guide, he mounts and takes the cells gradually, in their due course, till he reaches the very uppermost. Where having discharged his duty, he descends the same way, lighter by the load he carried up. This the poor stupid drudge fails not to do, day and night, at the stated hours.

Two gentlemen, who had joined me on the road, alike led by curiosity, seemed alike delighted, that the end of it was so well answered. I could easily discover in

their countenances a satisfaction, which,
if it did not give a sanction to my own,
much confirmed it, while they seemed to
allow with me that these reverend solitaries
were truly happy men : I then thought
them such ; and a thousand times since,
reflecting within myself, have wished, ba-
ting their errors, and lesser superstitions,
myself as happily stationed : for what can
there be wanting to a happy life, where all
things necessary are provided without care?
Where the days, without anxiety or troubles,
may be gratefully passed away, with an innocent variety of diverting and pleasing
objects, and where their sleeps and slum-
bers are never interrupted with any thing
more offensive, than murmuring springs,
natural cascades, or the various songs of
the pretty feathered quiristers ?

But their courtesy to strangers is no less
engaging than their solitude. A recluse
life, for the fruits of it, generally speaking,
produces moroseness ; pharisaical pride too
often sours the temper ; and a mistaken opi-

nion of their own merit too naturally leads such men into a contempt of others : but on the contrary, these good men (for I must call them as I thought them) seemed to me the very emblems of innocence ; so ready to oblige others, that at the same instant they seemed laying obligations upon themselves. This is self-evident, in that affability and complaisance they use in shewing the rarities of their several cells ; where, for fear you should slip any thing worthy observation, they endeavour to instil in you as quick a propensity of asking, as you find in them a prompt alacrity in answering, such questions of curiosity as their own have inspired.

In particular, I remember one of those reverend old men, when we were taking leave at the door of his cell, to which, out of his great civility, he accompanied us, finding by the air of our faces, as well as our expressions, that we thought ourselves pleasingly entertained ; to divert us afresh, advanced a few paces from the door, when, giving a whistle with his mouth, a surprising flock of pretty little birds, variegated, and of different colours, immediately flocked around him. Here you should see some alighting upon his shoulders, some on his awful beard; others took refuge on his snow-like head, and many feeding, and more endeavouring to feed, out of his mouth; each appearing emulous, and under an innocent contention, how best to express their love and respect to their no less pleased master.

Nor did the other cells labour under any deficiency of variety: every one boasting in some particular, that might distinguish it in something equally agreeable and entertaining. Nevertheless, crystal springs spouting from the solid rocks were, from the highest to the lowest, common to them all; and, in most of them, they had little brass cocks, out of which, when turned, issued the most cool and crystalline flows of excellent pure water. And yet what more affected me, and which I found near more cells than one, was the natural cascades of the same transparent element; these falling from one rock to another, in that warm, or rather hot climate, gave not more delightful astonishment to the eye, than they afforded grateful refreshment to the whole man. The streams falling from these, soften, from a rougher tumultuous noise, into such affecting murmurs, by distance, the intervention of groves, or neighbouring rocks, that it were impossible to see or hear them, and not be charmed.

Neither are those groves grateful only in a beautiful verdure ; nature renders them otherwise delightful, in loading them with clusters of berries of a perfect scarlet colour, which, by a beautiful intermixture, strike the eye with additional delight. In short, it might nonplus a person of the nicest taste, to distinguish or determine, whether the neatness of their cells within, or the beauteous varieties without, most exhaust his admiration. Nor is the whole, in my opinion, a little advantaged by the frequent view of some of those pyramidical pillars, which seem, as weary of their own weight, to recline and seek support from others in the neighbourhood.

When I mentioned the outside beauties of their cells, I must be thought to have forgot to particularize the glorious prospects presented to your eye from every one of them; but especially from that nearest the summit. A prospect, by reason of the purity of the air, so extensive, and so very entertaining, that to dilate upon it properly to one that never saw it, would baffle credit; and naturally to depaint it, would confound invention. I therefore shall only say, that on the Mediterranean side, after an agreeable interval of some fair leagues, it will set at defiance the strongest optics; and although Barcelona bounds it on the land, the eyes are feasted with the delights of such an intervening champaign, (where beauteous nature does not only smile but riot,) that the sense must be very temperate, or very weak, that can be soon or easily satisfied.

Having thus taken a view of all their refreshing springs, their grateful groves, and solitary shades under single trees, whose clusters proved that even rocks were grown fruitful; and having ran over all the variety of pleasures in their several pretty cells, decently set off with gardens round them, equally fragrant and beautiful, we were brought down again to the convent, which, though on a small ascent, lies very near the foot of this terrestrial paradise, there to take a survey of their sumptuous hall, much more sumptuous chapel, and its adjoining repository, and feast our eyes with wonders of a different nature; and yet as entertaining as any, or all, we had seen before.

Immediately on our descent, a priest presented himself at the door of the convent, ready to shew us the hidden rarities. And though, as I understood, hardly a day passes without the resort of some strangers to gratify their curiosity with the wonders of the place; yet is there, on every such occasion, a superior concourse of natives ready to see over again, out of mere bigotry and superstition, what they have seen perhaps a hundred times before. I could not avoid taking notice, however, that the priest treated those constant visitants with much less ceremony, or more freedom, if you please, than any of the strangers of what nation soever; or, indeed, he seemed to take as much pains to disoblige those, as he did pleasure in obliging us.

The hall was neat, large, and stately; but being plain and unadorned with more than decent decorations, suitable to such a society, I hasten to the other.

When we entered the chapel, our eyes were immediately attracted by the image of Our Lady of Montserat, (as they call it,) which stands over the altar-piece. It is about the natural stature; but as black and shining as ebony itself. Most would imagine it made of that material; though her retinue and adorers will allow nothing of the matter. On the contrary, tradition, which with them is, on some occasions, more than tantamount to religion, has assured them, and they relate it as undoubted matter of fact, that her present colour, if I may so call it, proceeded from her concealment, in the time of the Moors, between those two rocks on which the chapel is founded; and that her long lying in that dismal place changed her once lovely white into its present opposite. Would not a heretic here be apt to say, that it was great pity that an image, which still boasts the power of acting so many miracles, could no better conserve her own complexion? At least it must be allowed, even by a good catholic, to carry along with it matter of reproach to the fair ladies, natives of the country, for their unnatural and excessive affection of adulterating, if not defacing, their beautiful faces, with the ruinating dauberies of carmine?

As the custom of the place is, (which is likewise allowed to be a distinguishing piece of civility to strangers,) when we approach the black lady, (who, I should have told you, bears a child in her arms; but whether maternally black, or of the Mulatto kind, I protest I did not mind,) the priest, in great civility, offers you her arm to salute; at which juncture, I, like a true blue protestant, mistaking my word of command, fell foul on the fair lady's face. The displeasure in his countenance (for he took more notice of the rudeness than the good lady herself) soon convinced me of my error; however, as a greater token of his civility, having admitted no Spaniards along with my companions and me, it passed off the better; and his after civilities manifested, that he was willing to reform my ignorance by his complaisance.

To demonstrate which, upon my telling him that I had a set of beads, which I must entreat him to consecrate for me, he readily, nay eagerly complied; and having hung them on her arm for the space of about half, or somewhat short of a whole minute, he returned me the holy baubles with a great deal of address, and most evident satisfaction. The reader will be apt to admire at this curious piece of superstition of mine, till I have told him, that even rigid protestants have, in this country, thought it but prudent to do the like; and likewise having so done, to carry them about their persons, or in their pockets; for experience has convinced us of the necessity of this most catholic precaution; since those who have here, travelling or otherwise, come to their ends, whether by accident, sickness, or the course of nature, not having these sanctifying seals found upon them, have ever been refused Christian burial, under a superstitious imagination, that the corpse of a heretic will infect every thing near it.

Two instances of this kind fell within my knowledge; one before I came to Montserat, the other after. The first was of one Slunt, who had been bombardier at Monjouick; but being killed while we lay at Campilio, a priest, whom I advised with upon the matter, told me, that if he should be buried where any corn grew, his body would not only be taken up again, but ill treated, in revenge of the destruction of so much corn, which the people would on no account be persuaded to touch; for which reason we took care to have him laid in a very deep grave, on a very barren spot of ground. The other was of one Captain Bush, who was a prisoner with me on the surrender of Denia; who being sent, as I was afterwards, to Saint Clemente la Mancha, there died; and, as I was informed, though he was privately, and by night, buried in a corn field, he was taken out of his grave by those superstitious people, as soon as ever they could discover the place where his body was deposited. But I return to the convent at Montserat.

Out of the chapel, behind the high altar, we descended into a spacious room, the repository of the great offerings made to the Lady. Here, though I thought in the chapel itself I had seen the riches of the universe, I found a prodigious quantity of more costly presents, the superstitious tribute of most of the Roman Catholic princes in Europe. Among a multitude of others, they showed me a sword set with diamonds, the offering of Charles the Third, then King of Spain, but now Emperor of Germany. Though I must confess, being a heretic, I could much easier find a reason for a fair lady's presenting such a sword to a king of Spain, than for a king of Spain's presenting such a sword to a fair lady: and by the motto upon it, *Pulchra tamen nigra*, it was plain such was his opinion. That prince was so delighted with the pleasures of this sweet place, that he, as well as I, staid as long as ever he could; though neither of us so long as either could have wished.

But there was another offering from a king of Portugal, equally glorious and costly, but much better adapted; and therefore in its propriety easier to be accounted for. That was a glory for the head of her ladyship, every ray of which was set with diamonds, large at the bottom, and gradually lessening to the very extremity of every ray. Each ray might be about half a yard long; and I imagined in the whole, there might be about one hundred of them. In short, if ever her ladyship did the offerer the honour to put it on, I will, though a heretic, venture to aver, she did not at that present time look like a human creature.

To enumerate the rest, if my memory would suffice, would exceed belief. As the upper part was a plain miracle of nature, the lower was a complete treasury of miraculous art.

If you ascend from the lowest cell to the very summit, the last of all the thirteen, you will perceive a continual contention between pleasure and devotion; and at last, perhaps, find yourself at a loss to decide which deserves the pre-eminence : for you are not here to take cells in the vulgar acceptation, as the little dormitories of solitary monks: No! Neatness, use, and contrivance, appear in every one of them ; and though in an almost perfect equality, yet in such perfection, that you will find it difficult to discover in any one of them any thing wanting to the pleasure of life.

If you descend to the convent near the foot of that venerable hill, you may see more, much more of the riches of the world; but less, far less appearance of a celestial treasure. Perhaps, it might be only the sentiment of a heretic; but that awe and devotion, which I found in my attendant from cell to cell, grew languid, and lost, in mere empty bigotry and foggy superstition, when I came below. In short, there was not a greater difference in their heights, than in the sentiments they inspired me with.

Before I leave this emblem of the beatific vision, I must correct some thing like a mistake, as to the poor *borigo*. I said at the beginning, that his labour was daily; but the Sunday is to him a day of rest, as it is to the hermits, his masters, a day of refection. For, to save the poor faithful brute the hard drudgery of that day, the thirteen hermits, if health permit, descend to their Cœnobium, as they call it; that is, to the hall of the convent, where they dine in common with the monks of the order, who are Benedictines.

After seven days variety of such innocent delight, (the space allowed for the entertainment of strangers,) I took my leave of this pacific hermitage, to pursue the more boisterous duties of my calling. The life of a soldier is in every respect the full antithesis to that of a hermit; and I know not, whether it might not be a sense of that, which inspired me with very great reluctancy at parting. I confess, while on the spot, I over and over bandied in my mind the reasons which might prevail upon Charles the Fifth to relinquish his crown; and the arguments on his side never failed of energy, when I could persuade myself that this, or some like happy retreat, was the reward of abdicated empire.

Full of these contemplations, (for they lasted there,) I arrived at Barcelona; where

I found a vessel ready to sail, on which I embarked for Denia, in pursuance of my orders. Sailing to the mouth of the Mediterranean, no place along the Christian shore affords a prospect equally delightful with the castle of Denia. It was never designed for a place of great strength, being built, and first designed, as a seat of pleasure to the great Duke of Lerma. In that family it many years remained; though, within less than a century, that with two other dukedoms have devolved upon the family of the Duke de Medina Celi, the richest subject at this time in all Spain.

Denia was the first town, that, in our way to Barcelona, declared for King Charles; and was then by his order made a garrison. The town is but small, and surrounded with a thin wall; so thin, that I have known a cannon ball pierce through it at once.

When I arrived at Denia, I found a Spaniard governor of the town, whose name has slipt my memory; though his behaviour merited everlasting annals. Major Percival, an Englishman, commanded in the castle, and on my coming there, I understood it had been agreed between them, that in case of a siege, which they apprehended, the town should be defended wholly by Spaniards, and the castle by the English.

I had scarce been there three weeks before those expectations were answered. The place was invested by Count D'Alfelt, and Major General Mahoni; two days after which, they opened trenches on the east side of the town. I was necessitated, upon their so doing, to order the demolishment of some houses on that side, that I might erect a battery to point upon their trenches, the better to annoy them. I did so; and it did the intended service; for with that, and two others, which I raised upon the castle, (from all which we fired incessantly, and with great success,) the besiegers were sufficiently incommoded.

The governor of the town (a Spaniard as I said before, and with a Spanish garrison) behaved very gallantly; insomuch, that what was said of the Prince of Hesse, when he so bravely defended Gibraltar against the joint forces of France and Spain, might be said of him, that he was governor, engineer, gunner, and bombardier all in one: for no man could exceed him, either in conduct or courage. Nor were the Spaniards under him less valiant or vigilant; for in case the place was taken, expecting but indifferent quarter, they fought with bravery, and defended the place to admiration.

The enemy had answered our fire with all the ardour imaginable; and having made a breach, that, as we thought, was practicable, a storm was expected every hour. Preparing against which, to the great joy of all the inhabitants, and the surprise of the whole garrison, and without our being able to assign the least cause, the enemy suddenly raised the siege, and withdrew from a place, which those within imagined in great danger.

The siege thus abdicated, (if I may use

a modern phrase,) I was resolved to improve my time, and make the best provision I could against any future attack. To that purpose I made several new fortifications, together with proper casements for our powder, all which rendered the place much stronger, though time too soon shewed me that strength itself must yield to fortune.

Surveying those works, and my workmen, I was one day standing on the great battery, when, casting my eye toward the Barbary coast, I observed an odd sort of greenish cloud making to the Spanish shore; not like other clouds with rapidity or swiftness; but with a motion so slow, that sight itself was a long time before it would allow it such. At last, it came just over my head, and interposing between the sun and me, so thickened the air, that I had lost the very sight of day. At this moment it had reached the land; and though very near me in my imagination, it began to dissolve, and lose of its first tenebrity, when, all on a sudden, there fell such a vast multitude of locusts, as exceeded the thickest storm of hail or snow that I ever saw. All around me was immediately covered with those crawling creatures; and they yet continued to fall so thick, that with the swing of my cane I knocked down thousands. It is scarce imaginable the havoc I made in a very little space of time; much less conceivable is the horrid desolation which attended the visitation of those animalculæ. There was not, in a day or two's time, the least leaf to be seen upon a tree, nor any green thing in a garden. Nature seemed buried in her own ruins; and the vegetable world to be supporters only to her monument. I never saw the hardest winter, in those parts, attended with any equal desolation. When, glutton-like, they had devoured all that should have sustained them, and the more valuable part of God's creation, (whether weary with gorging, or over thirsty with devouring, I leave to philosophers,) they made to ponds, brooks, and standing pools, there revenging their own rape upon nature, upon their own vile carcases. In every one of these you might see them lie in heaps like little hills; drowned indeed, but attended with stenches so noisome, that it gave the distracted neighbourhood too great reason to apprehend yet more fatal consequences. A pestilential infection is the dread of every place, but especially of all parts upon the Mediterranean. The priests, therefore, repaired to a little chapel, built in the open fields, to be made use of on such like occasions, there to deprecate the miserable cause of this dreadful visitation. In a week's time, or thereabouts, the stench was over, and every thing but verdant nature in its pristine order.

Some few months after this, and about eight months from the former siege, Count D'Alfelt caused Denia to be again invested; and being then sensible of all the mistakes he had before committed, he now went about his business with more regularity and discretion. The first thing he set upon, and it was the wisest thing he could do, was to cut off our communication with the sea. This he did, and thereby obtained what he much desired. Next, he caused his batteries to be erected on the west side of the town, from which he plied it so furiously, that in five days time a practicable breach was made; upon which they stormed and took it. The governor, who had so bravely defended it in the former siege, fortunately for him, had been removed; and Francis Valero, now in his place, was made prisoner of war with all his garrison.

After the taking the town, they erected batteries against the castle, which they kept plied with incessant fire, both from cannon and mortars. But what most of all plagued us, and did us most mischief, was the vast showers of stones sent among the garrison from their mortars. These, terrible in bulk and size, did more execution than all the rest put together. The garrison could not avoid being somewhat disheartened at this uncommon way of rencounter; yet, to a man, declared against hearkening to any proposals of surrender, the governor excepted; who, having selected more treasure than he could properly or justly call his own, was the only person that seemed forward for such a motion. He had more than once thrown out expressions of such a nature, but without any effect. Nevertheless, having at last secretly obtained a peculiar capitulation for himself, bag, and baggage; the garrison was sacrificed to his private interest, and basely given up prisoners of war. By these means, indeed, he saved his money, but lost his reputation; and soon after, life itself. And sure every body will allow the latter loss to be least, who will take pains to consider, that it screened him from the consequential scrutinies of a council of war, which must have issued as the just reward of his demerits.

The garrison being thus unaccountably delivered up and made prisoners, were dispersed different ways: some into Castile, others as far as Oviedo, in the kingdom of

Leon. For my own part, having received a contusion in my breast, I was under a necessity of being left behind with the enemy, till I should be in a condition to be removed, and when that time came, I found myself agreeably ordered to Valencia.

As a prisoner of war, I must now bid adieu to the active part of the military life; and hereafter concern myself with descriptions of countries, towns, palaces, and men, instead of battles. However, if I take in my way actions of war, founded on the best authorities, I hope my interspersing such will be no disadvantage to my now more pacific Memoirs.

So soon as I arrived at Valencia, I wrote to our pay-master Mr Mead, at Barcelona, letting him know, that I was become a prisoner, wounded, and in want of money. Nor could even all those circumstances prevail on me to think it long before he returned a favourable answer, in an order to Monsieur Zoulicafre, a banker, to pay me on sight fifty pistoles. But in the same letter he gave me to understand, that those fifty pistoles were a present to me from General (afterwards Earl) Stanhope; and so indeed I found it, when I returned into England, my account not being charged with any part of it: but this was not the only test I received of that generous Earl's generosity. And where's the wonder, as the world is compelled to own, that heroic actions and largeness of soul ever did discover and amply distinguish the genuine branches of that illustrious family?

This recruit to me, however, was the more generous for being seasonable. Benefits are always doubled in their being easily conferred and well timed; and with such an allowance as I constantly had by the order of King Philip, as prisoner of war, viz. eighteen ounces of mutton *per diem* for myself, and nine for my man, with bread and wine in proportion, and especially in such a situation; all this, I say, was sufficient to invite a man to be easy, and almost forget his want of liberty, and much more so to me, if it be considered, that that want of liberty consisted only in being debarred from leaving the pleasantest city in all Spain.

Here I met with the French engineer, who made the mine under the rock of the castle at Alicant; that fatal mine, which blew up General Richards, Colonel Syburg, Colonel Thornicroft, and at least twenty more officers. And yet by the account that engineer gave me, their fate was their own choosing; the General, who commanded at that siege, being more industrious to save them than they were to be saved: he endeavoured it many ways: he sent them word of the mine, and their readiness to spring it; he over and over sent them offers of leave to come and take a view of it, and inspect it. Notwithstanding all which, though Colonel Thornicroft, and Captain Page, a French engineer in the service of King Charles, pursued the invitation, and were permitted to view it, yet would they not believe; but reported on their return, that it was a sham mine, a feint only to intimidate them to a surrender, all the bags being filled with sand instead of gunpowder.

The very day on which the besiegers designed to spring the mine, they gave notice of it; and the people of the neighbourhood ran up in crowds to an opposite hill in order to see it: nevertheless, although those in the castle saw all this, they still remained so infatuated, as to imagine it all done only to affright them. At length the fatal mine was sprung, and all who were upon that battery lost their lives; and among them those I first mentioned. The very recital hereof made me think within myself, who can resist his fate?

That engineer added further, that it was with an incredible difficulty, that he prepared that mine; that there were in the concavity thirteen hundred barrels of powder; notwithstanding which, it made no great noise without, whatever it might do inwardly; that only taking away what might be not improperly termed an excrescence in the rock, the heave on the blast had rendered the castle rather stronger on that side than it was before; a crevice or crack, which had often occasioned apprehensions, being thereby wholly closed and firm.

Some further particulars I soon after had from Colonel Syburg's gentleman; who, seeing me at the play-house, challenged me, though at that time unknown to me. He told me, that, the night preceding the unfortunate catastrophe of his master, he was waiting on him in the casement, where he observed, sometime before the rest of the company took notice of it, that General Richards appeared very pensive and thoughtful, that the whole night long he was pestered with, and could not get rid of a great fly, which was perpetually buzzing about his ears and head, to the vexation and disturbance of the rest of the company, as well as the General himself; that in the morning, when they went upon the battery, under which the mine was, the General made many offers of going off; but Colonel Syburg, who was got a little merry, and the rest out of a bravado, would stay, and would not let the General stir ; that at last it was proposed by Colonel Syburg to have the other two bottles to the queen's health, after which he promised they would all go off together.

Upon this my relater, Syburg's gentleman, said, he was sent to fetch the stipulated two bottles ; returning with which, Captain Daniel Weaver, within thirty or forty yards of the battery, ran by him, vowing, he was resolved to drink the queen's health with them ; but his feet were scarce on the battery, when the mine was sprung, which took him away with the rest of the company ; while Major Harding, now a justice in Westminster, coming that very moment off duty, exchanged fates.

If predestination, in the eyes of many, is an unaccountable doctrine, what better account can the wisest give of this fatality ? Or to what else shall we impute the issue of this whole transaction ? That men shall be solicited to their safety; suffered to survey the danger they were threatened with; among many other tokens of its approaching certainty, see such a concourse of people crowding to be spectators of their impending catastrophe; and, after all this, so infatuated to stay on the fatal spot the fetching up of the other two bottles; whatever it may to such as never think, to such as plead an use of reason, it must administer matter worthy of the sedatest consideration.

Being now pretty well recovered of my wounds, I was, by order of the governor of Valencia, removed to Sainte Clemente de la Mancha, a town somewhat more inland, and consequently esteemed more secure than a semi-seaport. Here I remained under a sort of pilgrimage upwards of three years. To me as a stranger, divested of acquaintance or friend, (for at that instant I was sole prisoner there,) at first it appeared such, though in a very small compass of time, I luckily found it made quite otherwise by an agreeable conversation.

Sainte Clemente de la Mancha is rendered famous by the renowned Don Michael Cervantes, who in his facetious but satirical romance, has fixed it the seat and birth-place of his hero Don Quixotte.

The gentlemen of this place are the least priest-ridden, or sons of bigotry, of any that I met with in all Spain ; of which, in my conversation with them, I had daily instances. Among many others, an expression that fell from Don Felix Pacheo, a gentleman of the best figure thereabout, and of a very plentiful fortune, shall now suffice. I was become very intimate with him ; and we used often to converse together with a freedom too dangerous to be common in a country so enslaved by the Inquisition. Asking me one day in a sort of a jocose manner, who, in my opinion, had done the greatest miracles that ever were heard of? I answered, Jesus Christ. " It is very true," says he, " Jesus Christ did great miracles, and a great one it was to feed five thousand people with two or three small fishes, and a like number of loaves : but Saint Francis, the founder of the Franciscan order, has found out a way to feed daily one hundred thousand lubbards with nothing at all ;" meaning the Franciscans, the followers of Saint Francis, who have no visible revenues ; yet in their way of living come up to, if they do not exceed, any other order.

Another day, talking of the place, it naturally led us into a discourse of the knight of la Mancha, Don Quixotte. At which time he told me, that, in his opinion, that work was a perfect paradox, being the best and the worst romance that ever was wrote. " For," says he, " though it must infallibly please every man, that has any taste of wit; yet has it had such a fatal effect upon the spirits of my countrymen, that every man of wit must ever resent ; for, continued he, before the appearance in the world of that labour of Cervantes, it was next to an impossibility for a man to walk the streets with any delight, or without danger. There were seen so many cavalieros prancing and curvetting before the windows of their mistresses, that a stranger would have imagined the whole nation to have been nothing less than a race of knight errants. But after the world became a little acquainted with that notable history, the man that was seen in that once celebrated drapery, was pointed at as a Don Quixotte, and found himself the jest of high and low. And I verily believe, added he, that to this, and this only, we owe that dampness and poverty of spirit, which has run through all our councils for a century past, so little agreeable to those nobler actions of our famous ancestors."

After many of these lesser sorts of confidences, Don Felix recommended me to a lodging next door to his own. It was at a widow's, who had one only daughter, her house just opposite to a Franciscan nunnery. Here I remained somewhat upwards of two years; all which time, lying in my bed, I could hear the nuns early in the morning at their matins, and late in the evening at their vespers, with delight enough to myself, and without the least indecency in the world in my thoughts of them. Their own divine employ too much employed every faculty of mine, to entertain any thing inconsentaneous or offensive.

This my neighbourhood to the nunnery gave me an opportunity of seeing two nuns invested; and in this I must do a justice to the whole country, to acknowledge, that a stranger, who is curious, (I would impute it rather to their hopes of conversion, than to their vanity,) shall be admitted to much greater freedoms in their religious pageantries, than any native.

One of these nuns was of the first quality, which rendered the ceremony more remarkably fine. The manner of investing them was thus: In the morning her relations and friends all met at her father's house; whence, she being attired in her most sumptuous apparel, and a coronet placed on her head, they attended her, in cavalcade, to the nunnery, the streets and windows being crowded, and filled with spectators of all sorts.

So soon as she entered the chapel belonging to the nunnery, she kneeled down, and, with an appearance of much devotion, saluted the ground; then rising up, she advanced a step or two farther; when on her knees she repeated the salutes: This done, she approached to the altar, where she remained till mass was over: after which, a sermon was preached by one of the priests in praise, or rather in an exalted preference, of a single life. The sermon being over, the nun elect fell down on her knees before the altar; and, after some short mental orisons, rising again, she withdrew into an inner room, where, stripping off all her rich attire, she put on her nun's weeds: in which making her appearance, she, again kneeling, offered up some private devotions; which being over, she was led to the door of the nunnery, where the lady and the rest of the nuns stood ready to receive her with open arms. Thus entered, the nuns conducted her into the quire, where after they had entertained her with singing, and playing upon the organ, the ceremony concluded, and every one departed to their proper habitations.

The very same day of the year ensuing, the relations and friends of the fair novitiate meet again in the chapel of the nunnery, where the Lady Abbess brings her out, and delivers her to them. Then again is there a sermon preached on the same subject as at first; which being over, she is brought up to the altar in a decent, but plain dress, the fine apparel, which she put off on her initiation, being deposited on one side of the altar, and her nun's weeds on the other. Here the priest in Latin cries, *Utrum horum mavis, accipe:* to which she answers, as her inclination, or as her instruction, directs her. If she, after this her year of probation, show any dislike, she is at liberty to come again into the world: but if awed by fear, (as too often is the case,) or won by expectation, or present real inclination, she makes choice of the nun's weeds, she is immediately invested, and must never expect to appear again in the world out of the walls of the nunnery. The young lady I thus saw invested was very beautiful, and sang the best of any in the nunnery.

There are in the town three nunneries, and a convent to every one of them; viz. one of Jesuits, one of Carmelites, and the other of Franciscans. Let me not be so far mistaken, to have this taken by way of reflection. No! whatever some of our rakes of the town may assert, I freely declare, that I never saw in any of the nunneries (of which I have seen many both in Spain and other parts of the world) any thing like indecent behaviour, that might give occasion for satire or disesteem. It is true, there may be accidents, that may lead to a misinterpretation; of which I remember a very untoward instance in Alicant.

When the English forces first laid siege to that town, the priests, who were apprehensive of it, having been long since made sensible of the profound regard to chastity and modesty of us heretics, by the ignominious behaviour of certain officers at Rota and Porta St Maria, the priests, I say, had taken care to send away privately all the nuns to Majorca. But that the heretic invaders might have no jealousy of it, the fair courtezans of the town were admitted to supply their room. The officers, both of land and sea, as was by the friars pre-imagined, on taking the town and castle, immediately repaired to the grates of the nunnery, tossed over their handkerchiefs, nosegays, and other pretty things; all which were, doubtless, very graciously received by those imaginary recluses. Thence came it to pass, that, in the space of a month or less, you could hardly fall into company of any one of our younger officers, of either sort, but the discourse, if it might deserve the name, was concerning these beautiful nuns; and you would have imagined the price of these ladies as well known as that of flesh in their common markets. Others, as well as myself, have often endeavoured to disabuse those gloriosos, but all to little purpose, till more sensible tokens convinced them, that the nuns, of whose favours they so much boasted, could hardly be perfect virgins, though in a cloister. And I am apt to think, those who would palm upon the world like vicious relations of nuns and nunneries, do it on much like grounds. Not that there are wanting instances of nunneries disfranchised, and even demolished, upon very flagrant accounts; but I confine myself to Spain.

In this town of La Mancha, the corrigidore always has his presidence, having sixteen others under his jurisdiction, of which Almanza is one. They are changed every three years, and their offices are the purchase of an excessive price, which occasions the poor people's being extravagantly fleeced, nothing being to be sold but at the rates they impose; and every thing that is sold, paying the corrigidore an acknowledgment in specie, or an equivalent to his liking.

While I was here, news came of the battle of Almanar and Saragosa; and giving the victory to that side, which they espoused, (that of King Philip,) they made very great rejoicings. But soon, alas, for them, was all that joy converted into sorrow: the next courier evincing, that the forces of King Charles had been victorious in both engagements. This did not turn to my present disadvantage; for convents and nunneries, as well as some of those Dons, whom afore I had not stood so well with, strove now how most to oblige me; not doubting, but if the victorious army should march that way, it might be in my power to double the most signal of their services in my friendship.

Soon after an accident fell out, which

had like to have been of an unhappy consequence to me. I was standing in company, upon the parade, when a most surprising flock of eagles flew over our heads, where they hovered for a considerable time. The novelty struck them all with admiration, as well as myself. But I, less accustomed to like spectacles, innocently saying, that, in my opinion, it could not bode any good to King Philip, because the eagle composed the arms of Austria; some busy body, in hearing, went and informed the corrigidore of it. Those most magisterial wretches embrace all occasions of squeezing money, and more especially from strangers. However, finding his expectations disappointed in me, and that I too well knew the length of his foot, to let my money run freely; he sent me next day to Alercon; but the governor of that place having had before intelligence, that the English army was advancing that way, refused to receive me, so I returned as I went; only the gentlemen of the place, as they had condoled the first, congratulated the last; for that corrigidore stood but very indifferently in their affections. However, it was a warning to me ever after, how I made use of English freedom in a Spanish territory.

As I had attained the acquaintance of most of the clergy and religious of the place; so particularly I had my aim in obtaining that of the provincial of the Carmelites. His convent, though small, was exceeding neat; but what to me was much more agreeable, there were very large gardens belonging to it, which often furnished me with sallading and fruit, and much oftener with walks of refreshment, the most satisfactory amusement in this warm climate. This acquaintance with the provincial was by a little incident soon advanced into a friendship, which was thus: I was one day walking, as I used to do, in the long gallery of the convent, when, observing the images of the Virgin Mary, of which there was one at each end, I took notice, that one had an inscription under it, which was this: *Ecce,*

Virgo peperit filium; but the other had no inscription at all; upon which, I took out my pencil, and wrote underneath this line;

Sponsa Dei, patrisque parens, et filis filii.

The friars, who at a little distance had observed me, as soon as I was gone, came up and read what I had writ; reporting which to the provincial, he ordered them to be writ over in letters of gold, and placed just as I had put them; saying, doubtless, such a fine line could proceed from nothing less than inspiration. This secured me ever after his and their esteem; the least advantage of which was a full liberty of their garden for all manner of fruit, sallading, or whatever I pleased: and, as I said before, the gardens were too fine not to render such a freedom acceptable.

They often want rain in this country; to supply the defect of which, I observed in this garden, as well as others, an invention not unuseful. There is a well in the middle of the garden, and over that a wheel with many pitchers, or buckets, one under another, which wheel being turned round by an ass, the pitchers scoop up the water on one side, and throw it out on the other into a trough, that by little channels conveys it, as the gardener directs, into every part of the garden. By this means their flowers and their sallading are continually refreshed, and preserved from the otherwise over-parching beams of the sun.

The inquisition, in almost every town in Spain, (and more especially, if of any great account,) has its spies, or informers, for treacherous intelligence. These make it their business to ensnare the simple and unguarded; and are more to be avoided by the stranger, than the rattlesnake; nature having appointed no such happy tokens in the former to foreshew the danger. I had reason to believe, that one of those vermin once made his attack upon me in this place: and as they are very rarely, if ever, known to the natives themselves, I being a stranger, may be allowed to make a guess by circumstances.

I was walking by myself, when a person, wholly unknown to me, giving me the civil salute of the day, endeavoured to draw me into conversation. After questions had passed on general heads, the fellow ensnaringly asked me, how it came to pass, that I showed so little respect to the image of the crucified Jesus, as I passed by it in such a street, naming it? I made answer, that I had, or ought to have him always in my heart crucified. To that he made no reply: but, proceeding in his interrogatories, questioned me next, whether I believed a purgatory? I evaded the question, as I took it to be ensnaring; and only told him, that I should be willing to hear him offer any thing that might convince me of the truth, or probability of it. " Truth ?" he replied in a heat : " there never yet was man so holy as to enter heaven without first passing through purgatory."—" In my opinion," said I, " there will be no difficulty in convincing a reasonable man to the contrary."—" What mean you by that?" cried the spy.—" I mean," said I, " that I can name one, and a great sinner too, who went into bliss without any visit to purgatory." —" Name him if you can," replied my querist. " What think you of the thief upon the cross," said I, " to whom our dying Saviour said, *Hodie eris mecum in paradiso?*" At which being silenced, though not convicted, he turned from me in a violent rage, and left me to myself.

What increased my first suspicion of him was, that a very short time after, my friend the provincial sent to speak with me ; and repeating all passages between the holy spy and me, assured me, that he had been forced to argue in my favour, and tell him, that I had said nothing but well : " For," says he, " all ought to have the holy Jesus crucified in their hearts. Nevertheless," continued he, " it is a commendable and good thing to have him represented in the high ways. For, suppose," said he, " a man was going upon some base or profligate design, the very sight of a crucified Saviour may happen to subvert his resolution, and deter him from committing theft, murder, or any other of the deadly sins." And thus ended that conference.

I remember upon some other occasional conversation after, the provincial told me, that in the Carmelite nunnery next to his convent, and under his care, there was a nun, that was daughter to Don Juan of Austria; if so, her age must render her venerable, as her quality.

Taking notice one day, that all the people of the place fetched their water from a well without the town, although they had many seemingly as good within; I spoke to Don Felix of it, who gave me, under the seal of secrecy, this reason for it: " When the seat of the war," said he, " lay in these parts, the French train of artillery was commonly quartered in this place; the officers and soldiers of which were so very rampant and rude, in attempting to debauch our women, that there is not a well within the town, which has not some Frenchmen's bones at the bottom of it; therefore the natives, who are sensible of it, choose rather to go farther afield."

By this well there runs a little rivulet, which gives head to that famous river called the Guadiana; which running for some leagues under ground, affords a pretence for the natives to boast of a bridge on which they feed many thousands of sheep. When it rises again, it is a fine large river, and after a currency of many leagues, empties itself into the Atlantic ocean.

As to military affairs, Almanar and Saragosa were victories so complete, that no body made the least doubt of their settling the crown of Spain upon the head of Charles the Third, without a rival. This was not barely the opinion of his friends, but his very enemies resigned all hope or expectation in favour of King Philip. The Castilians, his most faithful friends, entertained no other imagination; for after they had advised, and prevailed that the Queen with the Prince of Asturias should be sent to Victoria, under the same despondency, and a full dispiritedness, they gave him so little encouragement to stay in Madrid, that he immediately quitted the place, with a resolution to retire into his grandfather's dominions, the place of his nativity.

In his way to which, even on the last day's journey, it was his great good fortune to meet the Duke of Vendosme, with some few troops, which his grandfather Louis XIV. of France had ordered to his succour, under that Duke's command. The Duke was grievously affected at such an unexpected catastrophe; nevertheless, he left nothing unsaid or undone, that might induce that prince to turn back; and at length prevailing, after a little rest, and a great deal of patience, by the coming in of his scattered troops, and some few he could raise, together with those the Duke brought with him, he once more saw himself at the head of twenty thousand men.

While things were in this manner, under motion in King Philip's favour, Charles the Third, with his victorious army, advances forward, and enters into Madrid, of which he made General Stanhope governor. And even here the Castilians gave full proof of their fidelity to their prince; even at the time when, in their opinion, his affairs were past all hopes of retrieve, they themselves having, by their advice, contributed to his retreat. Instead of prudential acclamations therefore, such as might have answered the expectations of a victorious prince, now entering into their capital, their streets were all in a profound silence, their balconies unadorned with costly carpets, as was customary on like occasions; and scarce an inhabitant to be seen in either shop or window.

This, doubtless, was no little mortification to a conquering Prince; however, his Generals were wise enough to keep him from shewing any other tokens of resentment, than marching through the city with unconcern, and taking up his quarters at Villaverda, about a league from it.

Nevertheless King Charles visited, in his march, the chapel of the Lady de Atocha, where finding several English colours and standards, taken in the battle of Almanza, there hung up, he ordered them to be taken down, and restored them to the English General.

It was the current opinion then, and almost universal consent has since confirmed it, that the falsest step in that whole war, was this advancement of King Charles to Madrid. After those two remarkable victories at Almanar and Saragosa, had he directed his march to Pampeluna, and obtained possession of that place, or some other near it, he had not only stopt all succours from coming out of France, but he would, in a great measure, have prevented the gathering together of any of the routed and dispersed forces of King Philip: and it was the general notion of the Spaniards I conversed with while at Madrid, that had

King Philip once again set his foot upon French land, Spain would never have been brought to have re-acknowledged him.

King Charles with his army having staid some time about Madrid, and seeing his expectations of the Castilians joining him not at all answered, at last resolved to decamp, and return to Saragosa. Accordingly, with a very few troops, that Prince advanced thither; while the main body, under the command of the Generals Stanhope and Staremberg, passing under the very walls of Madrid, held on their march towards Arragon.

After about three days march, General Stanhope took up his quarters at Breuhiga, a small town half walled; General Staremberg marching three leagues farther, to Cifuentes. This choice of situation of the two several armies, not a little puzzled the politicians of those times; who could very indifferently account for the English General's lying exposed in an open town, with his few English forces, of which General Harvey's regiment of fine horse might be deemed the main; and General Staremberg encamping three leagues farther off the enemy. But to see the vicissitudes of fortune, to which the actions of the bravest, by an untoward sort of fatality, are often forced to contribute! None who had been eye-witnesses of the bravery of either of those Generals at the battles of Almanar and Saragosa, could find room to call in question either their conduct or their courage; and yet in this march, and this encampment, will appear a visible ill consequence to the affairs of the interest they fought for.

The Duke of Vendosme having increased the forces which he brought from France to upwards of twenty thousand men, marches by Madrid directly for Breuhiga, where his intelligence informed him General Stanhope lay, and that so secretly, as well as swiftly, that that General knew nothing of it, nor could be persuaded to believe it, till the very moment their bullets from the enemy's cannon convinced him of the truth.

Breuhiga, I have said, was walled only on one side, and yet on that very side the enemy made their attack. But what could a handful do against a force so much superior, though they had not been in want of both powder and ball; and, in want of these, were forced to make use of stones against all sorts of ammunition, which the enemy plyed them with? The consequence answered the deficiency; they were all made prisoners of war, and Harvey's regiment of horse among the rest; which, to augment their calamity, was immediately remounted by the enemy, and marched along with their army to attack General Staremberg.

That General had heard somewhat of the march of Vendosme, and waited with some impatience to have the confirmation of it from General Stanhope, who lay between, and whom he lay under an expectation of being joined with; however, he thought it not improper to make some little advance towards him: and accordingly, breaking up from his camp at Cifuentes, he came back to Villa Viciosa, a little town between Cifuentes and Breuhiga. There he found Vendosme ready to attack him, before he could well be prepared for him, but no English to join him, as he had expected; nevertheless, the battle was hot, and obstinately fought; although Staremberg had visibly the advantage, having beat the enemy at least a league from their cannon; at which time, hearing of the misfortune of Breuhiga, and finding himself thereby frustrated of those expected succours to support him, he made a handsome retreat to Barcelona, which in common calculation is about one hundred leagues, without any disturbance of an enemy, that seemed glad to be rid of him. Nevertheless, his baggage having fallen into the hands of the enemy, at the beginning of the fight, King Philip and the Duke of Vendosme generously returned it unopened, and untouched, in acknowledgement of his brave behaviour.

I had like to have omitted one material passage, which I was very credibly informed of; that General Carpenter offered to have gone, and have joined General Staremberg with the horse, which was refused him. This was certainly an oversight of the highest nature; since his going would have strengthened Staremberg almost to the assurance of an entire victory; whereas his stay was of no manner of service, but quite the contrary: for, as I said before, the enemy, by remounting the English horse, (which perhaps were the completest of any regiment in the world,) turned, if I may be allowed the expression, the strength of our artillery upon our allies.

Upon this retreat of Staremberg, and the surprise at Breuhiga, there were great rejoicings at Madrid, and every where else, where King Philip's interest prevailed. And indeed it might be said, from that day the interest of King Charles looked with a very lowering aspect. I was still a prisoner at La Mancha, when this news arrived; and very sensibly affected at that strange turn of fortune. I was in bed when the express passed through the town, in order to convey it farther; and in the middle of the night I heard a certain Spanish Don, with whom, a little before, I had had some little variance, thundering at my door, endeavouring to burst it open, with, as I had reason to suppose, no very favourable design upon me. But my landlady, who hitherto had always been kind and careful, calling Don Felix, and some others of my friends together, saved me from the fury of his designs, whatever they were.

Among other expressions of the general joy upon this occasion, there was a bullfeast at La Mancha; which being much beyond what I saw at Valencia, I shall here give a description of. These bull-feasts are not so common now in Spain as formerly, King Philip not taking much delight in them. Nevertheless, as soon as it was published here, that there was to be one, no other discourse was heard; and in the talk of the bulls, and the great preparations for the feast, men seemed to have lost, or to have laid aside, all thoughts of the very occasion. A week's time was allowed for the building of stalls for the beasts, and scaffolds for the spectators, and other necessary preparations for the setting off their joy with the most suitable splendour.

On the day appointed for the bringing the bulls into town, the cavalieroes mounted their horses, and, with spears in their hands, rode out of town about a league, or somewhat more, to meet them : if any of the bulls break from the drove, and make an excursion, (as they frequently do,) the cavaliero that can make him return again to his station among his companions, is held in honour, suitable to the dexterity and address he performs it with. On their entrance into the town, all the windows are filled with spectators; a pope passing in grand procession could not have more; for what can be more than all? And he, or she, who should neglect so rare a show, would give occasion to have his or her legitimacy called in question.

When they come to the Plaza, where the stalls and scaffolds are built, and upon which the feats of chivalry are to be performed, it is often with a great deal of difficulty that the brutes are got in; for there are twelve stalls, one for every bull, and as their number grows less by the enstalling of some, the remainder often prove more untractable and unruly: in these stalls they are kept very dark, to render them fiercer for the day of battle.

On the first of the days appointed, (for a bull-feast commonly lasts three,) all the gentry of the place, or near adjacent, resort to the Plaza in their most gaudy apparel, every one vieing in making the most glorious appearance. Those in the lower ranks provide themselves with spears, or a great many small darts in their hands, which they fail not to cast or dart, whenever the bull, by his nearness, gives them an opportunity. So that the poor creature may be said to fight, not only with the tauriro, (or bull-hunter, a person always hired for that purpose,) but with the whole multitude in the lower class at least.

All being seated, the uppermost door is opened first; and, as soon as ever the bull perceives the light, out he comes, snuffing up the air, and staring about him, as if in admiration of his attendants; and with his tail cocked up, he spurns the ground with his fore feet, as if he intended a challenge to his yet unappearing antagonist. Then, at a door appointed for that purpose, enters the tauriro all in white, holding a cloak in one hand, and a sharp two-edged sword in the other. The bull no sooner sets eyes upon him, but, wildly staring, he moves gently towards him; then gradually mends his pace, till he is come within about the space of twenty yards of the tauriro; when, with a sort of spring, he makes at him with all his might. The tauriro, knowing by frequent experience, that it behoves him to be watchful, slips aside just when the bull is at him; when casting his cloak over his horns, at the same moment he gives him a slash or two, always aiming at the neck, where there is one particular place, which if he hit, he knows he shall easily bring him to the ground. I myself observed the truth of this experiment made upon one of the bulls, who received no more than one cut, which, happening upon the fatal spot, so stunned him, that he remained perfectly stupid, the blood flowing out from the wound, till, after a violent trembling, he dropt down stone dead.

But this rarely happens, and the poor creature oftener receives many wounds, and numberless darts, before he dies. Yet whenever he feels a fresh wound, either from dart, spear, or sword, his rage receives addition from the wound, and he pursues his tauriro with an increase of fury and violence. And as often as he makes at his adversary, the tauriro takes care, with the utmost of his agility, to avoid him, and reward his kind intention with a new wound.

Some of their bulls will play their parts much better than others: but the best must die. For, when they have behaved themselves with all the commendable fury possible, if the tauriro is spent, and fail of doing execution upon him, they set dogs upon him; hough him, and stick him all over with darts, till, with very loss of blood, he puts an end to their present cruelty.

When dead, a man brings in two mules dressed out with bells and feathers, and, fastening a rope about his horns, draws off the bull with the shouts and acclamations of the spectators, as if the infidels had been drove from before Ceuta.

I had almost forgot another very common piece of barbarous pleasure at these diversions. The tauriro will sometimes stick one of their bull-spears fast in the ground, aslant, but levelled as near as he can at his chest; then presenting himself to the bull, just before the point of the spear, on his taking his run at the tauriro, which, as they assured me, he always does with his eyes closed, the tauriro slips on one side, and the poor creature runs with a violence often to stick himself, and sometimes to break the spear in his chest, running away with part of it till he drop.

This tauriro was accounted one of the best in Spain; and indeed I saw him mount the back of one of the bulls, and ride on him, slashing and cutting, till he had quite wearied him; at which time dismounting, he killed him with much ease, and to the acclamatory satisfaction of the whole concourse: for variety of cruelty, as well as dexterity, administers to their delight.

The tauriroes are very well paid, and in truth so they ought to be; for they often lose their lives in the diversion, as this did the year after in the way of his calling. Yet is it a service of very great profit when they perform dextrously; for, whenever they do any thing remarkable, deserving the notice of the spectators, they never fail of a generous gratification, money being thrown down to them in plenty.

This feast (as they generally do) lasted three days; the last of which was, in my opinion, much before either of the others. On this, a young gentleman, whose name was Don Pedro Ortega, a person of great quality, performed the exercise on horseback. The seats, if not more crowded, were filled with people of better fashion, who came from places at a distance to grace the noble tauriro.

He was finely mounted, and made a very graceful figure : but as, when the foot tauriro engages, the bull first enters ; so, in this contest, the cavaliero always makes his appearance on the Plaza before the bull. His steed was a maneged horse ; mounted on which, he made his entry, attended by four footmen in rich liveries ; who, as soon as their master had rid round, and paid his devoirs to all the spectators, withdrew from the dangers they left him exposed to. The cavaliero having thus made his bows, and received the repeated *vivas* of that vast concourse, marched with a very stately air to the very middle of the Plaza, there standing ready to receive his enemy at coming out.

The door being opened, the bull appeared; and, as I thought, with a fiercer and more threatening aspect than any of the former. He stared around him for a considerable time, snuffing up the air, and spurning the ground, without in the least taking notice of his antagonist. But, at last, fixing his eyes upon him, he made a full run at the cavaliero, which he most dexterously avoided, and, at the same moment of time, passing by, he cast a dart that stuck in his shoulders. At this, the shouts and *vivas* were repeated; and I observed a handkerchief waved twice or thrice, which, as I afterwards understood, was a signal from the lady of his affections, that she had beheld him with satisfaction. I took notice, that the cavaliero endeavoured all he could to keep aside the bull, for the advantage of the stroke; when, putting his horse on a full career, he threw another dart, which fixed in his side, and so enraged the beast, that he seemed to renew his attacks with greater fury. The cavaliero had behaved himself to admiration, and escaped many dangers, with the often repeated acclamations of *viva, viva;* when, at last, the enraged creature getting his horns between the horse's hinder legs, man and horse came both together to the ground.

I expected at that moment nothing less than death could be the issue; when, to the general surprise, as well as mine, the very civil brute, author of all the mischief, only withdrew to the other side of the Plaza, where he stood still, staring about him as if he knew nothing of the matter.

The cavaliero was carried off not much hurt, but his delicate beast suffered much more. However, I could not but think afterward, that the good-natured bull came short of fair play. If I may be pardoned the expression, he had used his adversary with more humanity than he met with; at least, since, after he had the cavaliero under, he generously forsook him, I think he might have pleaded, or others for him, for better treatment than he after met with.

For, as the cavaliero was disabled and carried off, the foot tauriro entered in white accoutrements, as before; but he flattered himself with an easier conquest than he found. There is always on these occasions, when he apprehends any imminent danger, a place of retreat ready for the foot tauriro; and well for him there was so; this bull obliged him over and over to make use of it. Nor was he able at last to dispatch him, without a general assistance; for I believe I speak within compass, when I say, he had more than an hundred darts stuck in him. And so barbarously was he mangled, and slashed besides, that, in my mind, I could not but think King Philip in the right, when he said, " that it was a custom deserved little encouragement."

Soon after this tauridore, or bull-feast, was over, I had a mind to take a pleasant walk to a little town, called Minai, about three leagues off; but I was scarce got out of La Mancha, when an acquaintance meeting me, asked where I was going? I told him to Minai; when, taking me by the hand, " Friend Gorgio," says he in Spanish, " come back with me; you shall not go a stride farther; there are Picarons that way; you shall not go." Inquiring, as we went back, into his meaning, he told me, that the day before, a man, who had received a sum of money in pistoles at La Mancha, was, on the road, set upon by some, who had got notice of it, and murdered him; that, not finding the money expected about him, (for he had cautiously enough left it in a friend's hands at la Mancha,) they concluded he had swallowed it; and therefore they ript up his belly, and opened every gut; but all to as little purpose. This diverted my walk for that time.

But some little time after, the same person inviting me over to the same place, to see his melon-grounds, which in that country are wonderful fine and pleasant, I accepted his invitation, and under the advantage of his company, went thither. On the road, I took notice of a cross newly erected, and a multitude of small stones around the foot of it: asking the meaning whereof, my friend told me, that it was raised for a person there murdered, (as is the custom throughout Spain,) and that every good catholic, passing by, held it his duty to cast a stone upon the place, in detestation of the murder. I had often before taken notice of many such crosses: but never till then knew the meaning of their erection, or the reason of the heaps of stones around them.

There is no place in all Spain more famous for good wine than Sainte Clemente de la Mancha; nor is it any where sold cheaper: for, as it is only an inland town, near no navigable river, and the people temperate to a proverb, great plenty, and a small vend, must consequently make it cheap. The wine here is so famous, that, when I came to Madrid, I saw wrote over the doors of most houses that sold wine,

Vino Sainte Clemente. As to the temperance of the people, I must say, that notwithstanding those two excellent qualities of good and cheap, I never saw, all the three years I was prisoner there, any one person overcome with drinking.

It is true, there may be a reason, and a political one, assigned for that abstemiousness of theirs, which is this, that if any man, upon any occasion, should be brought in as an evidence against you, if you can prove that he was ever drunk, it will invalidate his whole evidence. I could not but think this a grand improvement upon the Spartans. They made their slaves purposely drunk, to shew their youth the folly of the vice by the sottish behaviour of their servants under it: but they never reached to that noble height of laying a penalty upon the aggressor, or of discouraging a voluntary impotence of reason by a disreputable impotence of interest. The Spaniard, therefore, in my opinion, in this exceeds the Spartan, as much as a natural beauty exceeds one procured by art; for, though shame may somewhat influence some few, terror is of force to deter all. A man, we have seen it, may shake hands with shame; but interest, says another proverb, will never lie. A wise institution, therefore, doubtless is this of the Spaniard; but such as I fear will never take place in Germany, Holland, France, or Great Britain.

But though I commend their temperance, I would not be thought by any means to approve of their bigotry. If there may be such a thing as intemperance in religion, I much fear their ebriety in that will be found to be over-measure. Under the notion of devotion, I have seen men among them, and of sense too, guilty of the grossest intemperances. It is too common to be a rarity, to see their Dons of the prime quality, as well as those of the lower ranks, upon meeting a priest in the open streets, condescend to take up the lower part of his vestment, and salute it with eyes erected, as if they looked upon it as the seal of salvation.

When the Ave-bell is heard, the hearer must down on his knees upon the very spot; nor is he allowed the small indulgence of deferring a little, till he can recover a clean place; dirtiness excuses not, nor will dirty actions by any means exempt. This is so notorious, that even at the play-house, in the middle of a scene, on the first sound of the bell, the actors drop their discourse; the auditors supersede the indulging of their unsanctified ears, and all on their knees, bend their tongues, if not their hearts, quite a different way to what they just before had been employed in. In short, though they pretend in all this to an extraordinary measure of zeal and real devotion, no man, that lives among them any time, can be a proselyte to them, without immolating his senses and his reason: yet I must confess, while I have seen them thus deluding themselves with Ave Marias, I could not refrain throwing up my eyes to the only proper object of adoration, in commiseration of such delusions.

The hours of the Ave-bell, are eight and twelve in the morning, and six in the evening. They pretend, at the first, to fall down to beg that God would be pleased to prosper them in all things they go about that day. At twelve, they return thanks for their preservation to that time; and at six, for that of the whole day. After which, one would think that they imagine themselves at perfect liberty; and their open gallantries perfectly countenance the imagination: for, though adultery is looked upon as a grievous crime, and punished accordingly, yet fornication is softened with the title of a venial sin, and they seem to practise it under that persuasion.

I found here, what Erasmus ridicules with so much wit and delicacy, the custom of burying in a Franciscan's habit, in mighty request. If they can for that purpose procure an old one at the price of a new one, the purchaser will look upon himself a provident chap, that has secured to his deceased friend or relation, no less than heaven by that wise bargain.

The evening being almost the only time of enjoyment of company, or conversation, every body in Spain then greedily seeks it; and the streets are at that time crowded like our finest gardens, or most private walks. On one of those occasions, I met a Don of my acquaintance walking out with his sisters; and, as I thought it became an English cavalier, I saluted him: but, to my surprise, he never returned the civility. When I met him the day after, instead of an apology, as I had flattered myself, I received a reprimand, though a very civil one; telling me, it was not the custom in Spain, nor well taken of any one, that took notice of any who were walking in the company of ladies at night.

But, a night or two after, I found, by experience, that if the men were by custom prohibited taking notice, women were not. I was standing at the door, in the cool of the evening, when a woman, seemingly genteel, passing by, called me by my name, telling me she wanted to speak with me: she had her mantilio on; so that, had I had day-light, I could have only seen one eye of her. However, I walked with her a good while, without being able to discover anything of her business, nor passed there between us anything more than a conversation upon indifferent matters. Nevertheless, at parting, she told me she should pass by again the next evening; and if I would be at the door, she would give me the same advantage of a conversation, that seemed not to displease me. Accordingly, the next night she came, and, as before, we walked together in the privatest parts of the town: for, though I knew her not, her discourse was always entertaining and full of wit, and her enquiries not often improper. We had continued this intercourse many nights together, when my landlady's daughter, having taken notice of it, stopt me one evening, and would not allow me to stand at the usual post of intelligence, saying, with a good deal of heat, " Don Gorgio, take my advice; go no more along with that woman; you may soon be brought home deprived of your life if you do." I cannot say, whether she knew her; but this I must say, she was very agreeable in wit, as well as person. However, my landlady and her daughter took that opportunity of giving me so many instances of the fatal issues of such innocent conversations, (for I could not call it an intrigue,) that, apprehensive enough of the danger, on laying circumstances together, I took their advice, and never went into her company after.

Sainte Clemente de la Mancha, where I so long remained a prisoner of war, lies in the road from Madrid to Valencia; and the Duke of Vendosme being ordered to the latter, great preparations were made for his entertainment, as he passed through. He staid here only one night, where he was very handsomely treated by the corrigidore. He was a tall fair person, and very fat, and at the time I saw him wore a long black patch over his left eye; but on what occasion I could not learn. The afterwards famous Alberoni, (since made a cardinal,) was in his attendance; as, indeed, the Duke was very rarely without him. I remember that very day three weeks, they returned through the same place; the Duke in his hearse, and Alberoni in a coach, paying his last duties. That Duke was a prodigious lover of fish, of which having eat overheartily at Veneros, in the province of Valencia, he took a surfeit, and died in three days time. His corpse was carrying to the Escurial, there to be buried in the Pantheon among their kings.

The Castilians have a privilege by licence from the Pope, which, if it could have been converted into a prohibition, might have saved that Duke's life: in regard their country is wholly inland, and the river Tagas, famous for its poverty, or rather barrenness, their Holy Father indulges the natives with the liberty, in lieu of that dangerous eatable, of eating all Lent-time the inwards of cattle. When I first heard this related, I imagined, that the garbage had been intended; but I was soon after thus rectified,—by inwards, (for so expressly says the licence itself,) is meant the heart, the liver, and the feet.

They have here, as well as in most other parts of Spain, Valencia excepted, the most wretched music in the universe. Their guitars, if not their sole, are their darling instruments, and what they most delight in: though, in my opinion, our English sailors are not much amiss in giving them the title of strum-strums. They are little better than our Jews-harps, though hardly half so musical. Yet are they perpetually at nights disturbing their women with the noise of them, under the notion and name of serenadoes. From the barber to the grandee the infection spreads, and very often with the same attendant, danger; night quarrels and rencounters being the frequent result. The true-born Spaniards reckon it a part of their glory, to be jealous of their mistresses, which is too often the forerunner of murders; or, at best, attended with many other very dangerous inconveniences. And yet, bad as their music is, their dancing is the reverse. I have seen a country girl manage her castanets with the graceful air of a Duchess, and that not to common music, but to people's beating or drumming a tune with their hands on a table. I have seen half a dozen couple at a time dance to the like in excellent order.

I just now distinguished, by an exception, the music of Valencia, where alone I experienced the use of the violin; which, though I cannot, in respect to other countries, call good, yet, in respect to the other parts of Spain, I must acknowledge it much the best. In my account of that city, I omitted to speak of it; therefore now to supply that defect, I will speak of the best I heard, which was on this unfortunate occasion: several natives of that country, having received sentence of death for their adherence to King Charles, were accordingly ordered to the place of execution. It is the custom there, on all such occasions, for all the music of the city to meet near the gallows, and play the most affecting and melancholy airs, to the very approach of the condemned; and really the music was so moving, it heightened the scene of sorrow, and brought compassion into the eyes even of enemies.

As to the condemned, they came stript of their own clothes, and covered with black frocks, in which they were led along the streets to the place of execution, the friars praying all the way. When they came through any street, where any public images were fixed, they staid before them some reasonable time in prayer with the friars. When they are arrived at the fatal place, those fathers leave them not, but continue praying and giving them ghostly encouragement, standing upon the rounds of the ladder till they are turned off. The hangman always wears a silver badge of a ladder to distinguish his profession: but his manner of executing his office had somewhat in it too singular to allow of silence. When he had tied fast the hands of the criminal, he rested his knee upon them, and with one hand on the criminal's nostrils, to stop his breath the sooner, threw himself off the ladder along with the dying party. This he does to expedite his fate; though, considering the force, I wonder it does not tear head and body asunder; which yet I never heard that it did.

But, to return to La Mancha:—I had been there now upwards of two years, much diverted with the good humour and kindness of the gentlemen, and daily pleased with the conversation of the nuns of the nunnery opposite to my lodgings; when, walking one day alone upon the Plaza, I found myself accosted by a clerico. At the first attack, he told me his country; but added, that he now came from Madrid with a Potent, (that was his word,) from Pedro de Dios, dean of the inquisition, to endeavour the conversion of any of the English prisoners; that being an Irishman, as a sort of a brother, he had conceived a love for the English, and therefore more eagerly embraced the opportunity, which the holy inquisition had put into his hands, for the bringing over to mother church as many heretics as he could; that, having heard a very good character of me, he should think himself very happy, if he could be instrumental in my salvation: " it is very true," continued he, " I have lately had the good fortune to convert many; and besides the candour of my own disposition, I must tell you, that I have a peculiar knack at conversion, which very few, if any, ever could resist. I am going upon the same work into Murcia; but your good character has fixed me in my resolution of preferring your salvation to that of others."

To this very long, and no less surprising address, I only returned, that it being an affair of moment, it would require some consideration; and that by the time he returned from Murcia, I might be able to return him a proper answer. But not at all satisfied with this reply; " Sir," says he, " God Almighty is all-sufficient : this moment is too precious to be lost; he can turn the heart in the twinkling of an eye, as well as in twenty years. Hear me then ; mind what I say to you : I will convince you immediately. You heretics do not believe in transubstantiation, and yet did not our Saviour say in so many words, *Hoc est corpus meum ?* And if you do not believe him, do not you give him the lie ? Besides, does not one of the fathers say, *Deus, qui est omnis veritas, non potest dicere falsum ?*" He went on at the same ridiculous rate; which soon convinced me, he was a thorough rattle. However, as a clerico, and consequently, in this country, a man dangerous to disoblige, I invited him home to dinner; where, when I had brought him, I found I had no way done an unacceptable thing ; for my landlady and her daughter, seeing him to be a clergyman, received him with a vast deal of respect and pleasure.

Dinner being over, he began to entertain me with a detail of the many wonderful conversions he had made upon obstinate heretics; that he had convinced the most stubborn, and had such a *nostrum*, that he would undertake to convert any one. Here he began his old round, intermixing his harangue with such scraps and raw sentences of fustian Latin, that I grew weary of his conversation; so, pretending some business of consequence, I took leave, and left him and my landlady together.

I did not return till pretty late in the evening, with intent to give him time enough to think his own visit tedious; but, to my great surprise, I found my Irish missionary still on the spot, ready to dare me to the encounter, and resolved, like a true son of the church militant, to keep last in the field of battle. As soon as I had seated myself, he began again to tell me how good a character my landlady had given me, which had prodigiously increased his ardour of saving my soul; that he could not answer it to his own character, as well as mine, to be negligent; and therefore he had entered into a resolution to stay my coming, though it had been later. To all which, I returned him abundance of thanks for his good will, but pleading indisposition and want of rest, after a good deal of civil impertinence, I once more got rid of him; at least, I took my leave, and went to bed, leaving him again master of the field; for I understood next morning, that he staid some time after I was gone, with my good landlady.

Next morning, the nuns of the nunnery opposite, having taken notice of the clerico's ingress, long visit, and late egress, sent to know whether he was my countryman; with many other questions, which I was not then let into the secret of. To all which I returned, that he was no countryman of mine, but an Irishman, and so perfectly a stranger to me, that I knew no more of him than what I had from his own mouth, that he was going into Murcia. What the meaning of this enquiry was I could never learn ; but I could not doubt, but it proceeded from their great care of their vicino, as they called me ; a mark of their esteem, and of which I was not a little proud.

As was my usual custom, I had been taking my morning walk, and had not been long come home in order to dinner, when in again drops my Irish clerico : I was confounded, and vexed, and he could not avoid taking notice of it ; nevertheless, without the least alteration of countenance, he took his seat ; and on my saying, in a cold and indifferent tone, that I imagined he had been got to Murcia before this ; he replied, with a natural fleer, that truly he was going to Murcia, but his conscience pricked him, and he did find that he could not go away with any satisfaction, or peace of mind, without making me a perfect convert; that he had plainly discovered in me a good disposition, and had, for that very reason, put himself to the charge of man and mule, to the bishop of Cuenca for a licence, under his hand, for my conversion: for in Spain, all private missionaries are obliged to ask leave of the next bishop, before they dare enter upon any enterprise of this nature.

I was more confounded at this last assurance of the man than at all before; and it put me directly upon reflecting, whether any, and what inconveniences might ensue, from a rencounter that I at first conceived ridiculous, but might now reasonably begin to have more dangerous apprehensions of. I knew, by the articles of war, all persons are exempted from any power of the inquisition; but whether carrying on a part in such a farce, might not admit, or at least be liable to some dangerous construction, was not imprudently now to be considered. Though I was not fearful, yet I resolved to be cautious. Wherefore, not making any answer to his declaration about the bishop, he took notice of it; and, to raise a confidence he found expiring, began to tell me, that his name was Murtough Brennan, that he was born near Kilkenny, of a very considerable family. This last part indeed, when I came to Madrid, I found pretty well confirmed in a considerable manner. However, taking notice that he had altered his tone of leaving the town, and that, instead of it, he was advancing somewhat like an invitation of himself to dinner the next day, I resolved to shew myself shy of him; and thereupon abruptly, and without taking my leave, I left the room, and my landlady and him together.

Three or four days had passed, every one of which he never failed my lodgings; not at dinner-time only, but night and morning too; from all which I began to suspect, that, instead of my conversion, he had fixed upon a reconversion of my landlady. She was not young, yet, for a black woman, handsome enough; and her daughter very pretty: I entered into a resolution to make my observations, and watch them all at a distance; nevertheless carefully concealing my jealousy. However, I must confess, I was not a little pleased, that any thing could divert my own persecution. He was now no longer my guest, but my landlady's, with whom I found him so much taken up, that a little care might frustrate all his former impertinent importunities on the old topic.

But all my suspicions were very soon after turned into certainties in this manner: I had been abroad, and returning somewhat weary, I went to my chamber, to take, what in that country they call, a cesto, upon my bed: I got in unseen, or without seeing any body, but had scarce laid myself down, before my young landlady, as I jestingly used to call the daughter, rushing into my room, threw herself down on the floor, bitterly exclaiming. I started off my bed, and immediately running to the door, who should I meet there but my Irish clerico, without his habit, and in his shirt? I could not doubt, by the dishabille of the clerico, but the young creature had reason enough for her passion, which rendered me quite unable to master mine; wherefore, as he stood with his back next the door, I thrust him in that ghostly plight into the open street.

I might, with leisure enough, have repented that precipitate piece of indiscretion, if it had not been for his bad character, and the favourable opinion the town had conceived of me; for he inordinately exclaimed against me, calling me heretic, and telling the people, who were soon gathered round him, that, coming to my lodgings on the charitable work of conversion, I had thus abused him, stript him of his habit, and then turned him out of doors. The nuns, on their hearing the outcries he made, came running to their grates, to enquire into the matter; and when they understood it, as he was pleased to relate it, though they condemned my zeal, they pitied my condition. Very well was it for

me, that I stood more than a little well in
the good opinion of the town ; among the
gentry, by my frequent conversation, and
the inferior sort by my charitable distribu-
tions ; for nothing can be more dangerous,
or a nearer way to violent fate, than to in-
sult one of the clergy in Spain, and especially for such an oneas they entitle a heretic.

My old landlady, (I speak in respect to
her daughter,) however formerly my seeming friend, came in a violent passion, and,
wrenching the door out of my hands, opened it, and pulled her clerico in ; and, so
soon as she had done this, she took his part,
and railed so bitterly at me, that I had no
reason longer to doubt her thorough conversion, under the full power of his mission.
However, the young one stood her ground,
and, by all her expressions, gave her many
inquirers reason enough to believe, all was
not matter of faith that the clerico had advanced. Nevertheless, holding it advise-
able to change my lodgings, and a friend

confirming my resolutions, I removed that night.

The clerico, having put on his upper garments, was run away to the corrigidor, in a violent fury, resolving to be early, as well knowing, that he, who tells his story first, has the prospect of telling it to double advantage. When he came there, he told that officer a thousand idle stories, and in the worst manner; repeating how I had abused him, and not him only, but my poor landlady, for taking his part. The corrigidor was glad to hear it all, and with an officious ear fished for a great deal more; expecting, according to usage, at last to squeeze a sum of money out of me. However, he told the clerico, that, as I was a prisoner of war, he had no direct power over me; but if he would immediately write to the president Ronquillo, at Madrid, he would not fail to give his immediate orders, according to which he would as readily act against me.

The clerico resolved to pursue his old

maxim, and cry out first; and so taking the corrigidor's advice, he wrote away to Madrid directly. In the mean time, the people in the town, both high and low, some out of curiosity, some out of friendship, pursued their enquiries into the reality of the facts. The old landlady they could make little of to my advantage; but whenever the young one came to the question, she always left them with these words in her mouth, *El Diabolo en forma del Clerico*, which rendering things more than a little cloudy on the clerico's side, he was advised and pressed by his few friends, as fast as he could, to get out of town; nuns, clergy, and every body taking part against him, excepting his new convert, my old landlady.

The day after, as I was sitting with a friend at my new quarters, Maria (for that was the name of my landlady's daughter) came running in with these words in her mouth, *El clerico, el clerico, passa la calle*. We hastened to the window; out of which we beheld the clerico, Murtough Brennan, pitifully mounted on the back of a very poor ass; (for they would neither let nor lend him a mule through all the town,) his legs almost rested on the ground, for he was lusty, as his ass was little; and a fellow with a large cudgel marched afoot, driving his ass along. Never did Sancho Pancha, on his embassage to Dulcinea, make such a despicable out-of-the-way figure, as our clerico did at this time. And what encreased our mirth was, their teling me, that our clerico, like that squire, (though upon his own priest-errantry,) was actually on his march to Toboso, a place five leagues off, famous for the nativity of Dulcinea, the object of the passion of that celebrated hero Don Quixotte. So I will leave our clerico on his journey to Murcia, to relate the unhappy sequel of this ridiculous affair.

I have before said, that, by the advice of the corrigidor, our clerico had wrote to Don Ronquillo at Madrid. About a fortnight after his departure from La Mancha, I was sitting alone in my new lodgings, when two alguazils, (officers under the corrigidor, and in the nature of our bailiffs,) came into my room, but very civilly, to tell me, that they had orders to carry me away to prison ; but, at the same moment, they advised me not to be afraid ; for they had observed, that the whole town was concerned at what the corrigidor and clerico had done; adding, that it was their opinion, that I should find so general a friendship, that I need not be apprehensive of any danger. With these plausible speeches, though I afterwards experienced the truth of them, I resigned myself, and went with them to a much closer confinement.

I had not been there above a day or two, before many gentlemen of the place sent to me, to assure me, they were heartily afflicted at my confinement, and resolved to write in my favour to Madrid ; but as it was not safe, nor the custom in Spain, to visit those in my present circumstances, they hoped I would not take it amiss, since they were bent to act all in their power towards my deliverance; concluding, however, with their advice, that I would not give one real of Plata to the corrigidor, whom they hated, but confide in their assiduous interposal. Don Pedro de Ortega in particular, the person that performed the part of the tauriro on horseback, sometime before, sent me word, he would not fail to write to a relation of his, of the first account in Madrid, and so represent the affair, that I should not long be debarred my old acquaintance.

It may administer, perhaps, matter of wonder, that Spaniards, gentlemen of the staunchest punctilio, should make a scruple, and excuse themselves from visiting persons under confinement, when, according to all Christian acceptation, such a circumstance would render such a visit, not charitable only, but generous. But though men of vulgar spirits might, from the narrowness of their views, form such insipid excuses, those of these gentlemen, I very well knew, proceeded from much more excusable topics. I was committed under the accusation of having abused a sacred person, one of the clergy ; and though, as a prisoner of war, I might deem myself exempt from the power of the inquisition, yet how far one of that country, visiting a person, so accused, might be esteemed culpable, was a consideration in that dangerous climate, far from deserving to be slighted. To me, therefore, who well knew the customs of the country, and the temper of its countrymen, their excuses were not only allowable, but acceptable also ; for, without calling in question their charity, I verily believed I might safely confide in their honour.

Accordingly, after I had been a close prisoner one month to a day, I found the benefit of these gentlemen's promises and solicitations ; pursuant to which, an order was brought for my immediate discharge ; notwithstanding, the new convert, my old landlady, did all she could to make her appearing against me effectual, to the height of her prejudice and malice, even while the daughter, as sensible of my innocence, and acting with a much better conscience, endeavoured as much to justify me, against both the threats and persuasions of the corrigidor, and his few accomplices, though her own mother made one.

After receipt of this order for my enlargement, I was mightily pressed by Don Felix, and others of my friends, to go to Madrid, and enter my complaint against the corrigidor and the clerico, as a thing highly essential to my own future security. Without asking leave, therefore, of the corrigidor, or in the least acquainting him with it, I set out from La Mancha, and, as I afterwards understood, to the terrible alarm of that griping officer, who was under the greatest consternation, when he heard I was gone; for, as he knew very well that he had done more than he could justify, he was very apprehensive of any complaint; well knowing, that as he was hated as much as

I was beloved, he might assure himself of the want of that assistance from the gentlemen, which I had experienced.

So soon as I arrived at Madrid, I made it my business to enquire out and wait upon Father Fahy, chief of the Irish college. He received me very courteously; but when I acquainted him with the treatment I had met with from Brennan, and had given him an account of his other scandalous behaviour, I found he was no stranger to the man, or his character; for he soon confirmed to me the honour Brennan first boasted of, his considerable family, by saying, that scarce an assize passed in his own country, without two or three of that name receiving at the gallows the just reward of their demerits. In short, not only Father Fahy, but all the clergy of that nation at Madrid, readily subscribed to this character of him, that he was a scandal to their country.

After this, I had nothing more to do, but to get that father to go with me to Pedro de Dios, who was the head of the Dominican cloister, and dean of the inquisition. He readily granted my request; and when we came there, in a manner unexpected, represented to the dean, that having some good dispositions towards mother-church, I had been diverted from them, he feared, by the evil practices of one Murtough Brennan, a countryman of his, though a scandal to his country; that, under a pretence of seeking my conversion, he had laid himself open in a most beastly manner, such as would have set a catholic into a vile opinion of their religion, and much more one that was yet a heretic. The dean had hardly patience to hear particulars; but as soon as my friend had ended his narration, he immediately gave his orders, prohibiting Murtough's saying any more masses, either in Madrid, or any other place in Spain. This indeed was taking away the poor wretch's sole subsistence, and putting him just upon an equality with his demerits.

I took the same opportunity to make my complaints of the corrigidor; but his term expiring very soon, and a process being likely to be chargeable, I was advised to let it drop. So, having effected what I came for, I returned to my old station at La Mancha.

When I came back, I found a new corrigidor, as I had been told there would, by the dean of the inquisition, who, at the same time, advised me to wait on him. I did so, soon after my arrival, and then experienced the advice to be well intended; the dean having wrote a letter to him, to order him to treat me with all manner of civility. He shewed me the very letter, and it was in such particular and obliging terms, that I could not but perceive he had taken a resolution, if possible, to eradicate all the evil impressions, that Murtough's behaviour might have given too great occasion for. This served to confirm me in an observation that I had long before made, that a protestant, who will prudently keep his sentiments in his own breast, may command any thing in Spain; where their stiff bigotry leads them naturally into that other mistake, that not to oppose, is to assent. Besides, it is generally among them almost a work of supererogation to be even instrumental in the conversion of one they call a heretic. To bring any such back to what they call mother-church, nothing shall be spared, nothing thought too much : and if you have insincerity enough to give them hopes, you shall not only live in ease, but in pleasure and plenty.

I had entertained some thoughts on my journey back, of taking up my old quarters at the widow's; but found her so entirely converted by her clerico, that there would be no room to expect peace: for which reason, with the help of my fair vicinos, and Don Felix, I took another, where I had not been long before I received an unhappy account of Murtough's conduct in Murcia. It seems he had kept his resolution in going thither; where meeting with some of his own countrymen, though he found them staunch good catholics, he so far inveigled himself into them, that he brought them all into a foul chance for their lives. There were three of them, all soldiers, in a Spanish regiment; but in a fit of ambitious, though frantic zeal, Murtough had wheedled them to go along with him to Pedro de Dios, dean of the inquisition, to declare and acknowledge before him, that they were converted and brought over to motherchurch, and by him only. The poor ignorants, thus enticed, had left their regiment, of which the colonel having notice, sent after them, and they were overtaken on the road, their missionair with them. But notwithstanding all his oratory, nay, even the discovery of the whole farce, one of them was hanged for an example to the other two.

It was not long after my return before news arrived of the peace; which though they received with joy, they could hardly entertain with belief. Upon which, the new corrigidor, with whom I held a better correspondence than I had done with the old one, desired me to produce my letters from England, that it was true. Never did people give greater demonstrations of joy than they upon this occasion. It was the common cry in the streets, *Paz con Angleterra, con todo Mundo Guerra!* and my confirmation did them as much pleasure as it did service to me; for, if possible, they treated me with more civility than before.

But the peace soon after being proclaimed, I received orders to repair to Madrid, where the rest of the prisoners taken at Denia had been carried; when I, by reason of my wounds, and want of health, had been left behind. Others I understood lay ready, and some were on their march to Bayonne in France, where ships were ordered for their transportation into England. So, after a residence of three years and three months, having taken leave of all my acquaintance, I left a place, that was almost become natural to me, the delicious Sainte Clemente de la Mancha.

Nothing of moment, or worth observing,

met I with, till I came near Ocanna; and there occurred a sight ridiculous enough. The knight of the town I last came from, the ever renowned Don Quixotte, never made such a figure as a Spaniard, I there met on the road. He was mounted on a mule of the largest size, and yet no way unsizeable to his person: he had two pistols in his holsters, and one on each side stuck in his belt; a sort of large blunderbuss in one of his hands, and the fellow to it, slung over his shoulders, hung at his back. All these were accompanied with a right Spanish spado, and an attendant stilletto, in their customary position. The muletier that was my guide, calling out to him in Spanish, told him he was very well armed; to which, with a great deal of gravity, the Don returned answer, " By Saint Jago, a man cannot be too well armed in such dangerous times!"

I took up my quarters that night at Ocanna, a large, neat, and well built town. Houses of good reception, and entertainment, are very scarce all over Spain ; but that, where I then lay, might have passed for good in any other country. Yet it gave me a notion quite different to what I found ; for I imagined it to proceed from my near approach to the capital. But instead of that, contrary to all other countries, the nearer I came to Madrid, the houses of entertainment grew worse and worse; not in their rates do I mean, (for that with reason enough might have been expected,) but even in their provision, and places and way of reception. I could not, however, forbear smiling at the reason given by my muletier, that it proceeded from a piece of court policy, in order to oblige all travellers to hasten to Madrid.

Two small leagues from Ocanna we arrived at Aranjuez, a seat of pleasure, which the kings of Spain commonly select for their place of residence during the months of April and May. It is distant from Madrid about seven leagues; and the country round is the pleasantest in all Spain, Valencia excepted. The house itself makes but a very indifferent appearance; I have seen many a better in England, with an owner to it of no more than five hundred pounds per annum; yet the gardens are large and fine; or, as the Spaniards say, the finest in all Spain, which with them is all the world. They tell you at the same time, that those of Versailles, in their most beautiful parts, took their model from these. I never saw those at Versailles; but, in my opinion, the walks at Aranjuez, though noble in their length, lose much of their beauty by their narrowness.

The water-works here are a great curiosity; to which the river Tagus, running along close by, does mightily contribute. That river is let into the gardens by a vast number of little canals, which, with their pleasing meanders, divert the eye with inexpressible delight. These pretty wanderers, by pipes properly placed in them, afford varieties scarce to be believed or imagined; and which would be grateful in any climate, but much more where the air, as it does here, wants in the summer months perpetual cooling.

To see a spreading tree, as growing in its natural soil, distinguished from its pining neighbourhood by a gentle refreshing shower, which appears softly distilling from every branch and leaf thereof, while nature all around is smiling, without one liquid sign of sorrow, to me appeared surprisingly pleasing. And the more when I observed, that its neighbours received not any the least benefit of that plentiful effusion; and yet a very few trees distant, you should find a dozen together under the same healthful sudor. Where art imitates nature well, philosophers hold it a perfection: then what must she exact of us, where we find her transcendent in the perfections of nature?

The watery arch is nothing less surprising; where art, contending with nature, acts against the laws of nature, and yet is beautiful. To see a liquid stream vaulting itself for the space of threescore yards into a perfect semi-orb, will be granted by the curious to be rare and strange; but sure, to walk beneath that arch, and see the waters flowing over your head, without your receiving the minutest drop, is stranger, if not strange enough to stagger all belief.

The story of Actæon, pictured in water colours, if I may so express myself, though pretty, seemed to me but trifling to the other. Those seemed to be like nature miraculously displayed; this only fable in grotesque. The figures indeed were not only fine, but extraordinary; yet their various shapes were not at all so entertaining to the mind, however refreshing they might be found to the body.

I took notice before of the straitness of their walks; but though to me it might seem a diminution of their beauty, I am apt to believe to the Spaniard, for and by whom they were laid out, it may seem otherwise. They, of both sexes, give themselves so intolerably up to amouring, that, on that account, the closeness of the walks may be looked upon as an advantage rather than a defect. The grand avenue to the house is much more stately, and composed, as they are, of rows of trees somewhat larger than our largest limes, whose leaves are all of a perfect pea-bloom colour, together with their grandeur, they strike the eye with a pleasing beauty. At the entrance of the grand court we see the statue of Philip the Second; to intimate to the spectators, I suppose, that he was the founder.

Among other parks about Aranjuez there is one entirely preserved for dromedaries; an useful creature for fatigue, burden, and dispatch; but the nearest of kin to deformity of any I ever saw. There are several other enclosures for several sorts of strange and wild beasts, which are sometimes baited in a very large pond, that was shewn me about half a league from hence. This is no ordinary diversion: but when the court is disposed that way, the beast, or beasts, whether bear, lion, or tyger, are conveyed into a house prepared for that purpose;

whence he can no other way issue than by a door over the water, through, or over which, forcing or flinging himself, he gradually finds himself descend into the very depth of the pond by a wooden declivity. The dogs stand ready on the banks, and so soon as ever they spy their enemy, rush all at once into the water, and engage him. A diversion less to be complained of than their tauridores; because attended with less cruelty to the beast, as well as danger to the spectators.

When we arrived at Madrid, a town much spoken of by natives, as well as strangers, though I had seen it before, I could hardly restrain myself from being surprised to find it only environed with mud walls. It may very easily be imagined, they were never intended for defence, and yet it was a long time before I could find any other use, or rather any use at all, in them; and yet I was at last convinced of my error by a sensible encrease of expence. Without the gates, to half a league without the town, you have wine for twopence the quart; but within the place, you drink it little cheaper than you may in London. The mud walls, therefore, well enough answer their intent of forcing people to reside there, under pretence of security, but, in reality, to be taxed; for other things are taxable as well as wine, though not in like proportion.

All ambassadors have a claim or privilege of bringing in what wine they please tax-free; and the king, to wave it, will at any time purchase that exemption of duty at the price of five hundred pistoles per annum. The convents and nunneries are allowed a like licence of free importation; and it is one of the first advantages they can boast of; for, under that licence, having a liberty of setting up a tavern near them, they make a prodigious advantage of it. The wine drank and sold in this place is for the most part a sort of white wine.

But if the mud walls gave me at first but a faint idea of the place, I was pleasingly disappointed, as soon as I entered the gates.

The town then shewed itself well built, and of brick, and the streets wide, long, and spacious. Those of Atocha and Alcala are as fine as any I ever saw; yet it is situated but very indifferently : for, though they have what they call a river, to which they give the very fair name of La Mansuera, and over which they have built a curious, long, and large stone bridge ; yet is the course of it, in summer time especially, mostly dry. This gave occasion to that piece of raillery of a foreign ambassador, " that the king would have done wisely to have bought a river, before he built the bridge." Nevertheless, that little stream of a river which they boast of, they improve as much as possible; since down the sides, as far as you can see, there are coops, or little places hooped in, for people to wash their linen, (for they very rarely wash in their own houses,) nor is it really any unpleasing sight to view the regular rows of them at that cleanly operation.

The King has here two palaces; one

within the town, the other near adjoining. That in the town is built of stone; the other, which is called Bueno Retiro, is all of brick. From the town to this last, in summer time, there is a large covering of canvas, propt up with tall poles, under which people walk, to avoid the scorching heats of the sun.

As I was passing by the chapel of the Carmelites, I saw several blind men, some led, some groping the way with their sticks, going into the chapel. I had the curiosity to know the reason; I no sooner entered the door, but was surprised to see such a number of those unfortunate people, all kneeling before the altar, some kissing the ground, others holding up their heads, crying out *misericordia*. I was informed it was Saint Lucy's day, the patroness of the blind; therefore, all who were able came upon that day to pay their devotion: so I left them, and directed my course towards the King's palace.

When I came to the outward court, I

met with a Spanish gentleman of my acquaintance, and we went into the piazzas; whilst we were talking there, I saw several gentlemen passing by, having badges on their breasts, some white, some red, and others green: my friend informed me, that there were five orders of knighthood in Spain. That of the Golden Fleece was only given to great princes, but the other four to private gentlemen, viz. that of Saint Jago, Alcantara, Saint Salvador de Montreal, and Monteza.

The orders of knighthood in Spain.

He likewise told me, that there were above ninety places of grandees, but never filled up; who have the privilege of being covered in the presence of the King, and are distinguished into three ranks. The first is, of those who cover themselves before they speak to the King; the second, are those who put on their hats after they have begun to speak; the third, are those who only put on their hats, having spoke to him. The ladies of the grandees have also great respect shewed them. The queen rises up when they enter the chamber, and offers them cushions.

No married man, except the King, lies in the palace; for all the women who live there are widows, or maids of honour to the queen. I saw the Prince of Asturias' dinner carried through the court up to him, being guarded by four gentlemen of the Guards, one before, another behind, and one on each side, with their carbines shouldered; the Queen's came next, and the King's the last, guarded as before; for they always dine separately. I observed, that the gentlemen of the Guards, though not on duty, yet they are obliged to wear their carbine belts.

Saint Isodore, who, from a poor labouring man, by his sanctity of life arrived to the title of Saint, is the patron of Madrid, and has a church dedicated to him, which is richly adorned within. The sovereign court of the inquisition is held at Madrid, the president whereof is called the Inquisitor General. They judge without allowing any appeal for four sorts of crimes, viz.

heresy, polygamy, sodomy, and witchcraft, and when any are convicted, it is called the act of faith.

Most people believe, that the King's greatest revenue consists in the gold and silver brought from the West Indies, which is a mistake; for most part of that wealth belongs to merchants and others, that pay the workmen at the golden mines of Potosi, and the silver mines at Mexico; yet the King, as I have been informed, receives about a million and a half of gold.

The Spaniards have a saying, that the finest garden of fruit in Spain is in the middle of Madrid, which is the Plaza, or market place; and truly the stalls there are set forth with such variety of delicious fruit, that I must confess I never saw any place comparable to it; and, which adds to my admiration, there are no gardens or orchards of fruit within some leagues.

They seldom eat hares in Spain but whilst the grapes are growing; and then they are so exceeding fat, they are knocked down with sticks. Their rabbits are not so good as ours in England; they have great plenty of partridges, which are larger and finer feathered than ours. They have but little beef in Spain, because there is no grass; but they have plenty of mutton, and exceeding good, because their sheep feed only upon wild pot-herbs; their pork is delicious, their hogs feeding only upon chesnuts and acorns.

Madrid and Valladolid, though great, yet are only accounted villages: in the latter, Philip the Second, by the persuasion of Parsons, an English jesuit, erected an English seminary; and Philip the Fourth built a most noble palace, with extraordinary fine gardens. They say, that Christopher Columbus, who first discovered the West Indies, died there, though I have heard he lies buried, and has a monument at Sevil.

The King's palace. The palace in the town stands upon eleven arches, under every one of which there are shops, which degrade it to a mere exchange. Nevertheless, the stairs by which you ascend up to the guard room, (which is very spacious too,) are stately, large, and curious. So soon as you have passed the guard room, you enter into a long and noble gallery, the right hand whereof leads to the King's apartment, the left to the Queen's. Entering into the King's apartment, you soon arrive at a large room, where he keeps his levee; on one side whereof, (for it takes up the whole side,) is painted the fatal battle of Almanza. I confess the view somewhat affected me, though so long after, and brought to mind many old passages. However, the reflection concluded thus in favour of the Spaniard, that we ought to excuse their vanity in so exposing, under a French General, a victory, which was the only material one the Spaniards could ever boast of over an English army.

In this state room, when the King first appears, every person present receives him with a profound homage; after which, turning from the company to a large velvet chair, by which stands the father confessor, he kneels down, and remains some time at his devotion; which being over, he rising, crosses himself, and his father confessor having with the motion of his hand intimated his benediction, he then gives audience to all that attend for that purpose. He receives every body with a seeming complaisance, and with an air more resembling the French than the Spanish ceremony. Petitions to the King, as with us, are delivered into the hands of the secretary of state: yet in one particular they are, in my opinion, worthy the imitation of other courts; the petitioner is directly told what day he must come for an answer to the office; at which time he is sure, without any further fruitless attendance, not to fail of it. The audience being over, the King returns through the gallery to his own apartment.

I cannot here omit an accidental conversation, that passed between General Mahoni and myself in this place. After some talk of the bravery of the English nation, he made mention of General Stanhope, with a very peculiar emphasis. " But," says he,

" I never was so put to the nonplus in all my days as that General once put me in. I was on the road from Paris to Madrid, and having notice, that that General was going just the reverse, and that in all likelihood we should meet the next day, before my setting out in the morning, I took care to order my gayest regimental apparel, resolving to make the best appearance I could to receive so great a man. I had not travelled above four hours before I saw two gentlemen, who appearing to be English, it induced me to imagine they were forerunners, and some of his retinue. But how abashed and confounded was I, when putting the question to one of them, he made answer, ' Sir, I am the person !' Never did moderation put vanity more out of countenance : though, to say truth, I could not but think his dress as much too plain for General Stanhope, as I at that juncture thought my own too gay for Mahoni. But," added he, " that great man had too many inward great endowments to stand in need of any outside decoration."

Of all diversions, the King takes most delight in that of shooting, which he performs with great exactness and dexterity. I have seen him divert himself at swallow shooting, (by all, I think, allowed to be the most difficult,) and exceeding all I ever saw. The last time I had the honour to see him, was on his return from that exercise. He had been abroad with the Duke of Medina Sidonia, and alighted out of his coach at a back door of the palace, with three or four birds in his hand, which, according to his usual custom, he carried up to the Queen with his own hands.

The playhouses. There are two playhouses in Madrid, at both which they act every day; but their actors, and their music, are almost too indifferent to be mentioned. The theatre at the Bueno Retiro is much the best; but as much inferior to ours at London, as those at Madrid are to that. I was at one play, when both King and Queen were present. There was a splendid audience, and a great concourse of ladies; but the latter, as is the custom there, having lattices before them, the appearance lost most of its lustre. One very remarkable thing happened while I was there; the Ave-bell rung in the middle of an act, when down on their knees fell every body, even the players on the stage, in the middle of their harangue. They remained for some time at their devotion; then up they rose, and returned to the business they were before engaged in, beginning where they left off.

The ladies of quality make their visits in grand state and decorum. The lady-visitant is carried in a chair by four men; the two first, in all weathers, always bare. Two others walk as a guard, one on each side; another carrying a large lanthorn for fear of being benighted; then follows a coach drawn by six mules, with her women, and after that another with her gentlemen; several servants walking after, more or less, according to the quality of the person. They never suffer their servants to overload a coach, as is frequently seen with us; neither do coachmen or chairmen go or drive, as if they carried midwives in lieu of ladies. On the contrary, they affect a motion so slow and so stately, that you would rather imagine the ladies were every one of them near their time, and very apprehensive of a miscarriage.

I remember not to have seen here any horses in any coach, but in the King's, or an ambassador's; which can only proceed from custom, for certainly finer horses are not to be found in the world.

At the time of my being here, Cardinal Giudici was at Madrid; he was a tall, proper, comely man, and one that made the best appearance. Alberoni was there at the same time, who, upon the death of the Duke of Vendosme, had the good fortune to find the Princess Ursini his patroness; an instance of whose ingratitude will plead pardon for this little digression. That Princess first brought Alberoni into favour at court. They were both of Italy, and that might be one reason of that lady's espousing his interest; though some there are that assign it to the recommendation of the Duke of Vendosme, with whom Alberoni had the honour to be very intimate, as the other was always distinguished by that Princess. Be which it will, certain it is, she was Alberoni's first and sole patroness; which gave many people afterwards a very smart occasion of reflecting upon him, both as to his integrity and gratitude. For when Alberoni, upon the death of King Philip's first Queen, had recommended this present lady, who was his countrywoman, (she of Parma, and he of Placentia, both in the same dukedom,) and had forwarded her match with the King with all possible assiduity; and when that Princess, pursuant to the orders she had received from the King, passed over into Italy to accompany the Queen elect into her own dominions; Alberoni, forgetful of the hand that first advanced him, sent a letter to the present Queen, just before her landing, that if she resolved to be Queen of Spain, she must banish the Princess Ursini, her companion, and never let her come to court. Accordingly, that lady, to evince the extent of her power, and the strength of her resolution, dispatched that Princess away, on her very landing, and before she had seen the King, under a detachment of her own guards, into France; and all this without either allowing her an opportunity of justifying herself, or assigning the least reason for so uncommon an action. But the same Alberoni (though afterwards created cardinal, and for some time King Philip's prime minion) soon saw that ingratitude of his rewarded in his own disgrace, at the very same court.

I remember when at La Mancha, Don Felix Pachero, in a conversation there, maintained, that three women at that time ruled the world, viz. Queen Anne, Madam Maintenon, and this Princess Ursini.

Father Fahy's civilities, when last at Madrid, exacting of me some suitable acknowledgment, I went to pay him a visit; as to render him due thanks for the past, so to give him a further account of his countryman Brennan : but I soon found he did not much incline to hear any thing more of Murtough, not expecting to hear any good of him ; for which reason, as soon as I well could, I changed the conversation to another topic; in which some word dropping of the Count de Montery, I told him, that I heard he had taken orders, and officiated at mass : He made answer, it was all very true. And upon my intimating, that I had the honour to serve under him in Flanders, on my first entering into service, and when he commanded the Spanish forces at the famous battle of Seneff; and adding, that I could not but be surprised, that he, who was then one of the brightest cavalieroes of the age, should now be in orders, and that I should look upon it as a mighty favour barely to have, if it might be, a view of him ; he very obligingly told me, that he was very well acquainted with him, and that if I would come the next day, he would not fail to accompany me to the Count's house.

Punctually at the time appointed I waited on Father Fahy, who, as he promised, carried me to the Count's house: He was stepping into his coach just as we got there; but seeing Father Fahy, he advanced towards us. The father delivered my desire in as handsome a manner as could be, and concluding with the reason of it, from my having been in that service under him; he seemed very well pleased, but added, that there were not many beside myself living, who had been in that service with him. After some other conversation, he called his gentleman to him, and gave him particular orders to give us a frescari, or, in English, an entertainment; so, taking leave, he went into his coach, and we to our frescari.

Coming from which, Father Fahy made me observe, in the open street, a stone, on which was a visible great stain of somewhat reddish, and like blood. " This," said he, " was occasioned by the death of a countryman of mine, who had the misfortune to overset a child, coming out of that house; (pointing to one opposite to us ;) the child frighted, though not hurt, as is natural, made a terrible outcry ; upon which its father coming out in a violent rage, (notwithstanding my countryman begged pardon, and pleaded sorrow, as being only an accident,) stabbed him to the heart, and down he fell upon that stone, which to this day retains the mark of innocent blood, so rashly shed." He went on, and told me, the Spaniard immediately took sanctuary in the church, whence some time after he made his escape. But escapes of that nature are so common in Spain, that they are not worth wondering at. For even though it were for wilful and premeditated murder, if the murderer have taken sanctuary, it was never known that he was delivered up to justice, though demanded ; but in some disguise he makes his escape, or some way is secured against all the clamours of power or equity.

I have observed, that some of the greatest quality stop their coaches over a stinking nasty puddle, which they often find in the streets, and, holding their heads over the door, snuff up the nasty scent which ascends, believing that it is extremely healthful; when I was forced to hold my nose, passing by. It is not convenient to walk out early in the morning; they, having no necessary houses, throw out their nastiness in the middle of the street.

After I had taken leave of Father Fahy, and returned my thanks for all civilities, I went to pay a visit to Mr Salter, who was secretary to General Stanhope, when the English forces were made prisoners of war at Breuhiga. Going up stairs, I found the door of his lodgings a-jar; and knocking, a person came to the door, who appeared under some surprise at sight of me. I did not know him; but enquiring if Mr Salter was within, he answered, as I fancied, with some hesitation, that he was, but was busy in an inner room. However, though unasked, I went in, resolving, since I had found him at home, to wait his leisure. In a little time Mr Salter entered the room; and after customary ceremonies, asking my patience a little longer, he desired I would sit down and bear ensign Fanshaw company, (for so he called him,) adding, at going out, he had a little business that required dispatch; which being over, he would return, and join company.

The ensign, as he called him, appeared to me under a dishabille; and the first question he asked me, was, if I would drink a glass of English beer? Misled by his appearance, though I assented, it was with a design to treat, which he would by no means permit, but, calling to a servant, ordered some in. We sat drinking that liquor, which to me was a greater rarity than all the wine in Spain; when in dropt an old acquaintance of mine, Mr Le Noy, secretary to Colonel Nevil. He sat down with us, and before the glass could go twice round, told ensign Fanshaw, that his Colonel gave his humble service to him, and ordered him to let him know, that he had but threescore pistoles by him, which he had sent, and which were at his service, as what he pleased more should be as soon as it came to his hands.

At this I began to look upon my ensign as another guess person than I had taken him for; and Le Noy imagining, by our setting cheek by joul together, that I must be in the secret, soon after gave him the title of Captain. This soon convinced me, that there was more in the matter than I was yet master of; for, laying things together, I could not but argue within myself, that as it seemed at first a most incredible thing, that a person of his appearance should have so large credit, with such a compliment at the end of it, without some disguise; and as from an ensign he was risen to be a captain, in the taking of one bottle of English beer; a little patience would let me into a farce, in which at present I had not the honour to bear any part but that of a mute.

At last Le Noy took his leave, and as soon as he had left us, and the other bottle was brought in, ensign Fanshaw began to open his heart, and tell me who he was. " I am necessitated," said he, " to be under this disguise, to conceal myself, especially in this place. For you must know," continued he, " that when our forces were lords of this town, as we were for a little while, I fell under an intrigue with another man's wife: Her husband was a person of considerable account; nevertheless the wife shewed me all the favours that a soldier, under a long and hard campaign, could be imagined to ask. In short, her relations got acquainted with our amour, and knowing that I was among the prisoners taken at Breuhiga, are now upon the scout and enquiry, to make a discovery that may be of fatal consequence. This is the reason of my disguise; this the unfortunate occasion of my taking upon me a name that does not belong to me."

He spoke all this with such an openness of heart, that, in return of so much confidence, I confessed to him, that I had heard of the affair, for that it had made no little noise all over the country; that it highly behoved him to take great care of himself, since, as the relations on both sides were considerable, he must consequently be in great danger; that in cases of that nature, no people in the world carry things to greater extremities than the Spaniards. He returned me thanks for my good advice, which I understood, in a few days after, he, with the assistance of his friends, had taken care to put in practice; for he was conveyed away secretly, and afterwards had the honour to be made a peer of Ireland.

My passport being at last signed by the Count de las Torres, I prepared for a journey I had long and ardently wished for, and set out from Madrid in the beginning of September 1712, in order to return to my native country.

Accordingly I set forward upon my journey; but having heard, both before and since my being in Spain, very famous things spoken of the Escurial, though it was a league out of my road, I resolved to make it a visit. And I must confess, when I came there, I was so far from condemning my curiosity, that I chose to congratulate my good fortune, that had, at half a day's expence, feasted my eyes with extraordinaries, which would have justified a twelvemonth's journey on purpose.

The structure is entirely magnificent, beyond any thing I ever saw, or any thing my imagination could frame. It is composed of eleven several quadrangles, with noble cloisters round every one of them. The front to the west is adorned with three stately gates; every one of a different model, yet every one the model of nicest architecture. The middlemost of the three leads into a fine chapel of the Hieronomites, as

<small>Description of the Escurial.</small>

they call them, in which are entertained one hundred and fifty monks. At every of the four corners of this august fabric, there is a turret of excellent workmanship, which yields to the whole an extraordinary air of grandeur. The King's palace is on the north, nearest that mountain whence the stone it is built of was hewn; and all the south part is set off with many galleries, both beautiful and sumptuous.

This prodigious pile, which, as I have said, exceeds all that I ever saw, and which would ask of itself a volume to particularise, was built by Philip the Second. He laid the first stone, yet lived to see it finished; and lies buried in the Pantheon, a part of it set apart for the burial-place of succeeding princes, as well as himself. It was dedicated to Saint Lawrence in the very foundation; and therefore built in the shape of a gridiron, the instrument of that martyr's execution, and in memory of a great victory obtained on that Saint's day. The stone of which it is built, contrary to the common course, grows whiter by age; and the quarry, whence it was dug, lies near enough, if it had sense or ambition, to grow enamoured of its own wonderful production. Some there are, who stick not to assign this convenience as the main cause of its situation; and for my part, I must agree, that I have seen many other parts of Spain, where that glorious building would have shone with yet far greater splendour.

There was no town of any consequence presented itself in my way to Burgos. Here I took up my quarters that night; where I met with an Irish priest, whose name was White. As is natural on such rencounters, having answered his enquiry, whither I was going, he very kindly told me, he should be very glad of my company as far as Victoria, which lay in my road; and I with equal frankness embraced the offer.

Next morning, when we had mounted our mules, and were got a little distance from Burgos, he began to relate to me a great many impious pranks of an English officer, who had been a prisoner there a little before I came; concluding all, with some vehemence, that he had given greater occasion of scandal and infamy to his native country, than would easily be wiped off, or in a little time. The truth of it is, many particulars, which he related to me, were too monstrously vile to admit of any repetition here; and highly meriting that unfortunate end, which that officer met with some time after. Nevertheless, the just reflections, made by that father, plainly manifested to me the folly of those gentlemen, who, by such inadvertencies, to say no worse, cause the honour of the land of their nativity to be called in question. For though, no doubt, it is a very false conclusion, from a singular, to conceive a general character; yet, in a strange country, nothing is more common. A man, therefore, of common sense, would carefully avoid all occasions of censure, if not in respect to himself, yet out of a humane regard to such of his countrymen as may have the fortune to come after him; and, it is more than probable, may desire to hear a better and juster character of their country, and countrymen, than he perhaps might incline to leave behind him.

As we travelled along, Father White told me, that near the place of our quartering that night, there was a convent of the Carthusian order, which would be well worth my seeing. I was doubly glad to hear it, as it was an order most a stranger to me; and as I had often heard from many others, most unaccountable relations of the severity of their way of life, and the very odd original of their institution.

The next morning, therefore, being Sunday, we took a walk to the convent. It was situated at the foot of a great hill, having a pretty little river running before it. The hill was naturally covered with evergreens of various sorts; but the very summit of the rock was so impending, that one would at first sight be led to apprehend the destruction of the convent, from the fall of it. Notwithstanding all which, they have very curious and well-ordered gardens; which led me to observe, that, whatever men may pretend, pleasure was not incompatible with the most austere life. And indeed, if I may guess of others by this, no order in that church can boast of finer convents. Their chapel was completely neat, the altar of it set out with the utmost magnificence, both as to fine paintings, and other rich adornments. The building was answerable to the rest; and, in short, nothing seemed omitted, that might render it beautiful or pleasant.

When we had taken a full survey of all, we, not without some regret, returned to our very indifferent inn; where, the better to pass away the time, Father White gave me an ample detail of the original of that order. I had before-hand heard somewhat of it; nevertheless, I did not care to interrupt him, because I had a mind to hear how his account would agree with what I had already heard.

" Bruno," said the father, " the author or founder of this order, was not originally of this, but of another. He had a holy brother of the same order, that was his cell-mate, or chamber-fellow, who was reputed by all that ever saw or knew him, for a person of exalted piety, and of a most exact holy life. This man, Bruno had intimately known for many years; and agreed, in his character, that general consent did him no more than justice, having never observed any thing in any of his actions, that, in his opinion, could be offensive to God or man. He was perpetually at his devotions; and distinguishably remarkable for never permitting any thing but pious ejaculations to proceed out of his mouth. In short, he was reputed a saint upon earth.

" This man at last dies, and, according to custom, is removed into the chapel of the convent, and there placed with a cross fixed in his hands: soon after which, saying the proper masses for his soul, in the middle of their devotion, the dead man lifts up his head, and with an audible voice, cried out, *Vocatus sum*. The pious brethren, as any one will easily imagine, were most prodigiously surprised at such an accident, and therefore they earnestly redoubled their prayers; when, lifting up his head a second time, the dead man cried aloud, *Judicatus sum*. Knowing his former piety, the pious fraternity could not then entertain the least doubt of his felicity; when, to their great consternation and confusion, he lifted up his head a third time, crying out in a terrible tone, *Damnatus sum;* upon which they incontinently removed the corpse out of the chapel, and threw it upon the dunghill.

" Good Bruno, pondering upon these passages, could not fail of drawing this conclusion:—that if a person, to all appearance so holy and devout, should miss of salvation, it behoved a wise man to contrive some way more certain to make his calling and election sure. To that purpose he instituted this strict and severe order, with an injunction to them, sacred as any part, that every professor should always wear hair-cloth next his skin ; never eat any flesh, nor speak to one another, only as passing by, to say, *Memento mori.*"

This account I found to agree pretty well with what I had before heard ; but, at the same time, I found the redouble of it made but just the same impression it had at first made upon my heart. However, having made it my observation, that a spirit the least contradictory best carries a man through Spain, I kept Father White company, and in humour, till we arrived at Victoria; where he added one thing, by way of appendix, in relation to the Carthusians, that every person of the society is obliged every day to go into their place of burial, and take up as much earth as he can hold at a grasp with one hand, in order to prepare his grave.

Next day we set out for Victoria. It is a sweet, delicious, and pleasant town. It received that name in memory of a considerable victory there obtained over the

Moors. Leaving this place, I parted with Father White; he going where his affairs led him, and I to make the best of my way to Bilboa.

Entering into Biscay, soon after I left Victoria, I was at a loss almost to imagine what country I was got into. By my long stay in Spain, I thought myself a tolerable master of the tongue; yet here I found myself at the utmost loss to understand landlord, landlady, or any of the family. I was told by my muletier, that they pretend their language, as they call it, has continued uncorrupted from the very confusion of Babel; though, if I might freely give my opinion in the matter, I should rather take it to be the very corruption of all that confusion. Another rhodomontado they have, (for in this they are perfect Spaniards,) that neither Romans, Carthaginians, Vandals, Goths, or Moors, ever totally subdued them. And yet any man that has ever seen their country, might cut this knot without a hatchet, by saying truly, that neither Roman, Carthaginian, nor any victorious people, thought it worth while to make a conquest of a country so mountainous and so barren.

However, Bilboa must be allowed, though not very large, to be a pretty, clean, and neat town. Here, as in Amsterdam, they allow neither cart nor coach to enter; but every thing of merchandise is drawn and carried upon sledges: and yet it is a place of no small account as to trade, and especially for iron and wool. Here I hoped to have met with an opportunity of embarking for England ; but to my sorrow I found myself disappointed, and under that disappointment obliged to make the best of my way to Bayonne. *Bilboa described.*

Setting out for which place, the first town of note that I came to was Saint Sebastian. A very clean town, and neatly paved; which is no little rarity in Spain. It has a very good wall about it, and a pretty citadel. At this place I met with two English officers, who were under the same state with myself; one of them being a prisoner of war with me at Denia. They were going to Bayonne to embark for England as well as myself; so we agreed to set out together for Port Passage. The road from St Sebastian is all over a well paved stone causeway; almost at the end whereof, there accosted us a great number of young lasses. They were all prettily dressed, their long hair flowing in a decent manner over their shoulders, and here and there decorated with ribbons of various colours, which wantonly played on their backs with the wind. The sight surprised my fellow-travellers no less than me; and the more, as they advanced directly up to us, and seized our hands. But a little time undeceived us, and we found what they came for; and that their contest, though not so robust as our oars on the Thames, was much of the same nature; each contending who should have us for their fare. For it is here a custom of time out of mind, that none but young women should have the management and profit of that ferry. And though the ferry is over an arm of the sea, very broad, and sometimes very rough, those fair ferriers manage themselves with that dexterity, that the passage is very little dangerous, and in calm weather very pleasant. In short, we made choice of those that best pleased us; who, in a grateful return, led us down to their boat under a sort of music, which they, walking along, made with their oars, and which we all thought far from being disagreeable. Thus were we transported over to Port Passage; not undeservedly accounted the best harbour in all the Bay of Biscay.

We staid not long here after landing, resolving, if possible, to reach Fonterabia before night; but all the expedition we could use, little availed; for before we could reach thither, the gates were shut, and good nature and humanity were so locked up with them, that all the rhetoric we were masters of could not prevail upon the governor to order their being opened; for which reason, we were obliged to take up our quarters at the ferry house.

When we got up the next morning, we found the waters so broad, as well as rough, that we began to enquire after another passage; and were answered, that at the Isle of Conference, but a short league upwards, the passage was much shorter, and exposed to less danger. Such good reasons soon determined us: so, setting out, we got there in a very little time, and very soon after were landed in France. Here we found a house of very good entertainment; a thing we had long wanted, and much lamented the want of.

We were hardly well seated in the house, before we were made sensible, that it was the custom, which had made it the business of our host, to entertain all his guests at first coming in, with a prolix account of that remarkable interview between the two Kings of France and Spain. I speak safely now, as being got on French ground: for the Spaniard in his own country would have made me to know, that putting Spain after France had there been looked upon as a mere solecism in speech. However, having refreshed ourselves, to shew our deference to our host's relation, we agreed to pay our respects to that famous little isle he mentioned; which, indeed, was the whole burden of the design of our crafty landlord's relation.

When we came there, we found it a little oval island, overrun with weeds, and surrounded with reeds and rushes. "Here," said our landlord, (for he went with us,) "upon this little spot, were at that juncture seen the two greatest monarchs in the universe. A noble pavilion was erected in the very middle of it, and in the middle of that was placed a very large oval table; at which was the conference, from which the place received its title. There were two bridges raised; one on the Spanish side, the passage to which was a little upon a descent by reason of the hills adjacent; and the other upon the French side, which, as you see, was all upon a level. The music playing, and trumpets sounding, the two kings, upon a signal agreed upon, set forward at the same time; the Spanish monarch handing the Infanta, his daughter, to the place of interview. As soon as they were entered the pavilion, on each side, all the artillery fired, and both armies after that made their several vollies. Then the King of Spain advancing on his side the table with the Infanta, the King of France advanced at the same moment on the other; till meeting, he received the Infanta at the hands of her father, as his queen; upon which, both the artillery and small arms fired as before. After this was a most splendid and sumptuous entertainment; which being over, both kings retired into their several dominions; the King of France conducting his new Queen to Saint Jean de

Luz, where the marriage was consummated; and the King of Spain returning to Port Passage."

After a relation so very inconsistent with the present state of the place, we took horse, (for mule-mounting was now out of fashion,) and rode to Saint Jean de Luz, where we found as great a difference in our eating and drinking, as we had before done in our riding. Here they might be properly called houses of entertainment; though, generally speaking, till we came to this place, we met with very mean fare, and were poorly accommodated in the houses where we lodged.

A person that travels this way, would be esteemed a man of a narrow curiosity, who should not desire to see the chamber where Louis le Grand took his first night's lodging with his Queen. Accordingly, when it was put into my head, out of an ambition to evince myself a person of taste, I asked the question, and the favour was granted me, with a great deal of French civility.

Not that I found any thing here, more than in the Isle of Conference, but what tradition only had rendered remarkable.

<small>Saint Jean de Luz.</small> Saint Jean de Luz is esteemed one of the greatest village towns in all France. It was in the great church of this place, that Louis XIV., according to marriage articles, took before the high altar the oath of renunciation to the crown of Spain, by which all the issue of that marriage were debarred inheritance, if oaths had been obligatory with princes. The natives here are reckoned expert seamen, especially in whale fishing. Here is a fine bridge of wood; in the middle of which is a descent, by steps, into a pretty little island; where is a chapel, and a palace belonging to the bishop of Bayonne. Here the Queen Dowager of Spain often walks to divert herself; and on this bridge, and in the walks on the island, I had the honour to see that princess more than once.

This villa not being above four leagues from Bayonne, we got there by dinner-time, where, at an ordinary of twenty sous, we eat and drank in plenty, and with a gusto much better than in any part of Spain; where, for eating much worse, we paid very much more.

Bayonne is a town strong by nature; yet the fortifications have been very much neglected, since the building of the citadel, on the other side the river; which not only commands the town, but the harbour too. It is a noble fabric, fair and strong, and raised on the side of a hill, wanting nothing that art could furnish to render it impregnable. The Marshal Bouflers had the care of it in its erection; and there is a fine walk near it, from which he used to survey the workmen, which still carries his name. There are two noble bridges here, though both of wood, one over that river which runs on one side the town; the other over that which divides it in the middle. The tide runs through both with vast rapidity; notwithstanding which, ships of burden come up, and, paying for it, are often fastened to the bridge, while loading or unloading. While I was here, there came in four or five English ships laden with corn; the first, as they told me, that had come in to unlade there since the beginning of the war.

<small>Pont d'Esprit.</small> On that side of the river where the new citadel is built, at a very little distance, lies Pont d'Esprit, a place mostly inhabited by Jews, who drive a great trade there, and are esteemed very rich, though, as in all other countries, mostly very roguish. Here the Queen Dowager of Spain has kept her court ever since the jealousy of the present King reclused her from Madrid. As aunt to his competitor Charles, (now Emperor,) he apprehended her intriguing; for which reason, giving her an option of retreat, that princess made choice of this city, much to the advantage of the place, and in all appearance much to her own satisfaction. She is a lady not of the lesser size; and lives here in suitable splen-

dour, and not without the respect due to a person of her high quality, every time she goes to take the air, the cannon of the citadel saluting her as she passes over the bridge; and, to say truth, the country round is extremely pleasant, and abounds in plenty of all provisions, especially in wild fowl. Bayonne hams are, to a proverb, celebrated all over France.

We waited here near five months before the expected transports arrived from England, without any other amusements than such as are common to people under suspence. Short tours will not admit of great varieties; and much acquaintance could not be any way suitable to people that had long been in a strange country, and earnestly desired to return to our own. Yet one accident befel me here, that was nearer costing me my life, than all I had before encountered, either in battle or siege.

Going to my lodgings one evening, I unfortunately met with an officer, who would needs have me along with him, aboard one of the English ships, to drink a bottle of English beer. He had been often invited, he said ; " and I am afraid our countryman," continued he, " will hold himself slighted if I delay it longer." English beer was a great rarity, and the vessel lay not at any great distance from my lodgings ; so without any further persuasion I consented. When we came upon the bridge, to which the ship we were to go aboard was fastened, we found, as was customary, as well as necessary, a plank laid over from the ship, and a rope to hold by, for safe passage. The night was very dark, and I had cautiously enough taken care to provide a man with a lanthorn to prevent casualties. The man with the light went first, and, out of his abundant complaisance, my friend, the officer, would have me follow the light ; but I was no sooner stept upon the plank after my guide, but rope and plank gave way, and guide and I tumbled both together into the water.

The tide was then running in pretty strong; however, my feet in the fall touching ground, gave me an opportunity to recover myself a little; at which time I catched fast hold of a buoy, which was placed over an anchor on one of the ships there riding: I held fast, till the tide, rising stronger and stronger, threw me off my feet, which gave an opportunity to the poor fellow, our lanthorn-bearer, to lay hold of one of my legs, by which he held as fast as I by the buoy. We had lain thus lovingly at hull together, struggling with the encreasing tide, which, well for us, did not break my hold, (for if it had, the ships which lay breast-a-breast had certainly sucked us under,) when several on the bridge, who saw us fall, brought others with ropes and lights to our assistance; and especially my brother-officer, who had been accessary as well as spectator of our calamity; though at last a very small portion of our deliverance fell to his share.

As soon as I could feel a rope, I quitted

my hold of the buoy; but my poor drag at my heels would not on any account quit his hold of my leg. And as it was next to an impossibility, in that posture, to draw us up the bridge to save both, if either of us, we must still have perished, had not the alarm brought off a boat or two to our succour, who took us in.

I was carried as fast as possible to a neighbouring house hard by, where they took immediate care to make a good fire; and where I had not been long before our intended host, the master of the ship, came in very much concerned, and blaming us for not hailing the vessel before we made an attempt to enter. " For," says he, " the very night before, my vessel was robbed; and that plank and rope were a trap designed for the thieves, if they came again; not imagining that men in an honest way would have come on board without asking questions." Like the wise men of this world, I hereupon began to form resolutions against a thing, which was never again likely to

CAPTAIN CARLETON. 447

happen; and to draw inferences of instruction from an accident, that had not so much as a moral for its foundation.

One day after this, partly out of business, and partly out of curiosity, I went to see the mint here; and having taken notice to one of the officers, that there was a difference in the impress of their crown pieces, one having at the bottom the impress of a cow, and the other none: " Sir," replied that officer, " you are much in the right in your observation. Those that have the cow, were not coined here, but at Paw, the chief city of Navarre, where they enjoy the privilege of a mint as well as we. And tradition tells," says he, " that the reason of that addition to the impress was this: A certain King of Navarre, (when it was a kingdom distinct from that of France,) looking out of a window of the palace, spied a cow, with her calf standing aside her, attacked by a lion, which had got loose out of his menagerie. The lion strove to get the young calf into his paw; the cow bravely defended her charge; and so well, that the lion at last, tired and weary, withdrew, and left her mistress of the field of battle, and her young one. Ever since which," concluded the officer, "by order of that king, the cow is placed at the bottom of the impress of all the money there coined."

Whether or no my relator guessed at the moral, or whether it was fact, I dare not determine: but to me it seemed apparent, that it was no otherways intended, than as an emblematical fable to cover, and preserve the memory of the deliverance of Henry the Fourth, then the young King of Navarre, at that eternally ignominious slaughter, the massacre of Paris. Many historians, their own as well as others, agree, that the house of Guise had levelled the malice of their design at that great prince. They knew him to be the lawful heir; but as they knew him bred what they called a Huguenot, barbarity and injustice was easily concealed under the cloak of religion, and the good of mother-church, under the veil of ambition, was held sufficient to postpone the laws of God and man. Some of those historians have delivered it as matter of fact, that the conspirators, in searching after that young King, pressed into the very apartments of the Queen his mother; who having, at the toll of the bell, and cries of the murdered, taken the alarm, on hearing them coming, placed herself in her chair, and covered the young King her son with her farthingale, till they were gone. By which means she found an opportunity to convey him to a place of more safety; and so preserved him from those bloody murderers, and in them from the paw of the lion. This was only a private reflection of my own at that time; but I think carries so great a face of probability, that I can see no present reason to reject it. And to have sought after better information from the officer of the mint, had been to sacrifice my discretion to my curiosity.

While I staid at Bayonne, the Princess Ursini came thither, attended by some of the King of Spain's guards. She had been to drink the waters of some famous spaw in the neighbourhood, the name of which has now slipt my memory. She was most splendidly entertained by the Queen-dowager of Spain; and the Mareschal de Montrevel no less signalized himself in his reception of that great lady, who was at that instant the greatest favourite in the Spanish court; though, as I have before related, she was some time after basely undermined by a creature of her own advancing.

Bayonne is esteemed the third emporium of trade in all France. It was once, and remained long so, in the possession of the English; of which had history been silent, the cathedral church had afforded evident demonstration; being in every respect of the English model, and quite different to any of their own way of building in France.

<small>Pampelona.</small> Pampelona is the capital city of the Spanish Navarre, supposed to have been built

by Pompey. It is situated in a pleasant valley, surrounded by lofty hills. This town, whether famous or infamous, was the cause of the first institution of the order of the Jesuits: For at the siege of this place, Ignatius Loyola being only a private soldier, received a shot in his thigh, which made him incapable of following that profession any longer; upon which he set his brains to work, being a subtle man, and invented the order of the Jesuits, which has been so troublesome to the world ever since.

At Saint Stephen, near Lerida, an action happened between the English and Spaniards, in which Major General Cunningham, bravely fighting at the head of his men, lost his life, being extremely much lamented. He was a gentleman of a great estate, yet left it to serve his country; *dulce est pro patria mori.*

About two leagues from Victoria, there is a very pleasant hermitage placed upon a small rising ground; a murmuring rivulet running at the bottom, and a pretty neat chapel standing near it, in which I saw Saint Christopher in a gigantic shape, having a Christo on his shoulders. The hermit was there at his devotion; I asked him (though I knew it before) the reason why he was represented in so large a shape? The hermit answered with great civility, and told me, he had his name from Christo Ferendo; for when our Saviour was young, he had an inclination to pass a river, so Saint Christopher took him on his shoulders in order to carry him over, and as the water grew deeper and deeper, so he grew higher and higher.

At last we received news, that the Gloucester man-of-war, with two transports, was arrived at Port Passage, in order for the transporting of all the remaining prisoners of war into England. Accordingly, they marched next day, and there embarked. But I having before agreed with a master of a vessel, which was loaded with wine for

Amsterdam, to set me ashore at Dover, staid behind, waiting for that ship, as did that for a fair wind.

In three or four days time, a fine and fair gale presented; of which the master taking due advantage, we sailed over the bar into the bay of Biscay. This is with sailors, to a proverb, reckoned the roughest of seas; and yet on our entrance into it, nothing appeared like it. It was smooth as glass; a lady's face might pass for young, and in its bloom, that discovered no more wrinkles: yet scarce had we sailed three leagues, before a prodigious fish presented itself to our view. As near as we could guess, it might be twenty yards in length; and it lay sporting itself on the surface of the sea, a great part appearing out of the water. The sailors, one and all, as soon as they saw it, declared it the certain forerunner of a storm. However, our ship kept on its course, before a fine gale, till we had near passed over half the bay; when, all on a sudden, there was such a hideous alteration, as makes nature recoil on the very reflection. Those seas that seemed before to smile upon us, with the aspect of a friend, now in a moment changed their flattering countenance into that of an open enemy; and frowns, the certain indexes of wrath, presented us with apparent danger, of which little on this side death could be the sequel. The angry waves cast themselves up into mountains, and scourged the ship on every side from poop to prow: Such shocks from the contending wind and surges! such falls from precipices of water, to dismal caverns of the same uncertain element! Although the latter seemed to receive us, in order to screen us from the riot of the former, imagination could offer no other advantage than that of a winding-sheet, presented and prepared for our approaching fate. But why mention I imagination? In me it was wholly dormant. And yet those sons of stormy weather, the sailors, had theirs about them in full stretch; for seeing the wind and seas so very boisterous, they lashed the rudder of the ship, resolved to let her drive, and steer herself, since it was past their skill to steer her. This was our way of sojourning most part of that tedious night; driven where the winds and waves thought fit to drive us, with all our sails quite lowered and flat upon the deck. If Ovid, in the little Archipelagian sea, could whine out his *jam jam jacturus*, &c. in this more dismal scene, and much more dangerous sea, (the pitch-like darkness of the night adding to all our sad variety of woes,) what words in verse or prose could serve to paint our passions, or our expectations? Alas! our only expectation was in the return of morning: it came at last; yet even slowly as it came, when come, we thought it come too soon, a new scene of sudden death being all the advantage of its first appearance. Our ship was driving full speed towards the breakers on the Cabritton shore, between Bourdeaux and Bayonne; which filled us with ideas more terrible than all before, since those were past, and these seemingly as certain. Beside, to add to our distress, the tide was driving in, and consequently must drive us fast to visible destruction. A state so evident, that one of our sailors, whom great experience had rendered more sensible of our present danger, was preparing to save one, by lashing himself to the main mast, against the expected minute of desolation. He was about that melancholy work, in utter despair of any better fortune, when, as loud as ever he could bawl, he cried out, "a point, a point of wind!" To me, who had had too much of it, it appeared like the sound of the last trump; but to the more intelligent crew, it had a different sound. With vigour and alacrity they started from their prayers, or their despair, and with all imaginable speed unlashed the rudder, and hoisted all their sails. Never sure in nature did one minute produce a greater scene of contraries.

The more skilful sailors took courage at this happy presage of deliverance. And according to their expectation did it happen; that heavenly point of wind delivered us from the jaws of those breakers, ready open to devour us; and carrying us out to the much more welcome wide sea, furnished every one in the ship with thoughts as distant as we thought our danger.

We endeavoured to make Port Passage; but our ship became unruly, and would not answer her helm; for which reason we were glad to go before the wind, and make for the harbour of Saint Jean de Luz. This we attained without any great difficulty; and to the satisfaction of all, sailors as well as passengers, we there cast anchor, after the most terrible storm, (as all the oldest sailors agreed,) and as much danger as ever people escaped.

Here I took notice, that the sailors buoyed up their cables with hogsheads; enquiring into the reason of which, they told me, that the rocks at the bottom of the harbour were by experience found to be so very sharp, that they would otherwise cut their cables asunder. Our ship was obliged to be drawn up into the dock to be refitted; during which, I lay in the town, where nothing of moment or worth reciting happened.

I beg pardon for my error; the very movements of princes must always be considerable, and consequently worth recital. While the ship lay in the dock, I was one evening walking upon the bridge, with the little island near it, (which I have before spoke of,) and had a little Spanish dog along with me, when at the further end I spied a lady, and three or four gentlemen in company. I kept on my pace of leisure, and so did they; but when I came nearer, I found they as much out-numbered me in the dog, as they did in the human kind; and I soon experienced to my sorrow, that their dogs, by their fierceness and ill-humour, were dogs of quality; having, without warning, or the least declaration of war, fallen upon my little dog, according to pristine custom, without any honourable regard to size, interest, or number. However, the good lady, who, by the privilege of her sex, must be allowed the most competent judge of inequalities, out of an excess of condescension and goodness, came running to the relief of oppressed poor Tony ; and, in courtly language, rated her own oppressive dogs for their great incivility to strangers. The dogs, in the middle of their insulting wrath, obeyed the lady with a vast deal of profound submission ; which I could not much wonder at, when I understood, that it was a Queen-dowager of Spain who had chid them.

Our ship being now repaired, and made fit to go out again to sea, we left the harbour of Saint Jean de Luz, and, with a much better passage, as the last tempest was still dancing in my imagination, in ten days sail we reached Dover. Here I landed on the last day of March 1713, having not till then seen or touched English shore from the beginning of May 1705.

I took coach directly for London, where, when I arrived, I thought myself transported into a country more foreign than any I had either fought or pilgrimaged in. Not foreign, do I mean, in respect to others, so much as to itself. I left it, seemingly, under a perfect unanimity: the fatal distinctions of Whig and Tory were then esteemed merely nominal; and of no more ill consequence or danger, than a bee robbed of its sting. The national concern went on with vigour, and the prodigious success of the Queen's arms, left every soul without the least pretence to a murmur. But now on my return, I found them on their old establishment, perfect contraries, and as unlikely to be brought to meet as direct angles. Some arraigning, some extolling of a peace; in which time has shewn both were wrong, and consequently neither could be right in their notions of it, however an over-prejudiced way of thinking might draw them into one or the other. But Whig and Tory are, in my mind, the completest paradox in nature; and yet like other paradoxes, old as I am, I live in hope to see, before I die, those seeming contraries perfectly reconciled, and reduced into one happy certainty, the public good.

Whilst I staid at Madrid, I made several visits to my old acquaintance General Mahoni. I remember that he told me, when the Earl of Peterborough and he held a conference at Morvidro, his Lordship used many arguments to induce him to leave the Spanish service. Mahoni made several excuses, especially that none of his religion was suffered to serve in the English army. My Lord replied, that he would undertake to get him excepted by an act of parliament. I have often heard him speak with great respect of his Lordship; and was strangely surprised, that after so many glorious successes he should be sent away.

He was likewise pleased to inform me, that at the battle of Saragoza, it was his fortune to make some of our horse to give way, and he pursued them for a considerable time ; but at his return, he saw the Spanish army in great confusion : but it gave him the opportunity of attacking our battery of guns, which he performed with great slaughter, both of gunners and matrosses : he at the same time enquired who it was that commanded there in chief. I informed him it was Colonel Bourguard, one that understood the economy of the train exceeding well. As for that, he knew nothing of; but that he would vouch, he behaved himself with extraordinary courage, and defended the battery to the utmost extremity, receiving several wounds, and deserved the post in which he acted. A gentleman who was a prisoner at Gualaxara, informed me, that he saw King Philip riding through that town, being only attended with one of his guards.

Saragoza. Saragoza, or Cæsar Augusta, lies upon the river Ebro, being the capital of Arragon; it is a very ancient city, and contains fourteen great churches, and twelve convents. The church of the Lady of the Pillar is frequented by Pilgrims, almost from all countries; it was anciently a Roman colony.

Tibi laus, tibi honor, tibi sit gloria, O gloriosa Trinitas, quia tu dedisti mihi hanc opportunitatem, omnes has res gestas recordandi. Nomen tuum sit benedictum, per sæcula sæculorum. Amen.

THE END.

EDINBURGH :
Printed by James Ballantyne & Co.